Strip Club

INTERSECTIONS

Transdisciplinary Perspectives on Genders and Sexualities

General Editors: Michael Kimmel and Suzanna Walters

Sperm Counts: Overcome by Man's Most Precious Fluid
Lisa Jean Moore

The Sexuality of Migration:
Border Crossings and Mexican Immigrant Men
Lionel Cantú, Jr.
Edited by Nancy A. Naples and Salvador Vidal-Ortiz

Moral Panics, Sex Panics: Fear and the Fight over Sexual Rights
Edited by Gilbert Herdt

Out in the Country:
Youth, Media, and Queer Visibility in Rural America
Mary L. Gray

Sapphistries: A Global History of Love between Women
Leila J. Rupp

Strip Club: Gender, Power, and Sex Work
Kim Price-Glynn

Strip Club

Gender, Power, and Sex Work

Kim Price-Glynn

NEW YORK UNIVERSITY PRESS

New York and London

NEW YORK UNIVERSITY PRESS
New York and London
www.nyupress.org

Chapter 2 is reprinted with permission from *Gender & Society* 22/3 (June 2008)
by SAGE Publications Ltd. All rights reserved. © 2008.

Library of Congress Cataloging-in-Publication Data

Price-Glynn, Kim.
Strip club : gender, power, and sex work / Kim Price-Glynn.
p. cm. — (Intersections)
Includes bibliographical references and index.
ISBN-13: 978–0–8147–6760–3 (cl : alk. paper)
ISBN-10: 0–8147–6760–5 (cl : alk. paper)
ISBN-13: 978–0–8147–6761–0 (pb : alk. paper)
ISBN-10: 0–8147–6761–3 (pb : alk. paper)
[etc.]
1. Sex oriented businesses—Social aspects—United States—Case studies.
2. Stripteasers—United States—Case studies. 3. Power (Social sciences)—
Case studies. 4. Sex role—Case studies. I. Title.
HQ18.U5P74   2010
306.77—dc22   2010011997

New York University Press books are printed on acid-free paper,
and their binding materials are chosen for strength and durability.
We strive to use environmentally responsible suppliers and materials
to the greatest extent possible in publishing our books.

Manufactured in the United States of America

c   10 9 8 7 6 5 4 3 2 1
p   10 9 8 7 6 5 4 3 2 1

In remembrance of four strong women who
forged their own paths through the world,
Louise Walters Bowers, Lillian Gorell,
Kathryne Bowers Johnston, and Nell Simon Price.

Contents

Preface   ix

Acknowledgments   xiii

Introduction: A Typical Shift   1

1   Studying Strip Club Work: Context and Perspective   25

2   "Keeping the Dancers in Check":   47
    The Gendered Organization of Stripping in The Lion's Den

3   "It's a Nice Place to Hide, and It's Safe":   67
    The Making of Masculinities in The Lion's Den

4   Tradeoffs and Troubles: Managing Stripping Labor   101

5   Dollar Dances and Stage Dances: 143
    Strippers and Economic Exploitation

Postscript: The Lion's Den, 2005–2006   165

Appendix 1: Researching The Lion's Den   199

Appendix 2: Participant Descriptions of Life and Work   209

Notes   231

References   243

Index   255

About the Author   263

Preface

My introduction to The Lion's Den, a strip club featuring female nude performers for primarily male patrons, came during the spring of 2001 when I applied for and landed a job as a cocktail waitress.[1]

I entered The Lion's Den through the front door for the first (and last) time. I would never again use this entrance designed for patrons because I was, on my very first visit, to become an employee of the club. As an employee, I parked with the other workers and used the side entrance, often propped open with a black vinyl banquet chair. The employee entrance was backstage and led to the beer coolers, owner-manager's office, strippers' dressing rooms, and hallway leading to the bar and main room of the club. Empty beer boxes and trash were often scattered on the cement floor and sometimes all the way to the nearby dumpster. While I was not surprised to see the backstage areas in disarray—they are not designed for patrons to see, after all—I expected the front entrance to put on a better show. Despite my limited time in the front entryway, the space made an indelible impression. I noticed chipped and worn flat black paint on the walls dotted with tape and other remnants of old posters and advertisements. The charcoal gray carpet was worn to the threads and flattened down in places by large blobs of what looked like tar or blackened chewing gum. Once inside the club, a large windowless door shut out the daylight that made the entryway visible.

As darkness enveloped me, I stepped a few feet inside and approached a small counter to speak with Frank, the club's daytime doorman and bouncer (research participants' demographics are outlined in appendix 1 and appendix 2). A white man in his mid-fifties with thick, curly, salt and pepper hair, Frank was brawny from years of weightlifting, a passion he shared with anyone who would listen. Since I arrived for my interview before the evening shift (which began at 7:00), I saw Frank just before he left for the day. With a warm grin, Frank said, "How can I help you?" I explained that I had an interview with Steve, the club's owner-manager, for a cocktail waitressing position. Full of energy, Frank said, "Come on in" and motioned me around the doorman's cubicle and into the club. He escorted me past the deejay booth and VIP Room (the club's private dance performance space) down a narrow hallway behind the club's bar to Steve's small office.

When we arrived at his office, Steve's door, as usual, was open. He was online at his computer, reading. Before I could see the text, my attention was drawn to the adjacent black and white video monitors that displayed the club's two cash registers, one in the doorman's cubicle and the other behind the bar. The cameras zoomed in so close that during our interview I occasionally saw hands pass in front of the screen, open the drawers, remove and add bills, then close the drawers. Since the hands were not pictured with the bodies they belonged to, the images reminded me of "Thing," the disembodied hand from the *Addams Family*, depicted in cartoons, television, and film. Once I panned out from the video monitors, I noticed the office was sparsely decorated with only two chairs and a desk. The walls were a neutral tan and covered with paper signs and lists.

Steve was a tall, attractive, white man in his mid-thirties, with sandy hair, light eyes, and a wry smile. He enjoyed teasing women, and I was no exception. When my interview began, he asked me if I had ever worked in a strip club. I nervously smiled and said, "No, but I think you'll find I'm a quick study." He chuckled and told me, "No worries, very few people around here come with any experience." I explained that I learned about the job opening from Angela. He smiled and said, "Oh yeah, you're Angela's friend; she mentioned you'd be coming by." Angela was, in Steve's words, "the club's darling" and "his favorite." Angela was a student stripper and cocktail waitress I interviewed while still in the design phase of this research. She provided my connection and introduction to The Lion's Den, supplying me with information about the job opening, giving a strong recommendation to Steve, and vouching as my friend to other club workers. A beautiful young Portuguese college student with long brown hair and deep olive skin, Angela was indeed the darling of the club. Initially working as a cocktail waitress, this unassuming twenty-one-year-old was flattered right onto the stage. The perfect mix of youth, beauty, modesty, and earnestness, she had a proven track record and a stellar reputation.

Rather than focusing on job training, a task Steve left to Angela, the cocktail waitress on shift that evening, he asked me about myself. It turned out we had both lived in the Midwest during the 1970s and 1980s. Though I was nearly ten years younger than him and had no firsthand knowledge of top 40 and rock and roll clubs in those decades, he included me in his descriptions as an insider. He talked about running those clubs and the job insecurity associated with places that frequently closed after a year. Strip clubs by contrast, he argued, would always be in business. Ironically, in an industry known for high worker turnover, it was Steve's desire for steady employment that drew him to strip clubs.

Steve mentioned that he had an MBA and emphasized his desire for professionalism in the club. I presented him with a résumé; he was charmed by this. Though it was not unheard of for strip club workers to submit résumés, particularly deejays, it was uncommon for female workers to do so. In truth, my waitressing experiences were limited to two summer stints at local cafés in high school and college. My skills were even less remarkable, as those who know me will attest. I am just as likely to bobble a tray of food or drinks as I am to deliver it successfully. What I lacked in waitressing experience and skills I made up for in my level of schooling, my mostly conventional appearance, and my apparent earnestness.

On the topic of schooling I mentioned that I had a master's degree and was working toward my doctorate. Steve snorted, saying there were lots of other "students" in the club, particularly among the strippers. I sidestepped his sarcasm and launched into my pitch. Without hesitation I explained my desire to carry out research in the club for a dissertation that would turn, hopefully someday, into a book. Surprised and amused, he said he welcomed a researcher into the club and hoped I could address some of his nagging questions. In particular, he was interested in what he saw as a lack of work ethic among young people today. I explained that I was interested in exploring how the club operated through my own eyes, by doing participant observation, but also through the experiences of everyone in the club, including himself. He mentioned that he was interested in my findings and had lots of stories to tell. Steve was impressed enough with me that I was assigned to the coveted Thursday evening shift, a solo shift (by contrast, Friday and Saturday nights had three cocktail waitresses working) with larger numbers of patrons than on other weeknights. I was in. Within minutes of my interview, I was on the floor waitressing. My training came from Angela, and initially I was known for being "Angela's friend," though we were, in fact, only acquaintances.

I eventually became known for my research. I openly discussed my role as a researcher when asking questions of coworkers and patrons. Many may not have truly understood the scope of this study, though I did my best to explain it. I think some assumed I was writing an undergraduate paper. Indeed, some mentioned knowing or hearing about sociology or psychology students who had done similar research. Most responded to my inquiries with mild curiosity and seemed not to notice any disruptions they may have caused.[2]

I did little to alter or amplify my looks for the club. I dressed in casual slacks or jeans and a t-shirt, wore artsy black eyeglasses, long brown hair that I kept down, and minimal makeup. This presentation of self was conventional enough to satisfy the low expectations in The Lion's Den. My looks, coupled with my research and student status, soon earned me countless "sexy librarian" and "sleeper" remarks. "Sleeper" was a sexualized term used by white, middle-aged, male patrons to describe women who were conventional on the surface but probably extraordinary in other ways. These comments culminated in repeated dedications of the Van Halen song "Hot for Young Teacher." Van Halen's music video for the song features a teacher who, to her male students' delight, suddenly climbs atop students' desks and strips to a bikini. Though I never stripped in The Lion's Den or elsewhere, the possibility permeated my interactions in the club, particularly with patrons.

I also became well regarded for my dependability. In a place where turnover rates were high, someone who arrived to work early, always completed her tasks, and did not abuse drugs stood out. Early on, a single key event worked to my advantage, solidifying my reputation with strippers in the club. One night I found a large roll of rubberbanded bills (hundreds of dollars) that had been dropped by one of the dancers in the VIP Room. While I was speaking to Steve about finding the money, Roxanne came running in, screaming. Roxanne was in her early thirties and had worked in The Lion's Den longer than any of the other strippers. It was apparent that she was the owner of the money I had found. When I turned it over in full, she hugged me and handed over a few bills. As Roxanne relayed the story to other dancers, they approached me to praise my actions. I had proven myself as someone to be trusted.

The club was in many ways a ramshackle enterprise to be sure, but it had an internal logic that I was determined to uncover. When I first entered The Lion's Den, I expected to see far more solidarity than I found, based on previous research I had conducted in other clubs and, to be candid, my own personal-political hopes. Women in the sex industry do sometimes stick together to fight for better working conditions,[3] but here, time and again, what proved more true was that acts of solidarity were the exception rather than the rule. When I went to work, I carried nothing of value that I was not willing or planning to lose. Whether it was a stripper's wad of rolled-up bills left in the VIP Room, her belongings stored in the dressing rooms, or her purse left behind the bar—all were subject to possible thievery. When it came to items of personal value, even one's own self-worth, nothing was safe, and no one was to be fully trusted in The Lion's Den.

Acknowledgments

Thanks hardly seems enough for the strippers, employees, owner-manager, and patrons from The Lion's Den who welcomed me into their world and gave of their time so unselfishly. Since respect for their confidentiality prevents me from naming these individuals or the club where I met them, I can only provide my gratitude and say that without their assistance this work would have been impossible.

Many people have contributed helpful feedback at various stages of research and writing. At the University of Massachusetts–Amherst, the insightful comments of Margaret Cerullo, Naomi Gerstel, and Jackie Urla early on were a tremendous help to me. In particular, Robert Zussman's mentoring and enthusiasm for this project have been invaluable. Gratitude also goes to my UMass writing group, Amy Armenia, Pat Duffy, Ingrid Semaan, and Kathy Walker, whose feedback always made the research and writing process more robust. Semaan, a colleague who fortunately bridges two of my universities, has been a constant source of camaraderie and intellectual exchange, for which I am grateful. At the University of Connecticut, I thank my colleagues in Sociology on the Storrs campus, in Women's Studies on the Stamford campus, and in Urban and Community Studies on the Greater Hartford campus. Mary Bernstein, Mary Cygan, Michael Ego, Davita Glasberg, Nancy Naples, Bandana Purkayastha, Katherine Ratcliff, Stephen Ross, Clint Sanders, Gaye Tuchman, and David Williams all deserve special thanks for their interest and support.

Thank you to New York University Press and, in particular, executive editor Ilene Kalish, whose enthusiastic guidance and considerable understanding of sociology and sex work research helped make my manuscript into a book. I appreciate the supportive feedback and attention to detail I received from NYU editorial assistant Aiden Amos, managing editor Despina Papazoglou Gimbel, copyeditor Cynthia Garver, and the meticulous reviewers brought on board by NYU.

Writing has always been a collaborative process for me. At different stages of this project I have been fortunate to have the watchful eyes of two talented writers. Leslie Harris, a dear friend and thoughtful critic, provided detailed comments and copyediting on an earlier draft of this manuscript. Her hard work, kind words, and good humor are much appreciated. Alice Julier, sociologist, author, and editor, also provided feedback and copyediting on a subsequent draft. This manuscript has benefited tremendously from her careful review.

Ohio Wesleyan was my launching pad, and I would be remiss if I did not recognize Ted Cohen, John Durst, Jason Good, Mary Howard, and Jan Smith, who encouraged me to pursue qualitative research as an undergraduate. Thanks to Durst for continued support reviewing this work and sharing it with his classes.

An earlier version of the discussion presented in chapter 2 first appeared in print in *Gender & Society* in 2008, and I am grateful for the permission to present an extended version of that discussion here.

Throughout this project, my husband, Eric Price-Glynn, has listened and advised me about my work, provided detailed comments on each chapter, and sacrificed sleep to await my arrival home from late nights in The Lion's Den. His unwavering love and support remind me each day how lucky I am to have found him.

My parents, Christina and Ronald; my sisters, Cindy and Diana; my brothers-in-law, Brian and Doug; my nieces Christina and Maria; and my nephews Alexander, Nathaniel, Kyle, and Zachary are steady sources of happiness in my life. Their love, patience, and encouragement are always with me—my love and thanks to you all, as well as to my new family, Patricia, Dan, Patrick, Michael, Lisa, Lynn, Ashley, Ava, and Leah Glynn.

Steve Shraison, my friend, ally, and mentor, did not get to see the completion of my dissertation or this book, but he certainly envisioned them. His passion and intellect remain an inspiration to me.

My son, Lucas, I am saving my final words of thanks for you. Occasionally sleeping on my lap and later tinkering with the keyboard, you too have contributed to this book. You have made my life so full of joy. I love you fearlessly.

Introduction

A Typical Shift

As a sociologist interested in gender, I chose to study The Lion's Den for many reasons; chief among them was access. Beyond this practical consideration, The Lion's Den offered me a chance to write about something new—an ethnographic case study of a highly gendered organization, the strip club. By participating, observing, and interviewing, I examined the entire cast of club workers, strippers, and patrons, as well as the space itself, to explore issues of gender, power, and sex work. With regular access and approval from the club's owner-manager, Steve, I conducted my research openly. Over a fourteen-month period spanning 2001 and 2002, The Lion's Den occupied many of my waking hours: not only was I working there as a cocktail waitress; I was observing, researching, and analyzing—so both my feet and my brain sometimes hurt.

Readers may wonder, why study a strip club? What is interesting about such places, sociologically speaking? I contend that we can learn why people become sex workers, as well as sex patrons, by taking a closer look inside this club. We can learn about the underlying strengths and vulnerabilities that lure and frustrate women and men in such places. Further, I examine how the space itself is organized socially and economically. I show how women and men negotiate interactions with each other and the club itself, as well as whose interests strip clubs serve, why it serves them, and how. Often, the gendered, organizational, and economic outcomes cut both ways, leading to simultaneous benefits and drawbacks for those involved.

Stripping is frequently ghettoized as a topic irrelevant to the mainstream; as a result, popular assumptions about the stripping industry are often made on faulty premises. One may suppose that, as part of the sex work industry, strip clubs are inherently structured to men's advantage—men are the primary consumers and owners, after all. However, to assume a priori that women are necessarily oppressed in this industry would be a mistake. Not only does the assumption of women's oppression minimize women's agency, but also it glosses over the very process by which men secure and exercise power individually and collectively through particular clubs. The opposite viewpoint, however, emphasizes that women experience empowerment as sex symbols who unfasten men's desires, as well as their wallets. Focusing on the possible celebrity, glamour, money, and entertainment that can be associated with striptease performance, these accounts gloss over the often hazardous and unpredictable nature of this industry. In between these poles, there are countless individual stories of strippers' lives that have been bettered and worsened by the sex work industry.

America is often heralded as the land of opportunity, a place where one can pull oneself up by the bootstraps. Within this American story, strip clubs occupy a distinct place. Revenue estimates for "adult entertainment" vary considerably, but, according to industry experts, consumers spend between $8 and $13 billion annually on various performances and products.[1] From that total, strip clubs are estimated to draw on average between $500,000 to over $5 million.[2] As men are the industry's primary consumers, these numbers provide evidence of their frequent patronage. In addition, despite variation, revenue estimates demonstrate the potential financial gains that lure women and men to work in this industry. We see in strip clubs both continuity and transformation in femininity and masculinity, in what it means to be a woman and a man, and in what it means to be desirable, connected, prosperous, and powerful. They are sites that preserve vestiges of the past (women's deference and service to, as well as violence from, men) and reveal trajectories for the future (open spaces for women's sexual expression and the explosion of paid emotional labor). Through this inquiry, we gain a mirror onto women's bodies: how they are molded and expressed, understood, prized, and devalued. In a setting like The Lion's Den that was designed by and for men, although men often experience power, there is also considerable evidence of dependence and frustration for both patrons and coworkers. As such, strip clubs are a bellwether for permanence and change in contemporary gendered understandings, organization, and performances.

Rather than being an exception, sex work is better understood as part of a dramatic contemporary expansion in paid care and services. Increasingly, both domestic and international women are hired to clean, comfort, and care for various individuals inside and outside of private homes.[3] Sex work is best conceptualized as part of this trend precisely because it moves emotional, psychological, physical, and sexual care for individuals out of private households and into the public marketplace.[4] As increasing forms of paid care become more integrated and accepted as realities of American culture, the false dichotomies between authentic/fake and paid/free forms of caring are exposed. As anyone who has experienced quality child and elder care knows, relationships between caregivers and clients can involve long-term intimacy. Similarly, relationships between strippers and patrons may involve companionship over many years.[5]

Within strip clubs, the process by which men and women wield, negotiate, and contest power on a local level has not been well explored or understood. In the research reported in this volume, I explored one club in detail to hear multiple perspectives through the voices of club owners, managers, bartenders, deejays, bouncers, doormen, strippers, cocktail waitresses, and patrons. Through everyday practices and personal narratives, I explored The Lion's Den through those who know it best. This volume takes readers inside the club to become familiar with its organization and to fundamentally understand how it works and for whom. Other researchers have focused on collections of individual stories, emphasizing interactions between strippers and patrons.[6] By contrast, this research looks at the multiple layers of The Lion's Den as an organization—its hierarchy, rules, and practices. The kinds of questions that become possible through organizational analysis allow me to situate individual narratives in a wider context: How does a person's story fit with the workplace practices of others? How are decisions made? Who follows through on club practices? And, when necessary, who enforces club rules? It is my hope that what emerges from studying a strip club as an organization is an intimate portrait of life and work in The Lion's Den.

Situating The Lion's Den
Railton

The Lion's Den is located in a place I call Railton, which is a typical northeastern town. It is largely rural, with suburban enclaves and a quaint town center. Local businesses, smaller mom-and-pop shops, and occasional strip malls, anchored by big-box stores, dot the area. Small family and larger factory farms stretch out alongside park and recreational areas. Given the town's small size, even its Chamber of Commerce emphasizes the region as a whole rather than focusing on Railton. The broader region contains a few medium-sized cities where many of the residents work in small-scale manufacturing, agriculture, education, and health care. Since Railton and other nearby towns did not benefit from the technology booms of larger New England cities, it has kept the remnants of its mill-town working-class past without the veneer or economic benefits of tourism. The majority of Railton's residents are white and earn modest incomes. In 2000, the median household earnings were just under $50k.[7] Lower housing costs serve to offset limited earnings—the average single-family house sold for less than $140k that same year.[8]

Far from a hub for the sex work industry, Railton and surrounding areas are not known for their sex-oriented businesses. There are no adult bookstores, and The Lion's Den is the only strip club in town. In the area as a whole, almost a half-dozen strip clubs and as many adult bookstores are scattered in nearby cities. In this region, you are as likely to find new burlesque, artistic, or gay and lesbian adult performances in mainstream dance clubs and bars as you are to find straight strip club fare in adult-zoned businesses. Nearby strip clubs all feature female performers for primarily male patrons. One club boasts multiple themed rooms for drinking champagne and purchasing private dances. It also includes fine furnishings and dining. Other local clubs range from simple décor to ramshackle. Two clubs are well known for being even more rundown than The Lion's Den. One of those clubs, Hotties, had its bathroom catch fire due to faulty wiring. The other, Backwoods, is small and has a nondescript bar, some nude pinup posters, and minimal lighting. Since the late 1990s, ownership of most of these clubs, including The Lion's Den, has merged into the hands of Players. Despite this consolidation and some physical and personnel changes, area strip clubs have maintained most of their original character.

Given The Lion's Den's relative isolation, Railton residents seemed to tolerate its presence. Unlike other local clubs that have been the subject of media attention as a result of drug busts, shootings, and the bathroom fire, The Lion's Den managed to stay out of the fray. There were no local news stories featuring the club during my participant observation. This lack of attention continued with the club's new owners, who took over operations in the spring of 2004. The absence of negative news stories is important because, despite being a legal industry, strip clubs often come under attack by community organizations that do not want sex work businesses in their backyards. Community standards have placed some constraints on this club. For example, the club's marquee featured only "The Lion's Den" in neon lights, rather than images of nude women or the common adult business symbols "XXX." Actual interventions by police on behalf of community members' complaints were nonexistent. Even with the lack of community backlash, The Lion's Den insulated itself through preventive measures. The club actively cultivated a reputation for complying with laws against physical contact between strippers and patrons to facilitate its market and ward off possible crackdowns.[9]

In addition, the club made regular financial contributions, including huge donations to local police and fire department fundraising drives. No doubt this money facilitated open communication between club management and local officers. The Lion's Den also maintained individual police connections by giving officers free drinks and special introductions to female workers when they visited the club.

Inside The Lion's Den

A neighborhood of single-family houses seems an unlikely place for a strip club, but as the zoning faded from residential to light industrial, a lone neon sign for The Lion's Den beckoned would-be patrons. Flanked by several brightly painted aluminum buildings and empty lots, some with parked tractor trailers, The Lion's Den sat apart from other entertainment-oriented businesses along a wooded street where a suburban neighborhood meets a light industrial zone. On one side of the club's parking lot, an old chain-link fence guarded haphazard piles of scrap construction items and pallets of building materials. On the opposite side and across the street sat empty lots. Surrounded by a blacktop parking lot, The Lion's Den's two-story tan building had housed a bar for as long as anyone could remember, although it had been a strip club for only the past thirty years or so. The entrance sported a single window coated with a dark material that reflects the viewer's image. The Lion's Den was typical of other strip bars in this region: it served liquor, had fully nude female dancers, and catered to predominantly male patrons. In its prime during the 1980s, The Lion's Den touted the region's longest stage and featured acts that included famous pornographic models and actors, drawing patrons from all over the East Coast. Over the next two decades, the club downsized its stage and, at the time of my research, hosted local performers for mostly local patrons.

Like many of the workers, those in attendance were generally white men with blue-collar jobs and high school educations. On weekends, one was likely to see more middle-class professionals and college students. In an industry that is mostly white,[10] race operated in privileged and exclusionary ways.[11] In the absence of other races, the club's whiteness was invisible (as whiteness is normatively depicted); no one referred to The Lion's Den as a "white" club.[12] Whiteness, and race more generally, became visible precisely when the occasional African American, Asian, or Latina dancer arrived onstage or when African American, Asian, or Latino men were in the audience. Though racial lines were at times crossed in the club, such interactions were few and far between, given the club demographics. More often club practices made it evident to people of color that their presence was less than fully welcomed.

On the economic and cultural spectrum of nearly 2,800 nude dancing venues nationwide,[13] The Lion's Den fell toward the lower end. The absence of a dress code and the presence of a $5–$7 door fee helped distinguish this site from more elite clubs in major cities, where business attire is suggested and door fees can be $20 or more. To ensure that patrons did not become free-loaders, a one-drink minimum guaranteed that those in attendance would spend nearly $10 upon entering the club. Entrance fees for those under twenty-one included one soda. Rather than the microbrewed or imported beers and restaurant-style dining that one might find in a higher-end club, The Lion's Den had a menu of mostly domestic beers and vending machine food. The Lion's Den was a workingman's strip club. Patron reviews from a popular strip club website underscore this characterization: "[The Lion's Den] makes no pretense of being a gentleman's club," "This place is a total dive," and "[The Lion's Den] has gone downhill."[14]

Employees, Strippers, and Management

As a local club, The Lion's Den drew employees from surrounding towns. Given the club's difficulty filling shifts, both male and female workers were often recruited by friends. Male employees were also drawn from the ranks of regular patrons. In both cases, familiarity acted as a proxy for trustwor-thiness, despite possible conflicts of interest, particularly for patrons who became employees and found themselves in a completely different relation-ship with the strippers who used to entertain them. This overlap between workers and patrons contributed toward an environment of informality in the club. Male friends and boyfriends who patronized the club were often referred by women. Strippers working within the club also recruited them.

In all, The Lion's Den employed approximately twenty men across four positions—bartenders, bouncers, doormen, and deejays. On weeknights, the club had one bartender, bouncer, deejay, and doorman working. On bus-ier nights and weekends, the club increased the number of bartenders and bouncers to two. Drawing on a sample of one-half of these workers, most were white and ranged in age from nineteen to fifty-six, with an average age of thirty-four. All but one had finished high school, and many had taken college courses. Only two held a bachelor's degree: the owner-manager and a deejay. Nearly equal thirds were single, married, or living with a partner (table 3 in appendix 1). Despite the small size of this sample, it is important to note its comparability with the region as a whole.[15] Racially, club workers replicated the majority-white makeup of this area.[16] A comparison of male workers' education with regional averages shows that slightly more had completed high school, while fewer had completed college.[17] Since the work requires little experience or formal education, it makes sense that most employees would have no more than a high school education.

In terms of relationship status, one-half of the men in the region were married, while more than one-third had never been married.[18] Though the percentage of single men was relatively comparable across the club sample and the broader region, the percentage of married men was lower for the club workers.[19] It is plausible that adult entertainment may attract men seeking interactions with women precisely because women are largely absent from their lives. Men who seek employment in the adult entertainment industry may also have difficulty maintaining intimate relationships with women, as reported by many of the men interviewed.

Male workers divided control over club operations, with the greatest authority in the hands of bartenders. In addition to their responsibilities behind the bar, the bartenders acted as middle managers, overseeing other workers. Particularly when the club's owner-manager was absent, bartenders resolved conflicts, determined the closing time for the club, and enforced club rules. Bouncers leaned against the walls wearing a disciplined scowl as they watched the goings-on in the club. They were charged with verbally or physically intervening if there were fights between patrons or between patrons and strippers. They periodically left their posts to referee any issues that arose or to chat briefly with other workers. With physically large men serving as bouncers, the threat of expulsion from the club often loomed, though, in truth, bouncers rarely exercised this authority. Seated near the club's main entrance, doormen collected entry fees and checked identification; they also acted as bouncers during daytime shifts. Deejays provided music and ambiance for the club while also coordinating strippers' performances. They decided who should be onstage at any given time to provide patrons with an array of women's body types and hair colors. In addition to announcing each performer before she took the stage, deejays kept track of when strippers arrived for their shifts, when they were due onstage for their next rotation, and what music each dancer preferred.

All of the male employees were paid a wage of between $4.50 and $8.50 an hour. The highest wages went to bartenders. Both bartenders and deejays also received cash tips; however, partly these were not tips they acquired directly. Rather, the tipping system in the club was gendered: strippers and cocktail waitresses were required to share a portion of their tips with male workers. Strippers provided deejays with at least $10, and cocktail waitresses tipped bartenders 20 percent or at least $20, each shift.

At any given time, about fifty women worked across three positions in the club: cocktail waitresses, housemoms, and strippers. Most were strippers. There were six to twelve strippers at a time on shift, with lower numbers working on weekdays and greater numbers on weekends. Waitresses worked alone on weeknights and in teams of two or three on weekends. The one club housemom visited the club weekly to schedule strippers' shifts. In the industry, housemoms are veteran dancers hired by the club and its strippers for their experience and knowledge. Typically they act as middle managers in clubs, negotiating on behalf of strippers with management and between the strippers themselves. In exchange for strippers' tips, housemoms provide counsel and offer spare resources like costumes and personal hygiene products. Because The Lion's Den's occasional housemom held none of the typical characteristics associated with this job, she was not included in the interview portion of this research.

Based on interviews with twenty-one women working in the club, I discovered that female workers were mostly white and ranged in age from eighteen to thirty-seven, with an average age of twenty-three. Cocktail waitresses in The Lion's Den were, on average, two years older. Most female workers had completed high school (74%), though percentages were lower than the regional average.[20] Many had attended college (44%), nearly the same rate found in national census data.[21] Cocktail waitresses had relatively more education than strippers; all had completed high school, and most had some college background. Overall, differences in education may reflect the club's proximity to a large number of colleges and universities. In some ways, women's intimate partnerships closely paralleled those of other women in the area, with more than one-third reporting they were single or living with a partner.[22] However, only two of the women interviewed were married, a much lower rate than reported by other women in the region.[23] Drawing on strippers' explanations, it appears that adult entertainment is disruptive to long-term intimate relationships.

As part of their work, strippers performed scheduled stage rotations of between fifteen minutes and a half hour, depending on the number of dancers in attendance. The remainder of strippers' time across their seven-hour shift was their own to solicit private or table dances, performances typically for one or a small number of patrons. Strippers' pay came from both of these two sources; they were not paid a salary from the club. Minimum earnings for private performances were considerably more than for stage work: $10–$20 rather than $1 per performance, respectively. Despite inflation, patrons tipped $1 for stage dances that typically lasted less than one song; they were dubbed "dollar dances." Though they were longer (typically one song), private and table dances differed little in their content, though private dances might contain more seclusion and conversation than stage dances.

Though a couple of the dancers had been stripping for more than a decade, this was not their goal when they first started in the industry. Previous research on stripping has found much variation in the reasons women give for entering this line of work. Among the issues discussed are financial motivations, such as participation in low-wage or dead-end jobs; sexual activity and physical development at relatively young ages; abuse and low self-esteem in childhood; growing up in divorced or mother-only households; early childhood independence; and the desire to be found attractive, as well as an interest in exhibitionism and entertainment.[24] The strippers in this study emphasized that they danced "for the money." Indeed, stripping pays more than most of the jobs participants held before their work in The Lion's Den. However, incomes also varied greatly from stripper to stripper, club to club, night to night, and season to season. Most often, the women at The Lion's Den were stripping to pay off debts, support children, and finance schooling. As Faith, a thirty-seven-year-old stripper, explained: "I do this because it's the only way I can make a living as a single mother and have time with my kids." In all, six of the twenty-one strippers interviewed were supporting children from their incomes.

Cocktail waitresses were paid a salary of $3.50 an hour plus tips to work seven-hour daytime or evening shifts. Cocktail waitresses spent much of their time selling and filling drink orders, as well as chatting with patrons. Over the course of a shift, depending on the number of customers present and the number of waitresses working, a cocktail waitress might walk miles around the club. In addition to serving drinks, cocktail waitresses oversaw alcohol consumption among patrons and strippers. While, in theory, waitresses could cut someone off from receiving alcohol, these judgments were subject to the review of bartenders who might override them.

Despite the club's high degree of informality, Steve, the club's owner-manager, struggled to maintain a level of seriousness around the work performed. In his mid-thirties, Steve often drew attention to his undergraduate business degree to distinguish himself from most of the people in the club, who had less education. While this one-upmanship may have been simple vanity, Steve appeared to have another purpose: motivating others to make The Lion's Den a thriving business once again. His best efforts included a mandatory meeting of all club performers and employees, as well as an *Employee/ Entertainer Handbook* that outlined the roles, responsibilities, and rules for each job within the club.[25] Despite such bursts of zeal, Steve was burning out. Much of his time within the club was spent in his office playing computer games and surfing the Internet. From this vantage he could watch through two cameras positioned above the club's cash registers. When Steve ventured into the main room, he often sat behind the bar, talked with the bartender, and aired complaints about strippers and other club workers.

A Tour of The Lion's Den

Parking behind the building, club workers entered through an unmarked back door. Once inside, walking past the beer coolers, the owner-manager's office, and the side entrance behind the service bar, they entered the main room of the club.

The main room featured an aging, parquet-covered stage that was often missing squares and one or more dance poles. Surrounding the U-shaped stage were small, black vinyl banquet chairs with protruding tufts of stuffing. The club walls were flat black with a large mirrored midsection. A once state-of-the-art lighting system hung from the center of the ceiling to provide spotlights, strobe lights, and smoke in an effort to frame the dancers' performances in magic. Beer signs and black lights also helped illuminate the room. Throughout the club, but especially near the service bar, the years of spilled liquor and beer created a sticky, flypaper effect on the carpet.

Patrons entered the club through a door in the front corner and passed by a doorman who checked identification and collected the cover charge ($7 for those aged eighteen to twenty, and $5 for those twenty-one and over). Upon entering The Lion's Den, the first thing patrons noticed was the center stage, set at the eye level of patrons seated at and around the stage. This was where the strippers performed their stage dances. Patrons over twenty-one occupied this main area of the club; younger patrons had to stay in an area cordoned off at the front end of the stage adjacent to the entrance called the "sandbox" because of its designation as underage seating. The sandbox was situated between the doorman and deejay booth, presumably for closer observation. The deejay booth was a tiny, elevated room that afforded the deejays a view of the entire club.

Floor Plan of The Lion's Den

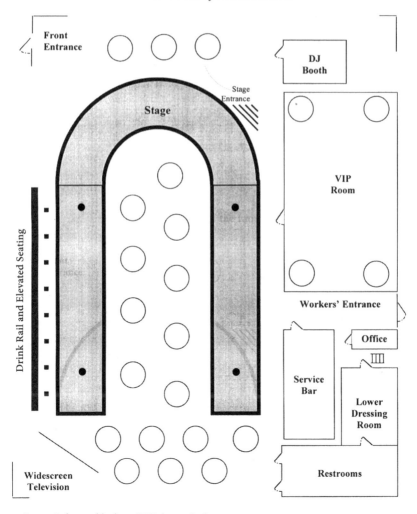

Large circles = table dance/VIP dance platforms

Black dots = strip poles

Stairs located between the Office and Lower Dressing Room

The VIP Room was a small private room next to the deejay booth with one door and a large picture window facing the main room of the club. The four private dance stations, located in each of the four corners, had a round, tan, particleboard platform for private dances; each platform was cordoned off by thick, black, vinyl cable from a pair of gray lounge chairs and a tall, pedestal drink table for the customer. Full-mirrored walls were decorated sparsely with drink special advertisements and pictures of nude women. Two artificial ficus trees rounded out the décor. Cocktail waitresses provided drinks (rather than patron self-service), so the small bar in the back left corner did not have any seating. It functioned more as a service bar where cocktail waitresses picked up orders from the bartender. Two sets of dressing rooms for the strippers were located on separate floors: one in a smaller downstairs room behind the service bar, and another in a larger room directly upstairs.

The club's interior had not changed until the summer of 2001, when the management remodeled. The main room's worn vinyl chairs were swapped for similar, but newer, gray cloth-covered seating. Throughout the main room of the club, the sticky, black carpet was replaced by one featuring primary colors in large geometric shapes over a black base. The middle of the room was enhanced by large, rounded, light-pink armchairs placed in paired or four-seat conversation groups around small, round, tan, particleboard platforms used for drinks and table dances. While these renovations improved the club's appearance, the changes only scratched the surface. In other sections, unsteady tables continued to make drink placement precarious. The dancers' dressing rooms retained the torn vinyl chairs and stained carpet. Chipped paint flaked off dressing tables and walls. Changes to the dancers' downstairs bathroom made the space available to any female patron, though hardly any were ever present. The men's bathroom remained unchanged, with its doorless toilet stall and the communal urinal that resembled a shallow horse trough.

A Typical Shift

Monday, Tuesday, and Wednesday, The Lion's Den opened at 7:00 PM; Thursday, Friday, and Saturday, it opened at noon. On Sundays, the club was closed. Despite the relatively late starting hours, strippers were frequently not on time for work. Dressed casually, often arriving in jeans and sweatshirts, dancers wheeled suitcases or duffle bags containing costumes, shoes, and toiletries to the dressing rooms. They added these items to things already housed in the rows of metal lockers positioned on the back walls of the two dressing rooms in the club. The upstairs dressing room was more social and frequently occupied by the in-house dancers (regular local dancers for the club). Traveling dancers or those looking for a quiet space to get ready often used the downstairs dressing room.

When The Lion's Den had trouble filling shifts, the owner-manager turned to contract dancers from a nearby state to work on weekends. Accompanied by a driver or their boss, this group of six to eight women worked their shifts at the club while spending the weekend in a nearby hotel. In response, the house girls feared the travelers were "stealing their money" or customers and initially shunned them. However, like all new dancers, the travelers became familiar over time, and their competitive edge, rooted in novelty, wore off, as did the resulting tensions with the house girls. While hostilities continued to flare up intermittently, they were limited to specific problems, without the generalized distrust in evidence when the traveling dancers first started working.

Once unpacked, the house girls and travelers chatted with other workers and readied themselves for the stage. Seated or standing in front of mirrors, they inspected their bodies, applied pancake makeup and deodorant, and covered themselves with lotion, glitter, and perfume. They applied eyeliner, mascara, and lipstick and brushed their hair or wigs. Though their underarm and pubic hair was often sparse and carefully manicured before each shift, they frequently used this opportunity for a last-minute shave. They swabbed between their legs with baby wipes and, depending on the time in their menstrual cycle, snipped and concealed tampon strings. Finally, they stepped into their costumes, frequently long, thin negligees over g-string underwear and bikini tops.

The dancers made conversation with each other while they awaited their call from the deejay. Some headed downstairs early to watch the evening's first performers. At this time, most of the strippers consumed their first of several alcoholic drinks. The exceptions were the traveling dancers, whose company had strict rules prohibiting alcohol consumption while at work. Their boss, who often sat in the club during their shifts, assured their compliance. Likewise, club employees (bouncers, bartenders, doormen, deejays, and cocktail waitresses) were not allowed to drink on shift.

While the strippers were getting ready, the cocktail waitresses began delivering the evening's first drinks, often to the dancers. Other early-shift tasks for the waitresses included setting up a "bank" of $20 from which they made change for any filled orders. This system made it the waitresses' responsibility to have bills tally correctly, since any mistakes came out of their own pockets.

Meanwhile, the bartenders were setting up the register, refilling beer coolers and liquor shelves, cutting limes and lemons for mixed drinks, and filling the dancers' first drink orders. By the front door, doormen and bouncers congregated, talking sports or gossiping over recent events.

The club was often quiet when it first opened, especially during dayshifts, when it better resembled a sports bar. The few strippers who worked daytime shifts were often late or absent. With the lack of dancers matching the lack of patrons, televised sports provided an important source of entertainment. With the music turned down, sporting events were broadcast from a large-screen television at the back of the club. While some dancers requested that the television be turned off, it often stayed on, providing a dizzying mix of competing sounds. The few men in attendance were typically regulars who visited the club often and desired more individualized attention from club workers. The rules around mandatory stage performances were often relaxed during the day, particularly when attendance was sparse. During these hours, dancers regularly sat on the stage or in seats by the television engaged in conversation rather than performing their stage rotations. Since the club often had trouble filling day shifts, the roles of dancer and waitress were sometimes one and the same.

In the early evening on weeknights, the club was thinly populated by a few regulars and a handful of other patrons. The main differences between the early evening and daytime shifts were the tendency to turn the television's volume down (though the set typically remained on) and to enforce the dancers' required stage rotations. Also during the early evening, club workers often pressed younger patrons into service to run errands, including fetching lemons or limes for the club's bartender or dinner for the strippers. The associated perks of running such errands often included free drinks and admission, as well as the title "gofer" and associated niceties (e.g., hearty thanks and friendly conversation).

A number of regular patrons were often in attendance. Jeff and his side-kick, Oscar, both white men in their mid fifties, were a rambunctious duo. They engaged in playful banter with strippers and cocktail waitresses and often referred to themselves as "the Odd Couple," emphasizing their similarities with the 1970s television sitcom of the same name. Joe, a white blue-collar worker in his early sixties, always showed up early, sitting in the corner near the service bar. He sat alone, drinking Budweiser from a glass with a dash of salt. Occasionally, a stripper or a waitress joined him briefly. Strippers learned quickly that Joe never bought dances and rarely bought anyone else a drink. Roger, a white blue-collar worker in his late fifties, often arrived early or hung around after his afternoon visit. Roger was the butt of many workers' jokes due to his considerable girth, sloppy dress, and huge square glasses. Many a night a bartender or another worker yelled out to nearby strippers or cocktail waitresses, "Don't get too close or be too nice—he'll get the wrong idea!"

Both management and patrons expected that female workers would be congenial and cater to men's needs within the context of services provided by the club. These needs included conversation and companionship, in addition to the more conventional tasks of delivering drinks and dances. Consider the following passage for cocktail waitresses from the *Employee/Entertainer Handbook*:

> Use yours and the customer's name. Reason—makes them feel like they are important to you, makes them feel like they belong to our "club," makes them feel like they're your "favorite" customer because you took the time to learn and remember their name. . . . Smile, Smile, Smile, I tried to explain the 10-5-1 rule at the last meeting, at 10 feet you make eye contact, at 5 feet smile, at 1 foot smile and say, "Hi"![26]

Management's clear demand for emotional labor on the part of cocktail waitresses made sense because the club's revenue depended largely on drink sales made by these women. Other female workers also advised each other about extending kindness to patrons since emotional labor can increase tips. As Kelly, a twenty-nine-year-old cocktail waitress and former stripper, explained: "You got to act and . . . make everybody happy and listen to all their problems. So I just do it because I make good money." The emotional labor performed by cocktail waitresses and strippers was similar in content to lots of women's work in service-oriented jobs. Like the flight attendants in sociologist Arlie Hochschild's influential study *The Managed Heart*,[27] cocktail waitresses and strippers in The Lion's Den were expected to cultivate feelings of friendliness to make customers feel "at home." Since the bar did not have its own seating, bartenders' ability to perform emotional labor (something that is conventionally associated with bartending) was greatly reduced. As such, emotional labor became gendered, and women performed the bulk of it.

As strippers climbed the horseshoe-shaped stage, they scanned the audience for patrons with tips. Patrons learned to set one bill, typically a dollar, on the stage to signal that a stripper's dance was desired. Patrons developed tricks to make their dollars stand out by folding them into football shaped triangles or little tents. In part, playing with money filled time between per-formances, as well as drew attention to the resources at hand. Patrons often sat themselves at the stage with dollar bills stacked inches high along a thin shelf that ran along the edge of the stage.

Other strip clubs in the state boast white-tableclothed dining rooms, leather furniture, flat-screen televisions, and upscale thematic cigar lounges and champagne rooms. Despite its relatively modest offerings, The Lion's Den found a way to specialize by crystallizing stripping to an essential compo-nent of its contemporary form: providing "spread shows," or eye-level views of women's genitals.[28] For these performances, the central horseshoe-shaped stage put a squatting dancer in the direct view of a seated patron. With lit-tle variation, performances at The Lion's Den took on an assembly line feel as dancers squatted for and chatted with patrons seated around the stage. Strippers' descriptions of men's reactions to the spread shows were fascinat-ing. Some men simply stared at women's genitals. Others perched forward in their seats for closer inspection; still others blew their breath or cigarette smoke onto the women's bodies, apparently designed to arouse the dancers and experience some physical interactions with them. Robin, a young, white stripper, explained she was disgusted "when a dirty man who's like sixty-five with no teeth is sitting there lookin' at you, and he blows his cigarette smoke on your crotch. You can be having the best day, and then something like that happens and you're just like—I've seen what nicotine does to my teeth, I don't want it doing anything to my crotch! What are you thinking?"

From Thursday to Saturday, the club filled up by around 10:00 PM. Patrons and dancers were drinking, talking, and milling about, creating a party atmo-sphere. The mixture of conversation and throbbing music was punctuated by the deejay's announcements of new dancers and repeated requests to "take care of our lovely entertainers and waitresses." The lights and cigarette smoke whirled around the club. Deejays orchestrated the music, sometimes taking requests but always getting final say on the night's fare. They often blared suggestive popular rock music, including Motley Crue's "Girls, Girls, Girls," Aerosmith's "Rag Doll," and Nine Inch Nails' "Closer" (with a chorus that echoes, "I want to fuck you like an animal"). •

Later in the evening or on weekend nights, the atmosphere became like a tailgate party, with patrons cheering as if for a sports team. They yelled for strippers to "take it off" and clamored for pole tricks. Pole tricks include doing the splits, climbing, and flipping upside down using long white poles that extend halfway to the ceiling at four points on the stage (see diagram). While pole tricks were crowd pleasers, most strippers simply hooked the poles in the crook of their elbow and spun around, scoping out the room. This may have been due, at least in part, to lack of skill or interest, but it was also because the poles often wobbled or might even be missing entirely, making pole tricks hazardous or impossible.

While spread shows were the club's centerpiece, scripted nude or seminude stage performances framed them. These performances included varying degrees of verbal interaction, from brief conversation to erotic storytelling. Strippers would lean forward and whisper directly into patrons' ears or speak loudly to be heard over the music. Strippers performed from a number of typical positions, including crouching, sitting, or lying on the stage. They modified these movements by lifting a leg, gyrating back and forth, or spanking themselves. Onstage, a stripper might whisper in a patron's ear during a dance to entice his purchase of a private performance. Offstage, dancers walked the club in search of private dances or companionship that might be accompanied by tips or free drinks. Since either party could initiate exchanges, patrons also requested dances. At times, dancers and patrons wooed each other with conversation, flirtation, and a few drinks before moving on to a private dance, making the club feel like a singles bar. On slower nights, strippers watched each other perform or sat together and complained about the lack of tips.

"Closing Time" began to play when it was nearly 2:00 AM. At the end of a shift, the smell of tobacco, alcohol, and perfume infused the club and its inhabitants. After the patrons left, the owner-manager or bartender emerged with bags to collect money from each of the registers. Strippers were often downstairs saying goodbye to patrons or making after-work plans. During this time, more often than not, dancers needed multiple reminders from the deejay to pack it up for the night. Bartenders handed out free beers to the other male workers and cocktail waitresses, who, unlike strippers, were not allowed to drink on shift. Strippers could purchase drinks before the bar closed, but they did not receive free drinks from the club. The club assumed strippers should be spending this time getting dressed and readied for home. Nearly all club employees drank during cleanup. As things wound down, workers chatted with each other about their night, how much money they made, the patrons in attendance, and any unusual events. Cocktail waitresses busily cleared drinks and ashtrays, while the deejay turned up the house lights and shut down the music. The bartender washed glasses, stocked beer coolers, and replaced empty bottles of liquor. After cleanup, the bartender and cocktail waitresses propped themselves near the bar to count their tips. On a good night, tips might total $120–$140 for cocktail waitresses and $70–$100 for bartenders. Both bartenders and cocktail waitresses also earned hourly wages from the club (of $8.50 and $3.50, respectively). Cocktail waitresses further supplemented bartenders' earnings by sharing their own tips, typically $20 a shift.

Laboring under the weight of bags crammed with clothing, shoes, and makeup, strippers thundered down the stairs from the upper dressing room. Though it would have been nearly impossible for any stripper to sneak out, the deejay often sat near the door to the employee entrance to be sure he received his cut of their night's tips. After the money changed hands, most female workers waited for a bartender or bouncer to walk them out to their car or at least watch them leave from the back doorway. Stories of female workers who were followed home from this and other clubs abound. While some female workers left in groups, others ignored club expectations and departed without an escort, taking the risk of entering the parking lot alone, often with a wad of cash in hand.

At the end of the evening, workers' hopes of big payoffs were either realized or dashed. Despite many nights of marginal earnings, the power of a profitable night held sway over all workers. For example, Summer, a twenty-year-old stripper, described her monetary expectations this way: "Some nights I make good money, like $400, and if I'd only done this and this I could have made more money." It is this potential for more—more income but also more power, more self-esteem, more celebrity—that keeps clubs in business and workers coming back. Strip clubs are often considered places of fantasy for patrons; the same could be said for workers, as many of their goals are often within reach for only a short time. Nevertheless, it was the possibility that men would be valued for their authority, women would be adored and rewarded, and patrons would experience their desires that fueled the club's gendered organization.

Worker, stripper, and patron ideals depended on overlapping organizational aspects of the club: (1) work roles, authority, and interactions; (2) club norms; and (3) the club's formal work rules.[29] Male coworkers continually asserted their influence over female workers through their work routines. They also used gender and sexuality stereotypes as ways to capitalize on their dominance. Given the club's formal work rules, there was little to inhibit or counterbalance male workers' authority. Women, as cocktail waitresses and strippers, hoped to gain both financial and emotional rewards from their work. Especially over time, this compensation was uneven and often declined, alongside mounting struggles to manage the burdens of stripping labor.[30] Patrons sought to experience themselves as desirable, connected, and

powerful. While their door fees, drink purchases, and tips to female workers afforded patrons access to erotic performance, alongside kindness from
female workers, this relationship was an exchange based on their ability to
pay and subject to interpretations of counterfeit intimacy.[31] The extent to
which patrons' interactions with strippers and other club workers were sat-
isfying largely depended on the patron's wants and needs, as well as his relationship with the club. As club workers', strippers', and patrons' narratives
demonstrate, strip clubs often hold out unfulfilled promises.

Stripping Strip Club Work

Like most strip clubs (and sex work) in the United States, The Lion's Den
featured female performers for primarily male patrons. A revolving number
of strippers rotated in and out; most did not remain for long. Besides being
financially advantageous to be a new face, The Lion's Den offered few incen-
tives for strippers to commit to long-term service and, assuming high turnover, demonstrated little value in its strippers. In an industry built on the
importance of new recruits, necessary to satisfy audiences' appetites for new
products, it is easy to discern how and why women are considered expendable. Take, for example, the pornography industry, with its emphasis on variety, churning out thousands of films a year that feature new and younger
actors. Strippers are subject to a similar reality by audiences who expect a
perpetual influx of young women. Common sex worker stereotypes also
emphasize their marginality. Sex workers are often portrayed as drug addicts,
vectors of disease, and, by definition, "bad girls"—in other words, not the
kind of women men should "bring home to their mothers." Male coworkers,
patrons, management, and the strippers themselves mobilize these stereotypes to undermine strippers' importance and emphasize their disposability.
Strippers and other sex workers often lack control over the context in
which their labor is performed. Since the early 1980s, sex industry scholars
have provided considerable documentation of third-party control over the
sex industry.[32] This constitutes a shift from the nineteenth century, when
women's work in prostitution was largely "unencumbered by third parties,"
like pimps or madams.[33] Today, the U.S. exception to third-party strip club
control is The Lusty Lady theater, a worker-owned collective peep show in
San Francisco, a well-known club that is often cited by sex work scholars.
The Lusty Lady has a sister club in Seattle that was under the same ownership until 2003, when the San Francisco workers purchased their club (www.
lustyladysf.com). Precisely because San Francisco's female employees own

The Lusty Lady, it stands in stark contrast to most other clubs in the industry. Within sex work, third-party control is largely gendered. Despite media attention on high-profile madams like Heidi Fleiss and CEOs like Hugh Hefner's daughter, Christie Hefner, most sex work businesses are owned and run by men.[34] Similarly, The Lion's Den was owned and operated by Steve, who also acted as the club's manager. The club's personnel included a typical cast of workers—bartenders, bouncers, deejays, doormen, and cocktail waitresses—who performed customary tasks. During my time in The Lion's Den, there were no roles available to women that broadened women's authority in the club, since housemoms there handled only stripper scheduling rather than a wider range of tasks as in other clubs.

In some ways, The Lion's Den was conventional. In this context, music and stripping were supplemented by televised sports events, a strip club staple. For this entertainment, strip club patrons in The Lion's Den, as in most other clubs, paid inflated alcohol prices and door fees (relative to nonstripping bars), which provided the bulk of the club's revenue. Two central features distinguished The Lion's Den from other strip clubs. First, it was once a high-end club with a state-of-the-art sound and light system and a well-known reputation in the region, attracting feature performers and hundreds of patrons. Since its heyday in the 1980s, the club had fallen on hard times. Besides small cosmetic maintenance, the club remained largely untouched. It now had more in common with other "dive" clubs than it did with elite competitors. Second, under Steve's direction, The Lion's Den maintained a strict division of labor by gender. In practice, this division of labor put power in the hands of men. Men were employed exclusively in positions with authority as managers, bouncers, bartenders, and deejays. Women's jobs—as strippers, cocktail waitresses, and housemoms—had little, if any, formal influence.

In other strip clubs, women may not be excluded from positions as managers, bartenders, and deejays, jobs that many times (though not always) carry some influence over operations. Strippers may also enjoy more authority over their performances by supplying or choosing their own music and developing creative routines with elaborate costumes and props, aspects that were absent from stripping labor in The Lion's Den. The broader sex industry, however, generally puts power in the hands of men. In prostitution, there are far greater numbers of pimps than there are madams. Across forms of sex work, authority is rarely assigned to female sex workers' jobs. This is particularly the case for stripping, where most dancers work as independent contractors and clubs avoid the social and economic benefits and obligations of employment.[35] This general disempowerment of female sex workers is what makes the often-mentioned Lusty Lady theater in San Francisco such an unusual and noteworthy business for being the nation's first unionized and, later, worker-owned peep show.

Given The Lusty Lady's exceptional status, let me say a bit more about it. The Lusty Lady is one of a kind. Often referred to as a strip club, it is really a peep show in which glass walls separate patrons from performers. Patrons view strippers through tiny rooms with doors instead of in open rooms. Patrons' tips are collected through cash machines. Rather than competing for tips, strippers' earnings are distributed based on a dancer's length of employment. Though some conversation is possible over the music and through the glass, it is not a primary part of strippers' onstage performances. The Lusty Lady theater has been the subject of numerous in-depth investigations throughout its transformations since the late 1990s.[36] After dancers in The Lusty Lady learned that patrons were filming them through one-way mirrors in the viewing booths, they organized to change club practices. After a protracted struggle, the strippers won representation with the Service Employees International Union in 1997.[37] In 2003, the peep show made news again when workers assumed ownership of the club.[38] Strippers, who are now co-owners in the collective, make club rules. As a result of this history, The Lusty Lady is an unusually safe and egalitarian place to work.

By contrast to The Lusty Lady, many other sex work contexts, from street prostitution to pornographic filmmaking, contain unsafe working conditions.[39] It is the convergence of a strict division of labor by gender, the consolidation of authority into the hands of men, and the club's disrepair that made The Lion's Den a particularly dangerous environment for women. Drawing on studies of gendered organizational theory,[40] these factors constitute what I call *gendered organizational jeopardy*. Understanding how gendered organizational jeopardy becomes normalized and even expected is important if we are to comprehend how inequalities and resulting dangers operated in this workplace.

Gendered outcomes in the club may at first seem illogical. For example, strippers were both adored and stigmatized, valued and devalued as physical sexual beings, and they simultaneously received the greatest incomes and held the least power compared with other club workers. These contradictory outcomes are part of what sociologist Judith Lorber calls a "paradox" of gender. As she points out, "much of what we take for granted about gender and its causes and effects either does not hold up or can be explained differently."[41] What we see in The Lion's Den is a manifestation of larger cultural processes and arrangements that position women in the world in relation to what their bodies offer to men. Few (if any) women and girls are exempt from cultural pressures to be attractive, thin, and desirable. Critiques of beauty, diet, and fashion industries have spoken volumes about the harmful effects these external and internal expectations have on girls and women, leading to low self-esteem, depression, and eating disorders.[42] These are the gendered realities of our time, not just for strippers but for all girls and women. When the pressures of the beauty myth collide with a rigid division of labor between men and women, we find the gendered organizational jeopardy reflected within the experiences and stories I outline in this book. In the pages that follow, I explore these gendered contradictions as they emerged at The Lion's Den.

Overview of the Book

In chapter 1, I situate this book within a broader cultural, legal, and socio-historical framework, elaborating on how this research was conducted and my role as a researcher. Building from a gendered organization-of-work perspective, in chapter 2, I demonstrate how strippers were stigmatized, excluded from positions of authority, and put in danger by club rules and practices. Rather than simply the isolated acts of disgruntled workers, women's exclusion and mistreatment were systematic in the club. Indeed, they were woven into the text of the owner-manager's *Employee/Entertainer Handbook,* his blueprint for how the club should operate. In chapter 3, I show patrons' demands for affirmation and group affiliation, as well as the deeply rooted aggression and violence they exhibited toward women. The resulting emotional and physical burdens on strippers did not end there. Workers' and management's lax safety standards and disdain for strippers compounded the risks strippers faced from all men in the club. In chapter 4, I describe the way the gendered organization of work and men's behaviors took a toll on strippers. Strippers detailed a range of (often unsuccessful) strategies and coping mechanisms for negotiating their work. In chapter 5, I explore the economic contradictions strippers faced in the club. Examining the club's organizational form, I show that strippers, in contrast with other workers, experience both economic autonomy and dependence, one of many gender paradoxes associated with stripping work.

After completing my participant observation in The Lion's Den, I frequently wondered what happened to the club and research participants outlined in these pages. To further study The Lion's Den, I made a virtual reentry four years later by examining a popular strip club website's discussion board pertaining to the club. The postscript, "The Lion's Den, 2005–2006," draws on these new data to chart changes in the club and continued troubles for strippers.

Further details on my methodology are in appendix 1. The table in appendix 1 outlines each participant's socioeconomic information. In appendix 2, I briefly describe each participant's entrance into The Lion's Den, as well as the consequences of their work and patronage. I encourage readers to explore this appendix to learn more about Steve, Frank, Roxanne, Faith, and others.

I visited my first two strip clubs in 1993, over a decade and a half ago. Both were rather small, rundown places in central Ohio. The first setting was steeped in dreariness and featured a drunken dancer staggering around the stage. The second club had a vintage look, complete with musty velvet draperies and a small, wooden, spotlighted stage with a tall, brass dance pole. The place was shabby, but it showcased a woman performing something more reminiscent of Cirque de Soleil than striptease. Little did I know then how much these two examples had to say about stripping labor. Reminiscent of these images, within the pages of this book there is much sadness; however, there are also glimmers of strength and talent.

Studying Strip Club Work

Context and Perspective

Working as a cocktail waitress, I felt like Gloria Steinem going undercover as a Playboy bunny—I was playing hostess in the ultimate male playground.[1] I understood the drudgery and physical labor associated with waitressing, even before reading Steinem's famous firsthand account. Less than two months on the job, I wrote in my field notes that I left work "pickled with cigarette smoke, sticky from alcohol and Windex, and physically and mentally exhausted." Remembering drink orders and patrons' names alongside research questions and observations fully consumed my mind. My body ached from walking, lifting, bending, and carrying. Beyond the physical and mental work of waitressing, I knew strip clubs accentuated the burdens all waitresses may face, as Steinem's bunny shift description details: "Somehow the usual tail pullings and propositions and pinching and oogling seemed all the more depressing when, outside this windowless room of perpetual night, the sun was shining."[2] The Lion's Den was also always shrouded in darkness and hazy smoke. Another cocktail waitress described the club as a "cave" due to the absence of natural light and fresh air.

As in Steinem's experience, my interactions with men were rife with come-ons and sexual overtones. Comments about my body and my looks, as well as requests for clothing removal, were standard fare. Men would invite me home or out on dates. By far the most common remark was, "You should be onstage!" The repetition normalized these exchanges for me and other female workers. This was, after all, a strip club. Instead of understanding these statements as distinct from men's verbal and physical aggression, however, we should consider more fully the particular setting where they occurred. By doing so we can locate these come-ons in relationship to men's and women's practices in clubs, as well as the broader character of strip club work. Behind patrons' comments loomed the assumption that women working in strip clubs were ready to comply, were resisting the urge to comply, or could be pressured to comply. As explored in later chapters, seemingly innocuous and expected comments like those described here are part of a larger set of club rules and practices that systematically objectify and marginalize women.

Before working in the club, I was keenly aware of the abuses men brought on female workers, particularly in the sex work industry. I read about them in Steinem's and others' firsthand accounts of sex work research. For example, sociologist Eleanor Miller, in her book *Street Women,* recounted intimidation and fear, particularly when confronted with male prisoners and pimps.[3] At one point during Miller's research on female hustlers, she had her car's tires slashed. Miller's and others' sense of danger stuck with me throughout my research. Fortunately, my concerns over my personal safety were not realized, though I did have my car scratched by someone's keys while I was working. Many of the women I worked with were not as lucky, as their stories will describe.

Given these considerations, I faced many questions about how to study a strip club. Should I observe? conduct interviews? participate? Each method entailed certain risks for my physical and emotional safety. If I chose to participate, I would embody the research, rather than relying on secondhand accounts. In the end, the need to acquire information through a variety of means proved compelling. Methodologically speaking, observations, interviews, and participation each provided a way of seeing and not seeing. For example, I wanted information not easily observed, like patrons' self-concepts, strippers' identity management, and coworkers' attitudes toward strippers, so observations alone would not suffice. Similarly, interviews provided detailed individual information, but only when they were combined with observations and participation could I corroborate and contextualize people's stories. Like lots of ethnographers, researchers who study groups of people and places from the inside out, I knew that firsthand experience with strip club work combined with observations and in-depth interviews would provide a treasure trove of information. Given my deliberations, it should come as no surprise that a variety of different approaches have emerged for investigating places like The Lion's Den. Several authors, in particular, have shaped recent methods of inquiry.

Researching Sexual Subcultures

Sexual subcultures have long fascinated sociologists. Over the past several decades, sex researchers have reasoned different ways for studying groups that may be secretive, dangerous, and uncooperative to outsiders. Access has been a key concern for them. While there have been many engaged projects since the 1970s, here I focus on three sociologists' work to highlight their particular standpoints and strategies.[4] The examination of these authors and their books contextualizes this and other research on places where "sex" in its many different forms is offered and exchanged. Their research creates a framework for examining other entries into the field, modes of connection, and the relationship between fieldwork, access, and findings.

In 1970, Laud Humphreys published *Tearoom Trade*, his now infamous study of men's impersonal sex with other men in public parks. Humphreys wanted the world to better understand closeted homosexuality and reduce the stigma associated with same-sex sexual practices. Widely criticized for his unwitting participants' lack of informed consent, Humphreys brought us into a previously hidden world through observations and surveys. In effect, he became an insider serving as a watch queen, or lookout, for tearoom participants. His emphasis was on the men who made use of the "tearooms" rather than those we might consider sex workers. As a participant observer, Humphreys was able to study tearoom practices in detail, but how could he find out more about the men outside of the tearoom? As a watch queen, he was able to record participants' license plate numbers. With the help of a local motor vehicles department, he got access to tearoom participants' addresses. After changing his appearance, he approached these men at home with a health-related study. As a result of these covert actions, Humphreys suggested that he was able to uncover otherwise unavailable information about the more than fifty largely middle-class Catholic married men purchasing anonymous sex from other men. However, the deception of his participants makes his study a ubiquitous lesson in research ethics.

In 1986, Eleanor Miller produced the before-mentioned *Street Women*, a study of prostitution and other forms of street hustling. An outsider, Miller gained access to Chicago street women through a bar job, courthouse visits, and interviews with halfway house residents and prison inmates. She explains that her initial fascination with street women came while she was working in a local Chicago bar. After seeing some female street hustlers, she began to question then-current notions about women and crime. One argument posed that the Women's Movement and women's liberation had opened up space for women to participate more fully in not just formal but informal economies as well. However, the women Miller met hardly seemed liberated; rather, they seemed to be making ends meet under duress. These initial experiences paved the way for her fieldwork in homes and area businesses. Early contacts familiarized her with the language and practices of street women and enabled her to snowball sample and recruit over sixty participants.

Miller describes being an accepted outsider who did not share the same background, race, or dialect of those she studied. She connected with her participants through demonstrated interest and professionalism over shared food and conversation. Participants even occasionally made her the butt of their jokes. These relationships were nevertheless fragile because of the difficult circumstances under which these women lived. Despite these differences, Miller's access to information, especially regarding illegal work, makes her ethnography compelling. Drawing on both feminist and crime and deviance perspectives, Miller was able to consider the entirety of street hustlers' lives rather than reducing them to their illegal activities.

In 1997, Wendy Chapkis's *Live Sex Acts* ushered in a new approach to sex worker research by situating the author as both an outsider and an insider. As a feminist researcher, Chapkis was familiar with the "sex wars" debates over whether strippers, prostitutes, and pornography actresses are empowered or oppressed through their work. She sought to address this polarizing debate through the voices of nearly two-dozen sex workers from the United States and abroad. Based on their reports of difficult working conditions, she argued for decriminalization and greater attention to context. To understand sex work as a consumer, she later decided to couple this study with participation. Embodying her research, she paid for and participated in Annie Sprinkle's co-taught sexual massage class. The class instructed participants in various sensuous massage techniques they would later perform on other women. Placing herself on the purchasing end, Chapkis concluded, "I strongly suspected I would have liked the whole experience more if I had been paid for it."[5] With this ending, Chapkis foreshadowed recent books by stripping veterans who have examined various facets of the industry from the inside.[6]

Authors like Humphreys, Miller, and Chapkis all situate themselves differently with regard to their "insiderness" and "outsiderness."[7] For ethnographic research, it is common to elaborate on one's biography so readers can understand the researcher's relationship with her or his subject. While this is a staple of ethnography, it is also paramount to sex work research. The study of sex frequently prompts intimate questions regarding a researcher's identity and involvement. On the one hand, these questions reflect frequent connections between biography and research. Researchers often study facets of society to which they have an intimate connection. On the other hand, however, they reflect titillation that is peculiar to sex work research and indicate both our fascination and discomfort with the study of sex and sexuality. Humphreys, Miller, and Chapkis each provide the reader with a different perspective in terms of their identity, connection, and involvement. Though

Humphreys strongly defended his work, his approach has not been looked on favorably over time. The approaches of Miller and Chapkis, however, are emblematic of current research strategies. Most research on stripping adopts some combination of observation, participant observation, and interviews.

The strategy I adopted borrows from both Miller and Chapkis. I was, in part, an outsider with a professional relationship to those I met and interviewed, much like Miller. However, as a cocktail waitress, I became a colleague and comrade through my participation, much like Chapkis. This combination of participation, observation, and in-depth interviewing provides three central components of this research. My access would have been greatly limited had I not worked within the club I studied, since strangers to The Lion's Den were not trusted. I add to these methods a fourth component, an examination of associated texts, in particular, the club's *Employee/Entertainer Handbook* and online posts to a discussion board associated with The Lion's Den, Strip Club List.[8] Bringing together these four resources produces what I hope is a nuanced organizational analysis of The Lion's Den.

Stripping in Popular Representations

Stripping over Time

Stripping, with its simultaneous cultural attraction and repulsion, has its ancestry in burlesque, a popular form of entertainment that had its U.S. heyday in the mid-nineteenth through the early twentieth centuries. Today, burlesque is commonly associated with twentieth-century striptease, or the seductive removal of clothing. However, the content of striptease performances and the amount of nudity has varied over the years. Historian Mark Caldwell explains that nudity may have largely been in the eye of the beholder: "Systematic stripping down to bare flesh didn't become an inevitable burlesque feature until the 1920s," and even then performers often flashed body parts covered with pasties, g-strings disguised as pubic hair, or bodies caked with heavy white stage makeup.[9]

During the early to mid-nineteenth century, burlesque consisted of comedy, political satire, and striptease dancing that drew primarily middle-class and working-class audiences.[10] Notable acts included Lydia Thompson and her troupe, the Beautiful Blondes, who performed comedic operas and played dominant roles clad in costumes that revealed flesh-colored tights, a spectacle for the times. Women adopted men's and women's roles with strong sexual overtones, even performing as sexual aggressors in parodies of well-known and lesser-known plays and musicals, like *Ixion* and the adaptation of *Ben Hur* into *Bend Her*.[11] This combination of women's roles and dress was radical relative to mainstream conceptions of femininity. This more permissive cultural climate changed in the later nineteenth and early twentieth centuries, however, and burlesque performance lost favor with the middle class, a transformation that took place as women became regular audience members. The simultaneous onstage presence of bawdy performers like Lydia Thompson clashed with the offstage presence of "respectable" middle-class women. Both government and church officials led the rallying cry against burlesque.[12] Cultural historian Robert C. Allen argues that along with this change of audience came a change in performance.[13] Burlesque morphed into something akin to the stripping of today, with more emphasis on women's bodies and less on speaking or theatrical skill. This change meant women were seen but not heard.[14]

The most familiar aspect of burlesque—the cooch, hootchy-kootchy, or belly dance—debuted in the United States during the Chicago World's Columbian Exposition in 1893.[15] The Columbian Exposition was a world's fair featuring a number of different venues. Along what was called the Midway Plaisance, there were concessions and sideshows organized thematically and geographically as world venues. The Egyptian and Algerian exhibits featured women in baggy pants, short tops, and sometimes bare midriffs who belly danced for throngs of fairgoers.[16] Researcher Lucinda Jarrett describes:

> In the theater of the "Street of Cairo" the six belly dancers comprised three Algerians, one Syrian, one Turk and one handkerchief dancer of unknown racial origin. The racial difference of the dancers [to the white onlookers] meant that they were watched as an exotic attraction and not as individuals with names.[17]

Audience reception of the cooch dance, like later burlesque, was mixed. Fair attendees flocked to performances; Jarrett reports, "in the first six months the fair drew between 25 and 39 million visitors who went straight for the Street of Cairo."[18] Politicians and reporters railed against the shows as obscene.[19] Mark McDonald, in a *San Francisco Chronicle* article from the summer of 1893, lamented, "Their dance was the most vulgar thing I have ever seen. . . . When one of those women commenced to wriggle herself I was amazed for a moment, but the feeling soon gave way to disgust."[20]

The arrival of the cooch dance is credited with giving rise to modern-day stripping.[21] Following the close of the Columbian Exposition, the cooch dance was picked up in New York burlesque performances. Theaters owned by the Minsky Brothers began to feature scantily clad women per-forming cooch and shimmy dances on runway-like stages.[22] The runway was engineered for completely practical reasons. The Minskys' theaters were former movie houses with associated dim lighting, and stage con-struction was less expensive than wiring for new lights.[23] Morton Minsky described club performances "as definitely 'Not a Family Show!' Burlesque as practiced here, was 'a popular and inexpensive form of entertainment whose basic ingredients were girls, gags, and music.' And in that order."[24] Alongside men's venues in New York (like Minskys'), tamer versions of burlesque also appeared in East Side variety shows.[25] However, it was the Minsky brothers who "offered even more daring burlesque shows until they were put out of business by the license commissioner" under Mayor Fiorello H. LaGuardia.[26] Despite the Minsky brothers' best efforts, New York was to be a difficult place for burlesque for years to come, due to a series of legal battles.[27]

The ebb and flow of striptease performances and venues continued over the next several decades across the United States. During the 1940s, "the war buoyed the burlesque industry and striptease. The influx of men in port cities and army bases in the Midwest created a demand for strip shows."[28] Dur-ing the 1950s, mainstream American culture recoiled from stripping because "popular culture presented the idea of aggressive female desire—which strip-tease often suggested—as hostile."[29] The 1960s ushered in a new era with the creation of venues for suggestive and nude female performance such as Hugh Hefner's Playboy Club in Chicago and the Condor Club in San Francisco. Simultaneously, many of the old burlesque venues were closing their doors. Rachel Shteir explains:

> For the last decade, none of the twenty or so decrepit grind theatres across the country had survived by simply featuring striptease. Forced to com-pete with X-rated movies, topless bars, and an increasing number of men's magazines, burlesque theatres were scrambling to add 16-millimeter adult movies and peep shows, as well as continuing to hire a few strippers and aging comics.[30]

As the mix of proliferating pornographic films and magazines, peep shows, and sex shows continued through the 1980s, stripping underwent another set of dramatic changes. Because of the increasing availability of more-explicit media and entertainment materials, clubs were under increasing pressure to compete, creating the space for topless and bottomless performances.[31] At the same time, striptease, long performed by women, began to be performed by men like the Chippendales.[32] As stripping became more closely associated and in direct competition with other forms of sex work, it has maintained its emphasis on closeup nude or semi-nude performance.[33]

Legal Context

Although all sex work has historically been subject to legal and social debates, the particular context of stripping has placed it in an unusual position relative to other types of sex work. In contrast to prostitution, which falls under criminal codes, laws pertaining to stripping fall under commercial statutes, most specifically those governing the zoning of businesses and the distribution, sale, and consumption of alcohol.[34] These laws create and maintain an important and implied distinction between various forms of sex work based on legal or illegal location. In effect, the state creates a hierarchy in which stripping is privileged over prostitution through its status as a commercial business enterprise and a legal form of work. Statutes vary from state to state regarding the legality of alcohol consumption and amounts of nudity (i.e., topless versus fully nude performance).

The physical zoning of clubs into particular parts of towns or cites makes this work, though legal, appear not quite legitimate. Consider, for example, the Combat Zone in Boston, the Sunset Strip in Los Angeles, the Tenderloin in San Francisco, or the 8 Mile Road in Detroit. Red-light districts are commonly associated with prostitution, as in Amsterdam, Netherlands, perhaps the most famous red-light district in the world. As Michel Foucault argues, Western cultures have historically created segregated spaces for *illegitimate* sexualities.[35] In other words, sex work is tolerated as long as it remains reasonably separated from mainstream life. Urban renewal projects are often associated with the re-creation and movement of these segregated spaces. For example, the Combat Zone in Boston was created through the transformation of Scollay Square into Government Center, which displaced burlesque theatres like the Old Howard.[36] U.S. Supreme Court decisions have further separated adult entertainment through zoning laws that support a city's ability to consolidate or scatter adult businesses, as well as forbid their location anywhere proximate to homes, places for children, and places of worship.[37]

In addition to the role of zoning's oversight, sex-oriented businesses are governed by laws regulating the labor performed in strip clubs, including amounts of nudity, physical proximity, and contact between strippers and patrons, as well as whether alcohol consumption is permitted. These laws may vary considerably from city to city, resulting in a plethora of local ordinances. Given the specificity of the laws to various locations, in this overview the focus is on federal cases that affect the entire industry. Several Supreme Court cases dating back to the early 1970s have shaped the current status of stripping under federal law. First Amendment protection has been at stake in all of these cases. Namely, does nude performance constitute protected expression? The Supreme Court's answer is a moderated "yes." The Supreme Court has consistently protected nude dance, albeit with lots of ambiguity, disagreement, and possibilities for legal challenges and constraints.

Public and governmental fears regarding secondary effects—seen as related to adult businesses—loom like a specter over nude-dancing debates. Secondary effects include nearby property devaluation, the creation of red-light districts that concentrate sex-oriented businesses, and the potential for related illegal activities like prostitution and illicit drug use. One of the first cases, *California v. LaRue* (1972), regulated both alcohol use and the content of strip club performances. In this case, the California Department of Alcohol and Beverage Control aimed to render full nudity and sex performances (or the acting out of such, including sexual touching of one's own body) illegal. These performances were seen as related to other illegal activities, like prostitution, illicit drug use, and alcoholism. The Supreme Court agreed with their decision (6–3). This early case outlines much of the terrain of continued litigation.

In two more-recent cases, *Barnes v. Glen Theatre, Inc.* (1991) and *City of Erie v. Pap's A.M.* (2000), the Supreme Court upheld that cities can outlaw fully nude dance based on concerns regarding public moral standards and fears regarding secondary effects. *Barnes* involved Indiana club owners and dancers who sought to perform fully nude in the Kitty Kat Lounge and Glen Theatre. Indiana's public-indecency law prohibited fully nude performance and required strippers to cover their breasts and genitals.[38] After flip-flopping outcomes in the lower courts, the Supreme Court's 5–4 decision protected Indiana's right to regulate the amount of nudity permitted in striptease performances.[39] *City of Erie* involved a comparable Pennsylvania law that banned public nudity. In this case, the owner of Kandyland sought to overturn Pennsylvania's prohibition of fully nude performance. As in *Barnes*, the Supreme Court's 6–3 ruling supported Pennsylvania's requirement that strippers cover their breasts and genitals. Drawing common threads from the early case in California, both Indiana and Pennsylvania laws emphasize the secondary effects at stake in each state's decision.

The Supreme Court in these cases (and others) has supported a state's decision to regulate the content of nude performance, as well as the possibilities of associated negative effects. First Amendment activists and those seeking to protect nude dancing fear that the cumulative weight of these decisions could eventually eradicate nude dance and other forms of erotic or artistic expression.[40] The Court has been clear through the cases outlined here that some (though not all) of striptease content is protected under law. The Court specifically addressed the eradication question in *Schad v. Borough of Mount Ephraim* (1981) when it overturned (7–2) a New Jersey town's mandate outlawing adult entertainment. Nevertheless, the ambiguities through numerous lawsuits may leave stripping legally "corseted."[41] While the overarching legal context for stripping has been fairly consistent, the U.S. cultural response has shifted radically.

Stripping and Mainstream Culture

Since the late 1990s, print media and film have lavished attention on stripping and erotic dance performances, collapsing the space between deviant activities and everyday life. Integrating stripping into mainstream life further distinguishes the activity from other forms of sex work. Mainstream consumption of stripping includes cable programs like *The Girls Next Door* (2005–), *The Man Show* (1999–2004), *Howard Stern* (1994–2005), *Wild on E* (1997–2003), and *G-String Divas* (2000); Hollywood films such as *Bachelor Party 2: The Last Temptation* (2008), *The Sunday Morning Stripper* (2003), *Dancing at the Blue Iguana* (2000), *The Players Club* (1998), *Showgirls* (1995), *Striptease* (1996), and *Exotica* (1994); documentaries like *Live Nude Girls UNITE!* (2000); as well as countless other incidental images in shows and advertising. News media coverage includes more glamorous stripping reports from The Lusty Lady's unionization and the growing popularity of new burlesque in the *New Yorker*[42] to *New York Times* stories about club expansion in Texas and striptease work in Las Vegas.[43]

Today, stripping is high-selling entertainment for people across the economic and social spectrum. In 2003, *USA Today* announced that "stripping itself, once a forbidden topic in polite circles, is now strutting into the mainstream, propelled by pop culture and the loosening of societal taboos."[44] Conventional media is inundated with advertisements for stripping-related products. The message (for women): You, too, can dress like a stripper; perform striptease in your home, or at your local gym. "Get fit, stay in shape and be sexy," raves Carmen Electra's aerobic striptease DVD advertisement.[45] Even Oprah Winfrey has gotten on board by hosting Sheila Kelley's *S Factor* (the "S" is for striptease) workout *seven* times, according to Kelley's website.[46] Celebrity "strippercise" enthusiasts like Terri Hatcher have also performed on Oprah's show. This cultural mainstreaming of stripping has normalized facets of performance—clothes, music, and dance—as well as some striptease venues. Clubs are now publicly traded on the NASDAQ. All of these developments make stripping seem familiar to conventional audiences.

Journalist Ariel Levy, in her book *Female Chauvinist Pig,* laments, "because the only sign of sexuality we seem to be able to recognize is a direct allusion to red-light entertainment, we have laced the sleazy energy and aesthetic of a topless club or a *Penthouse* shoot throughout our entire culture."[47] Though I share Levy's unease over the lack of sexual diversity afforded to women who are continually repackaged in the same ways, her words about the sex industry reproduce the stigma associated with stripping labor as "sleazy." As Levy's writing suggests, stripping has hit the mainstream, but not in all forms. In the form of paid work, stripping and strippers are still discredited. Despite the stigma associated with stripping in many venues, there is at least one location that is exalted.

The Lusty Lady Theater

Some of the media attention directed at stripping focuses on particular kinds of striptease entertainment, such as that found in The Lusty Lady theater. In addition to print, television, and documentary film coverage, there are three firsthand accounts about the San Francisco and Seattle locations that follow life and work in these now famous peep shows.[48] One reason for the widespread attention is the San Francisco site's unique status as the first unionized stripping venue that is also a worker-owned collective. However, The Lusty Lady's uniqueness does not end there; like its sister club of the same name in Seattle, it is a peep show (not a strip club).

The distinction between peep shows and strip clubs is paramount in understanding the mainstreaming of this form of sex work. By contrast with strip clubs, peep shows place a glass barrier between strippers and patrons and as such remove any possibility for physical contact. Rather than perform in the same room with patrons, strippers are separated into their own room, which is encircled by smaller rooms occupied by patrons. Patrons do not even tip strippers directly; instead, they place money into a slot that goes directly to the club and only later gets distributed to the dancers. It is no surprise, then, that The Lusty Lady is offered as evidence of stripping as safe, potentially feminist, and sexually liberating work.[49]

New Burlesque

In addition to peep show work at The Lusty Lady, other emerging forms of stripping also encompass ideals of sexual liberation, like "new burlesque."[50] New burlesque performances reinvent the playful striptease acts of a bygone era with their subversive gender performances.[51] These shows build on a pop culture ideal of stripper-chic, which is closely associated with sex-positive notions of sexuality as a source of empowerment and pleasure for women.[52] Self-described fat performers, like those in the troupes Fat Bottom Revue and the Glamazons, as well as drag performers and female-female and male-female impersonators, parody striptease.[53] The cumulative effect of these varied stripping portrayals is to make nude or semi-nude performance accessible to wider-ranging groups of spectators and participants. Shedding the association of mainstream female stripping as a show for male-only audiences by entering different venues, incorporating comedic elements, and allowing a greater array of performances and bodies, new burlesque has contributed to the mainstreaming of nude performance.[54]

Amateur Stripping

Alongside new burlesque are products that feature female nude performances by amateurs, who are displaying their bodies for free on the Internet on YouTube and in films like *The Real Cancun* (2003) and the video series *Girls Gone Wild* (1998–). Both the variety of participants and the proliferation of images of stripping suggest a shift toward greater accessibility of the act, if not the industry, ushering it into the mainstream. The variety of performances also makes visible the simultaneous celebration and scorn associated with nude or semi-nude performance. For example, public outrage over Janet Jackson's costume being torn off during the Super Bowl halftime show of 2004 suggests a more complicated mainstream reaction, depending on the context and the act. In this case, the Super Bowl is intended to be family-friendly entertainment, free of actual nudity, even though commercials are often highly sexually suggestive.

The trend toward more amateur stripping and stripping for free may affect strippers who work for pay. In part, strippers' earnings depend on the special services they provide (live nude or topless performances). The ushering of stripping into the mainstream may draw more amateurs into paid work. Alternatively, as these performances are more accessible, they may reduce patrons' attendance or strippers' pay. A similar effect can be seen in video pornography, for which sales have "been falling by 15 percent a year since 2005 . . . now that Web sites such as RedTube and PornHub basically give it away."[55] Patrons may expect strippers to remove their clothing as "fun," rather than "work." This possibility is not far-fetched. During workers' union contract negotiations at The Lusty Lady, lawyers on behalf of the club wanted stripping documented as "fun" employment as a way to whittle down workers' demands.[56] At the same time, if the proliferation of nude dancing franchises across the country in the last ten years is taken as an indicator, men's consumption of strip club industry products has been on the rise. According to Rob Abner, publisher of the trade journal *Stripper*, in a recent five-year period, the number of strip clubs in the United States roughly doubled.[57] Regardless of whether the sex work industry is currently expanding or contracting, it is nonetheless here to stay.

The Paradox of Stripping

A popular face of stripping, as done by celebrities, amateurs, and new burlesque performers, hides another side of the industry, one that is far less glamorous. While stripping may be constructed as fun, mainstream entertainment, it depends on minimizing perceptions of riskiness and deviance in other less-visible contexts. This dual perception amounts to a risky shell game. Under one shell, there are the possibilities for women's sexual self-expression. Under another shell, there are dangerous working conditions for women that are fostered by men's aggression and violence. The shell game conditions mean that one is never certain which possibilities will win. But the rules of gambling dictate the house almost always wins. The question is, who controls the house?

Most stripping as work remains on the sidelines of mainstream society and, as such, is a context in which women's self-expression is contained by the occupational risks of male-dominated spaces. The risks are higher on the side of the stripping industry documented here at The Lion's Den, a rundown club produced by and for men. It was a place where women were compelled to strip out of economic need rather than a means of liberation; stripper narratives often reflect drudgery and dismay. The club was owned and operated by a man who enjoyed near complete control over operations. He described his work as "professional babysitting," reflecting his disdain for the strippers. Following suit, cynical male coworkers adopted similar views and often resented the "protection" they provided. Unfortunately, there are no large-scale studies of strip clubs that can speak reliably to industry-wide trends. Nevertheless, existing studies of strip clubs with female performers for primarily male patrons suggest a potent form of gendered organization.

Stripping has much in common with other feminized occupations. It is not uncommon for women to work in female-dominated jobs, as sex segregation is typical across various forms of employment in the United States.[58] According to the 2000 census, women are concentrated in fields like "health care practitioner and technical occupations" and "office and administrative support occupations."[59] Within these female-dominated occupations, some commonalities exist: workers typically receive low pay and prestige, they have little authority over their own work or the work of others, and there are scant opportunities for advancement.[60] Stripping shares all of these characteristics except low pay.

The labor performed by strippers is also similar to that of women in other feminized workplaces, like nursing homes and beauty salons. For all of these workers, relationships with clients may be long term, entailing emotional labor and physical proximity. Nursing assistants, hair and nail stylists, and strippers all may have regular customers they see often over many years. Emotional labor, a concept developed by sociologist Arlie Hochschild, involves a worker's demonstrating feelings as part of his or her job, with the intention of cultivating feelings in a customer or client.[61] Emotional labor is expected and often required across many jobs, but it is perhaps most conspicuous in the service industry. Think of a Wal-Mart greeter who smiles and welcomes "guests" into the store, or a Trader Joe's employee who chats with customers about their groceries. Both employees are trained to foster a particular kind of friendly environment to enhance shoppers' experiences. In addition to emotional labor, these workers' jobs involve what sociologist Miliann Kang calls "body labor."[62] Kang's research on nail salons builds on Hochschild's concept of emotional labor, arguing that women working in nail salons perform physical and emotional labor around their own and customers' bodies: "Body labor not only demands that the service worker present and comport her body in appropriate fashion but also that she induces customers' positive feelings about their own bodies."[63]

Stripping is distinctive among feminized jobs because in a strip club one expects to see women in roles defined by, working for, and serving men. Both the clientele and women's levels of authority are varied in other settings. Nevertheless, women's earnings in The Lion's Den are typically greater than those of other women's jobs, given the number of hours worked. Based on self-reported data from 2001 to 2002, strippers earned about $26,000 annually, with a range of over $60,000 to under $10,000, for an average of three working days a week (the range was two to six days with a mode of two days). By contrast, in female-dominated jobs like registered nursing and elementary school teaching, workers earned $38,158 and $35,204, respectively, for forty-hour weeks in 2000.[64] Likewise, similar to manicurists, strippers experience close physical proximity and contact with customers. Strippers' work is also performed nude or semi-nude, however, and most clients are of the opposite gender.

These peculiarities of stripping place it in a contradictory position relative to other feminized jobs. It is both highly paid and low-prestige work, characteristics that do not typically go hand in hand. Strippers in The Lion's Den have little authority and few opportunities for advancement. Indeed, strippers' careers are generally short lived, as they reach employment ceilings in "young adulthood."[65] Given these associated difficulties with stripping work, it is puzzling that stripper-chic arguments often go unchallenged. This stripper-chic sleight of hand is possible, in part, because an organizational focus has been largely absent from analyses. However, this deception is commonplace, not just in the sex industry but in the broader U.S. culture. It is part of a larger paradox of gender.

Gender is a paradox because so many of its assumed attributes are based on misinformation and mythology.[66] In the sex industry, for the most part, women are workers and men are customers. However, this is not due to inherent gender difference, biological or social. The facts supporting far greater similarities than differences across genders are well documented.[67] Sociologist Judith Lorber explained this phenomena in her book *Paradoxes of Gender*: "This paradox is resolved if gender is conceptualized as a social institution often rooted in conflict over scarce resources and in social relationships of power."[68] Using the example of procreation, Lorber continues: "Gender inequality structures the unequal conditions of procreation, not the other way round."[69] We move a long way toward understanding why strippers' troubles are intractable when we substitute stripping or sex work for procreation in Lorber's passage above. It is in contexts like The Lion's Den, where gender rules are entrenched, where performers are seen and not heard, and where work, as a result, can be dangerous, that the exploration of stripping begins.

Stripping in Scholarly Representations

Stripping often exists in a context of legal and social limbo: it is tolerated but constrained as a "safe" form of sex work, as long as it is still constructed as a deviant activity. In keeping with this perspective, many scholars have examined stripping through the lens of deviance.[70] These authors present stripping as a marginal occupation that draws women in by preying on those with lifelong patterns of gender abuse. In other words, only the most socially marginalized individuals would subject themselves to the stigma associated with stripping. It is useful to recall parallel claims made through culture-of-poverty arguments that hypothesize inequality as a circumstance actively reproduced by the poor, rather than broader social and structural phenomena. Similarly, strippers are seen as reproducing their own gender exploitation as women who come from "unhappy," "broken," "abusive," "unstable" homes with "little parental attention or affection" and "an absent or ineffective father," or those who have experienced childhood emotional and sexual abuse.[71] Contemporary accounts have recognized the limitations inherent in these assumptions and subsequently challenged earlier deviance approaches through interaction-based perspectives.

Interaction-Based Perspectives

Interaction-based perspectives, which dominate the literature on stripping, showcase the industry's central product—women's erotic and expressive labor performed for men.[72] Interactionist perspectives are concerned with how social actors understand and create their worlds through their interactions with others and their subjective thoughts.[73] Shaped by the feminist sex wars beginning in the 1980s[74] and continuing today,[75] interactionist perspectives on stripping (and the sex industry more generally) are influenced by two main perspectives—that of the radical feminists and that of the sex radicals. Briefly, radical feminists, such as Catharine Mackinnon, a legal scholar, and the late writer and activist Andrea Dworkin, argue that stripping, prostitution, and pornography are inherently oppressive products of patriarchy.[76] Sex radicals like Carole Vance and Gayle Rubin counter that sex work is not inherently oppressive but a site for investigation in which one may find oppressive working conditions but also resistance and empowerment.[77]

A number of sociologists have worked to resolve these polarizing positions. In 1997, Wendy Chapkis made a major contribution toward reconciliation by emphasizing the need for empirical study in *Live Sex Acts*. Building on sociologist Arlie Hochschild's concept of emotional labor, Chapkis compared stripping and other forms of sex work to the "deep acting" performed by flight attendants in Hochschild's study *The Managed Heart*. Drawing on interviews with women across the sex industry, Chapkis reasoned that strippers, like flight attendants and other service and sex workers, cultivate feelings of empathy and friendliness to give customers a congenial and more-personalized transaction. What these workers are selling is their emotional labor on behalf of themselves and their employers. Based on this argument, an analysis of stripping must begin with an understanding of sex work as *work* and, in so doing, must present the perspectives of the women who actually perform the work, rather than gazing from afar and determining a perspective a priori. In Chapkis's words, feminist analysis of stripping must examine "mundane concerns like status differences between worker and client, employee/employer relations, and negative cultural attitudes toward the work performed, [which] may be at the root of the distress and damage experienced by some workers."[78]

Part of Chapkis's call has been heard. Building on her writings, as well as those of Foucault, Rubin, and Hochschild,[79] interactionist studies examine the actual practices of strippers, addressing them as active agents in their workplace. For example, sociologist Bernadette Barton interviewed strippers working in Hawaii, Kentucky, and San Francisco, California. Based on this research, she argues strippers' experiences are best seen through a Möbius strip, a metaphor from mathematics for a continuous loop with a half twist, on which strippers precariously attempt to balance early rewards with later costs.[80] Other studies take a similar approach, using interaction-based perspectives that focus on strippers' or patrons' narratives regarding their experiences with each other as an entry point for examinations of empowerment and disempowerment.[81] These analyses are critical to further empirical study and offer substantive insights into the lives of strippers and patrons. In further response to Chapkis, my research broadens the focus from strippers and patrons to the entire cast of club workers and the owner-manager by studying the larger workplace dynamics in The Lion's Den.

The literature on stripping has not questioned the industry's gendered organization because it seems overt. What is generally typical of workplaces where sex work is done is that men own, boss, work, and patronize; women perform. Note that women's performance, which is the heart of the actual labor done at clubs (other than serving drinks and possibly food), is not constructed as work but as "performance." While this stereotype may prove true in examining clubs, little is actually known about the gendered organizational forms strip clubs take in terms of their policies, practices, interactions, and identities.[82] While strippers and patrons have been the subject of numerous analyses, a much smaller literature addresses the cast of support workers, including bartenders, bouncers, deejays, doormen, cocktail waitresses, and housemoms.[83] Similarly, club owners and managers—those who formulate, dictate (alongside local laws and police), and profit from particular work roles, regulations, and club culture—appear infrequently in academic writing.

The Gendered Organization of Strip Club Work

It may seem obvious that strip clubs are highly gendered settings. However, Joan Acker argues that past research in the literature on organizations began with the opposite assumption—that hierarchies, practices, and tasks were gender neutral. Organizations and jobs were seen as gender neutral because they were studied in "abstract," disembodied, and universalized forms.[84] Acker contends there was little investigation into gendered organizations because there was little dispute: "The link between masculinity and organizational power was so obvious that no debate was needed."[85] Fortunately, many feminist scholars recognized the need for debate.

Context greatly influences organizational structure and culture.[86] As Dana Britton argues, "the gendering process is clearly affected by the context of the organization itself."[87] Since organizations are products of their culture, they reproduce normative social patterns "shaped in particular by those who have acquired the symbolic power to define the situation."[88] Within any organization, the power to define the situation and shape institutions is often held and exercised by men.[89] Many organizations reproduce gender inequalities that privilege men and marginalize women through the interactions of social actors and the larger organizational structure and culture, broad-based global and institutional, or macrostructural, gendered realities that affect social groups and institutions like families, economies, governments, and religious organizations. In other words, on the micro level, social actors "do gender,"[90] and at the meso level, particular organizations reproduce a "gendered organizational logic,"[91] both of which occur within the context of macrolevel social structures, all of which may simultaneously construct inequalities based on gender, race, class, and sexuality.

In this research, I apply a gendered organizations perspective to one particular strip club in order to broaden the understanding of organizational forms and the reproduction of inequalities therein. To understand The Lion's Den, this research draws on Acker's framework for studying gendered organizations.[92] I explore the club's *gendered processes,* including work roles, authority, and interactions among workers and patrons. With regard to these processes, I examine how those who do each job—deejays, bouncers, doormen, bartenders, cocktail waitresses, and strippers—reproduce the club's hierarchy. Rather than adopting an assumption of gender neutrality within the club, I argue that work roles and authority exhibit divisions along lines of gender. I also examine the use of *gender and sexuality as organizational resources.* In The Lion's Den, coworkers use stereotypes of strippers to create a culture of women's inferiority and men's superiority. Lastly, I investigate the *gendered substructure* of The Lion's Den through which management formulates work rules and roles. These three facets interact to produce gendered organizational jeopardy for strippers in which they are subject to dangers by the very organization of their work. This organization, however, is not without its inconsistencies: while strippers do not enjoy formal authority in the club, their work simultaneously produces economic outcomes that make them the highest earners (outside of club owners and managers) with the responsibility for providing income to male support workers.

Race and Class Dynamics

Without a doubt, The Lion's Den is a haven for white, working-class men. Also, almost all of the strippers and workers are white and working class. Because of this homogeneity, it might appear that gender is the predominant organizing principle of inequality in this type of setting. However, even here, identities are produced by the intersections of race, class, and gender.[93] In addition to shaping the culture and character of places, identities are, in turn, shaped by the organizations they re-create. In particular, identities are subject to organizational hierarchies and resulting status differences. Looking at a wealth of cross-cultural research on work, Acker argues that facets of identity interact in organizations as "inequality regimes" that concentrate or mitigate access to power.[94] Summing up her findings, she writes that "inequality regimes still seem to place white men in advantaged positions in spite of the erosion of advantages for middle and lower-level men workers."[95] Acker's argument is well illustrated by The Lion's Den, in which white men hold the authority. In terms of race and class, most of the strippers, other workers, and patrons are white and from similar lower-middle, working-class backgrounds. Though race plays an exclusionary role in the club, it is gender that is more central to The Lion's Den's organizational structure. As a result, here

I concentrate on organizational meanings produced through gender. Nevertheless, it is important to discuss how class and race operate in conjunction with gender.

In most work sites, status, workplace culture, and the experiences of workers themselves can be understood through identity-based characteristics. Previous research has distinguished a club's social class by its strippers, patrons, and the type of performance offered.[96] For example, anthropologist Katherine Frank draws on Bourdieu's concept of cultural capital, arguing that the resources (economic, educational, and social) available to female performers shape their class identities and, in turn, the relative standing of particular clubs in which they perform.[97] Among elite strippers (as well as others), indicators of status include having designer clothes, perfecting the art of conversation, and knowing the etiquette around fine dining. However, it is not just a club's strippers who influence the club's status characteristics. Some trends are industry wide, as Frederick Schiff details, and differentiate not just a club's offerings but also its relative standing.[98] For Schiff, the strip club hierarchy is built on the type of performance, specifically nude versus topless.[99] He explains: "Customers at topless bars are mostly white-collar[;] . . . customers at the nude cabarets are mostly blue collar men."[100] The social class position of The Lion's Den as a site is partly understood through identity-based characteristics. Its status as a working-class club stems from all of these factors—strippers' and patrons' identities, as well as the club's fully nude performances.

Race is also constructed, at least in part, through identity-based characteristics. Like much of the stripping industry,[101] the club's racial makeup—management, most workers, performers, and patrons—was predominantly white. However, it was not described as "white." Instead, race was rendered largely invisible unless African Americans, Asian Americans, or Latinas/Latinos were present. Nevertheless, race operated structurally through the active barriers to racial diversity created by coworkers, patrons, and management. The first form was racism. It was common to hear white male patrons and workers engaged in racist dialogue about Latino and African American men. Comments linking crime, bad neighborhoods, and other social ills with Latino and African American men abounded. Such open racism created a hostile environment that mitigated diversity. That second form, diversity, was limited by the owner-manager's perspective on race. Because he enjoyed nearly complete control over decision-making in The Lion's Den, he affected the organization's racial climate. When asked about how race plays out in the club, Steve offered the following:

This is on tape. This is not good [*laughs*]. Just like there's white trash and there's white people, there's black people and there's black people that have that little attitude that we owe them the world. Then there's the Puerto Ricans that are absolutely wonderful people and then there's the Puerto Ricans, the ones that we see [a nearby city] trying to clean off the streets, so it all depends on the person, I think.

Judging from the club's employment practices, far more African American and Latinas/Latinos seemed to occupy Steve's "undesirable" categories. As the participant information table in appendix 1 illustrates, only two strippers and one bouncer self-identified as African American, and one stripper self-identified as Latina. For the most part, Asian American men and women were invisible in discussions of race with management, workers, and patrons.

If identity was seen as a discrete characteristic, this analysis would miss part of the racial dynamics of The Lion's Den. Additional patterns emerge when viewed through an intersectional approach that simultaneously examines race, class, and gender.[102] This is because race and class play out differently for men and women in the club. While white men subjected Latino and African American men to racist dialogue behind their backs, they refrained from such behaviors involving Latina and African American women. In part, this may have been since Latina (and, to a lesser extent, African American) dancers worked in the club; their presence may have mitigated the space for such dialogue, even if done surreptitiously. The presence of women of color may have also counterbalanced racist stereotypes, as they were seen as friends and comrades. Further, since these women were performers, they may have been the subject of fantasy and desire rather than derision. White men's lack of outward racism toward African American and Latina women in the club also stemmed from simultaneous gendered and economic realities. White male patrons' and workers' racism toward African American men and Latinos seemed to rest on economic issues: African American men and Latinos are scapegoats for an economy that leaves behind many of the white, predominantly working-class males in the club. Susan Faludi's 1999 book *Stiffed* explored a similar refrain from white men who felt disenfranchised by a culture that no longer clearly advantaged them. In the club, white men's tolerance for more diversity among strippers was due to chronic stripper shortages, as well as the sex industry's trend toward appealing to diverse attractions. Since female performers lacked authority in the club, they did not pose the same kind of threat as male coworkers.

At the intersections of race, class, and gender, we also see some of the diverging practices and understandings at work in The Lion's Den. Clearly, identity characteristics do not contain the same meanings across different groups of actors. Adopting a gendered organizations approach to our study of The Lion's Den enables us to examine issues of gender, race, and class as they are produced and reflected through four sources of information—interviews, direct observation, participation, and a workplace handbook written by the club's owner. These materials provide a detailed basis for evaluation. Though I am not the sole author of the materials I studied, I am solely accountable for the analysis that follows. It is my hope that readers will understand and view The Lion's Den through both critical and sensitive eyes. Indeed, that is the way I came to understand this club and its inhabitants.

"Keeping the Dancers in Check"

The Gendered Organization of
Stripping in The Lion's Den

Nothing has mainstreamed stripping quite like the *Girls Gone Wild* DVD series (1998–). These multimillion-dollar documentary-style films have a reality feel, though they are often staged. They present countless young, thin, mostly white women (and now men, too) who strip off their clothes. Reporter Claire Hoffman followed front man Joe Francis and his crew to a Chicago "shoot" on the back of the *Girls Gone Wild* tour bus with 18-year-old Jannel Szyszka: "Following a cameraman's instructions, [Szyszka] shows her breasts and says, 'Girls Gone Wild.' She seems shy but willing. She smiles. The unseen cameraman asks her to take off her shirt, her skirt, then her under-wear."[1] Though the title suggests girls "go wild" for the camera, Hoffman's description sounds more like scripted clothing removal. Products like *Girls Gone Wild* should prompt readers to question what the sex work industry includes and excludes, how it is defined, and how differences and similarities in the kinds of performances matter. The key to understanding is found by examining the gendered organization of different performances and sites. Of course, the major difference between the acts described above and those in The Lion's Den is that the former is not a job. *Girls Gone Wild* performers do receive compensation, however, in the form of free drinks, hats, tank tops, and underwear, but the only employment is on the other side of the camera.[2] Still, scripted nudity is at the center of both performances.

Images like those from *Girls Gone Wild* fuel widespread expectations that stripping should be effortless. These ideas shape strippers' expectations and misrepresent work-related challenges. Layla, a twenty-one-year-old college student, believed stripping would be "really easy" and she would "catch on quick." The realities she faced onstage were far more challenging. She struggled with coordination: "It's really hard, and I've messed up so many times. I've spilled [patrons'] drinks in their laps. I've kicked them in the head."

Tamara, a twenty-five-year-old, white, married dancer, discussed how stripping taxed her body: "I've had injuries at work. I think I got water on the knee for a while. . . . I've had bruises all over my back from being onstage. . . . My body takes a hard toll."

Emotionally, strippers worked to express empathy and patience toward patrons while also flirting, arousing desire and intrigue, and engaging in patrons' sexual fantasies. As an embodiment of both visual and interactive fantasies, strippers mingled with patrons to earn tips that reward both the physical and emotional components of their labor. Kelly, who had worked as both a dancer and a cocktail waitress, described the support she provided to patrons: "You have to listen to more of [the patrons'] problems than anything. . . . Some of them do need more attention." Sometimes the emotional aspect of the work required strippers to manage their own troubled feelings that stemmed from patrons' comments. Layla explained:

> It upsets me . . . I'm very weak, and that's the reason I'm probably having such a hard time. Because when somebody says something to me, it shouldn't offend me, but it does, and I let it get to me, and I let it ruin my night, which makes it so that I don't make any money.

Other studies report evidence of strippers' "psychological and social estrangement"[3] and identity problems.[4] As William Thompson et al. and Eleanor Maticka-Tyndale et al. observe, strippers experience "a heavy emotional toll on their personal and social lives."[5] Beyond the physical and psychological labor involved, scholars have tried to disentangle why stripping is difficult. The literature suggests that time spent in the industry is one factor, since the emotional burdens associated with stripping increase over time. Nova Sweet and colleagues contend that the work-related costs of stripping accumulate after a few years in the industry and outweigh rewards[6] that simultaneously diminish.[7]

To fully understand both stripping's costs and rewards, we must situate individual performances within their local surroundings and broader macrostructural trends. Strip clubs' central product—women's erotic and expressive labor performed for men—may vary dramatically with its context. *Where* strippers work shapes everything: from the particulars of striptease performances to management's practices and the likely types of clientele and coworkers. Likewise, broader cultural norms of gender, race, and economic inequalities shape strippers' experiences with management, coworkers, and patrons.

Looking at The Lion's Den, we see it is a club run by men, for men. It is a space in which the gendered division of labor is palpable. Male workers, regardless of their role in the club, made decisions and oversaw female workers. The exclusion of women from positions of power and authority, combined with explicit policies that formalized male surveillance and the disparagement of strippers, skewed the balance of power toward management's agenda. This arrangement underwrote a hostile work environment and ensured men's dominance. Evidence from both women's and men's work demonstrated that the entire cast of the club's workers contributed to the gendered organization of The Lion's Den. In sum, conventional workplace understandings of how and which workers engaged in regular tasks were gendered processes, the first component of The Lion's Den's gendered organization discussed here.

Gendered Processes in The Lion's Den

In virtually every aspect of their work, other club workers monitored what strippers were doing. Bouncers had the primary task of overseeing stripper-patron interactions,[8] but all workers (both men and women) in The Lion's Den played a role in such oversight. This organization affected how work was divided in the club, relationships between strippers and other club workers, characterizations of the work performed (e.g., whether it was valued or devalued), and the self-concepts of the workers themselves. For male workers, success depended heavily on their ability to keep the dancers in check through monitoring stage rotations, alcohol consumption, and interactions with patrons. Generally three to five workers watched the same or double the number of strippers. In other clubs and peep shows, women may serve as bartenders, managers, and even co-owners, as strippers do in the San Francisco Lusty Lady theater. In The Lion's Den, the gendered division of labor was seldom violated. On rare occasions, a woman took a (usually slow) daytime bartending shift. In those cases, the owner-manager always supervised her work. The Lion's Den is not alone in rigidly segregating work between men and women. Jacqueline Lewis's study of Ontario strip clubs found similar gendered job segregation.[9] These work roles, authority, and interactions among workers constitute the gendered processes in the club. Gendered processes are commonplace workplace activities that, in the case of The Lion's Den, reproduced gendered inequalities by patterning men's dominance and women's subordination.[10]

Deejays

Deejays oversaw strippers' stage shifts, set the number of dancers performing, and determined the length of each set, depending on how many patrons were in the club, as well as the number of dancers working. In addition to having deejays organize strippers' shifts, the club structured formal oversight of dancers in other ways. Steve required that deejays submit a form ("The Dancer Daily Report") documenting each stripper's arrival and the duration of her stage performances for each shift. As Steve demanded in the *Employee/Entertainer Handbook,* "'The Dancer Daily Report' is important to me; it doesn't take rocket science to figure out how to fill it out, I want it done, I want to see the set rotation, and I want to see times for fining purposes."[11] It was also the deejay's responsibility to announce each stripper's stage name twice before actually calling her to perform. In some cases, the deejay physically went to the dressing room to get dancers who were late.

One of the deejays, Marcus, a twenty-six-year-old college student, emphasized his oversight of dancers. When asked to describe his work, he replied, "To be a babysitter for everybody—for the drunk people, the girls." Leo, a twenty-year-old deejay, substantiated this account: "You have to stay on your toes with them, or they'll try to get off early or get on late." He concluded: "There's not much else to my job besides keeping the crowd happy and keeping the dancers in check." Since becoming a deejay, it took Marcus time to learn strippers' preferences: "You've got all the headaches of the girls yelling at you for playing the wrong kind of music when they're onstage and putting [strippers] up with the wrong girl." Losing track of these details meant "[getting] chewed out all the time" by dancers. In contrast to the strippers, dealing with patrons seemed easy to Marcus. He explained that, unless patrons were drunk, they were not impolite. Regulars, he knew, were easy to comfort. The beer stein in the deejay booth window filled with $1 tips as long as Marcus learned which songs a regular liked to hear and played those soon after his arrival.

As Leo and Marcus illustrate, oversight of strippers was laced with suspicion of wrongdoing and anticipation of conflict. More than simply the words of frustrated workers, the language (e.g., "babysitting") that developed around this oversight reinforced the subordination of strippers and the dominance of men. They were, in effect, infantilizing strippers by employing a term typically used with children. Strip clubs are not alone in fostering "control mechanisms for women . . . [that] resemble those used with children."[12] Acker and Van Houten's reexamination of the historic Hawthorne and Crozier studies produced similar findings. Male managers in both workplaces adopted a "paternalistic" approach, referring to adult women as "girls" to foster compliance.[13]

Bouncers and Doormen

Just as the deejays' work entailed several simultaneous tasks, bouncers and doormen also usually had multiple job responsibilities. Despite being separate jobs, in practice, management often combined the doorman and bouncer positions, especially during daytime shifts or at times when the club was short on workers. When the club was fully staffed, doormen checked identification, collected door fees, and directed patrons to the appropriate section. They steered underage patrons toward the "sandbox," the section reserved for eighteen- to twenty-year-olds (in which the club did not serve alcohol), and guided those aged twenty-one and over in the opposite direction toward the rest of the club.

A bouncer's primary role was to oversee and monitor club interactions. Frank filled most daytime shifts, acting as both doorman and bouncer. He summed up his bouncer responsibilities this way: "[I] . . . keep an eye on the girls, make sure they're behaving onstage, . . . mak[e] sure [the dancers are] not breaking the rules, and [make] sure the guys aren't breaking the rules, that's all." Frank also monitored patrons. In his words, "[I] stop [patrons] if they look like they're drunk or causing problems [and] shut them off. . . . If they give me any trouble, I have to throw them out, but I ask them to leave first."

Bouncers, who oversaw and monitored club interactions, were often picked for their imposing physical size. Darrel, a thirty-eight-year-old African American bouncer, explained how his size created challenges in his work: "A lot of people, when you weigh 250 . . . don't really feel open to you. If you're the [bouncer], you want [strippers] to approach you—feel open to you, 'cause I'm their safety, and I like that. It makes me feel wanted," he said, laughing. James, a bartender and bouncer, said he hated bouncing: "I'm too smart for it. I really am. I think that's a very demeaning job for a guy. They hire you on your size; I don't like it." Being physically large, bouncers were formidable figures when called to intervene in problematic situations between patrons or between patrons and strippers. However, their power also stemmed from cultural understandings of masculinity and men's roles as women's "gatekeepers" and "protectors." As sociologists Matthew DeMichele and Richard Tewksbury argue, bouncers draw on "stereotypical notions of masculinity that are attached to power and sexuality, which bolsters bouncers' abilities to enforce organizational rules."[14]

Bartenders

In addition to making drinks and stocking coolers, bartenders were in charge when the owner-manager was away; in effect, they were middle managers. In the absence of the owner-manager, bartenders oversaw strippers, club workers, and patrons; resolved disputes; decided if and when employees could leave; and shut down the club at the end of the night. Ted, a thirty-three-year-old bartender, bouncer, doorman, and patron, explained: "I'm supposed to make sure dancers follow the rules, that the bouncers or the doormen enforce the rules, make sure the customers are not doing anything wrong, and that they're following the rules. I guess I'm ultimately in charge of shutting people off for alcohol." Regulating alcohol consumption was an important facet of a bartender's job that extended not just to patrons but also to strippers.

Sometimes bartenders took on additional tasks to fill a gap left by another worker. James complained: "[I have to] make sure the girls don't get out of hand again because our bouncer's outside all the time." His reference to the bouncer being outside refers to the bouncer's visits to the barbecue trailer that parked by the club's front entrance during evening hours. Club workers and patrons often congregated outside chatting and getting food. James concluded: "Basically, I'm the bouncer, and lots of times I'm the waitress and the bartender." The climate of informality in the club often meant many workers did as they pleased on shift, leaving the diligent few to carry their load.

Having deejays, bouncers, doormen, and bartenders fill multiple roles makes business sense during slow day shifts when there were few patrons, but it exacerbated the trend toward greater workloads. It also put dancers at risk since it overtaxed workers who had to fulfill numerous tasks simultaneously. Not only were they assigned to "protect" dancers from harassment and physical aggression at the hands of patrons, but these workers safeguarded the club from strippers or patrons who engaged in physical contact, underage drinking, or intoxication (and thus the risk of drinking and driving) or who caused a disturbance, all of which might provoke police intervention. The club's drive for efficiency compromised these workers' ability to execute any of these tasks effectively since workers were already frequently carrying out the duties of others. Take Frank, the fifty-six-year-old daytime jack-of-all-trades doorman/bouncer, for instance: he simultaneously checked identification, collected door fees, entertained patrons, trained and socialized dancers, and monitored stripper-patron interactions in the main and VIP rooms of the club. Not only was he required to be in three places at once (front door, main room, and VIP Room), he had at least five concurrent responsibilities. Nonetheless, these examples demonstrate that all male coworkers policed strippers and their interactions with patrons. Rather than focusing on the need to regulate patrons' behaviors through the strippers—maintaining the notion that strippers were allies in these tasks—male workers often underscored stripper stereotypes that amplified the need for oversight in the first place. By contrast, male coworkers viewed cocktail waitresses more as (unequal) partners in their labor.

Cocktail Waitresses

Strippers' inequalities were reflected not just relative to male coworkers in The Lion's Den but also in relation to women working as cocktail waitresses. In addition to serving drinks, cocktail waitresses also oversaw strippers. In their limited authority, cocktail waitresses made decisions regarding whether or not to serve a stripper or a patron. However, these decisions were always subject to the review of bartenders, who could override them.

In addition to selling and overseeing alcohol, cocktail waitresses, like strippers, performed a great deal of emotional labor for patrons and contributed to the fantasy environment that strip clubs produce for men. In addition to selling drinks and looking out for intoxication in the club, cocktail waitresses provided friendly conversation and a sympathetic ear for patrons. Often this involved chatting with patrons about their evening, what they did for work, how groups of men knew each other, or why an individual patron was having a bad day. Kelly explained: "When [they] walk into this place, you want all of the customers to think that you're in love with them, that you're there to make them happy and stuff. Because obviously they're not happy at work, or they're not happy at home." Female employees behaving like each patron is special contributes to the fantasy environment strip clubs produce for men. Along with strippers, cocktail waitresses provided this kind of companionship for patrons.

Despite some similarities between cocktail waitressing and stripping, cocktail waitresses were not subject to the same surveillance or distrust. In part, this may be due to small but important demographic differences between these two groups of women. Cocktail waitresses in The Lion's Den were, on average, two years older (twenty-five versus twenty-three years in age), the majority held down multiple jobs (strippers most often had no other employment), all had completed high school, and most had some college background (by contrast, four strippers had not completed high school, seven had a GED or high school diploma, and the remainder reported some college).

Differences in treatment also resulted from a good-girl/bad-girl dichotomy operating in the club, a mechanism for dividing and ranking women into mutually exclusive groups based on feminine virtue. My exchange with Roxanne, a cocktail waitress and stripper, highlights this point:

> ROXANNE: As a waitress . . . you get to keep your clothes on. . . . So, I tend to think the club treats the waitresses way better than the girls.
> KP-G: Do you think it has to do with being clothed versus being unclothed?
> ROXANNE: Oh yeah, I just think the club thinks that because you get naked for money that you're stupid, so that's how they treat you.

My experience as a cocktail waitress underscored these differences. On countless occasions, patrons asked me, "What's a nice girl like you doing in a place like this?" The contrast in my case—I often wore a t-shirt, jeans, and eyeglasses—was perhaps more dramatic than for other waitresses who dressed provocatively. Most cocktail waitresses wore tight, low-cut shirts and pants in which their bra and g-string underwear were visible. Later, when the club introduced uniforms, cocktail waitresses were instructed to wear pink tank tops and black pants of their choosing. In compliance with these new club rules, most women opted for spaghetti-strapped tops or cropped tops (displaying their stomachs) and stretch pants.

Given the large number of cocktail waitresses who were former strippers (five of the six cocktail waitresses I interviewed either currently or previously worked as strippers), one can see that the club's good-girl/bad-girl hierarchy was built on contradictions. Complicating matters further, cocktail waitresses may actually have experienced more physical contact with patrons than strippers did, since the club did not prohibit these kinds of interactions. Patrons frequently greeted waitresses by putting their arms around them or offering hugs. This physical contact was something Kelly disliked about waitressing compared with dancing: "Sometimes I think waitressing is worse because . . . [patrons are] more apt to touch you." These kinds of oversimplifications are common across the sex industry, as the false dichotomy of good girls and bad girls suggests. Owners, coworkers, and patrons often represent women, especially strippers, in uncomplicated ways, despite evidence to the contrary.

Housemoms

Housemoms occupy another position in the workplace hierarchy. Similar to sorority and fraternity housemothers on college campuses, strip club housemoms also supervise or "mother" those in their charge. As such, this position retains some of its infantilizing connotations. Housemoms are typically ex-dancers. In many clubs, they advocate on behalf of strippers to improve working conditions, negotiate conflicts between strippers, and provide resources such as costumes and equipment. Paid through tips from the strippers, housemoms are often women who no longer want (or are able) to dance.

In The Lion's Den, the term "housemom" was a misnomer since the position involved few of the typical responsibilities of the job. Appearing with a clipboard and signup sheet, The Lion's Den's housemom spent much of her time in the dressing rooms collecting strippers' schedules. She only appeared in the club to locate dancers who were in between stage and private dance performances. The housemom typically stayed less than an hour—just long enough to schedule the week's shifts.

An outside agency run by Steve paid low wages to housemoms. Management was openly ambivalent about what to do with the position. Steve recognized that some of the dancers liked the idea of a housemom, and they hoped the actual position would be reestablished. However, former housemoms who broke the rules, played favorites with some of the strippers, and were not reliable discouraged management from reinstating the position. The housemoms I met were slightly older than the average dancers and remained in the club too briefly to have an impact or to be well known by other workers.

By limiting the role of housemoms, The Lion's Den narrowed women's work options in the club and denied them the chance to hold a position with some authority. While housemoms can act as tools of management—for example, operating as informants regarding "problem" strippers—they are also in a position to negotiate with and keep strippers informed about management's plans. Housemoms who align themselves with strippers rather than management could advocate for change.

Since The Lion's Den did not employ women as bartenders or deejays, as do other clubs, women had no access to recognized authority. As a result, strippers had to rely on their own abilities to protect themselves and their interests. This individualized strategy had limitations, since strippers had to struggle simultaneously with a difficult job, an entrenched gendered organization of work, hostility and belittlement from male coworkers, and social stigma. The odds were, in effect, stacked against them.

Strippers

Strippers' earnings came from stage, private, and table dances. All performances involved physical and emotional labor. Strippers' physical labor included crouching their bodies low to the stage to show and fondle their breasts, slap their butts, and display their genitals for patrons. In addition to physical labor, strippers also provided conversation, companionship, support, and erotic storytelling. As part of their job, strippers simultaneously fostered and fended off men's attention. Jen, a twenty-six-year-old cocktail waitress and stripper, explained how she had to be the subject of—but not consummate—men's desires: "When I'm table dancing, I will touch your shoulders, I will touch your knees, that's it, and you are not allowed to even touch my kneecap." Despite clear restrictions, strippers anticipated problems from patrons and developed their own strategies for dealing with them. Consider Tamara's explanation of how she "protected" herself:

> I state my limits, my boundaries, really strongly. And if a guy tries to touch me, I'll make a joke out of it. I'll be like [*in a singsong voice*], "No touching. You'll turn me on too much," or something like that, and make it a joke. But, I've stated my limit, I haven't been rude about it, so they know what's clear, and they usually don't push too much after that. I also don't usually ask for dances from people that I think are too inebriated. If I don't feel safe, I won't ask them for a dance.

While Tamara claimed to have the ability to detect inebriated patrons, hers is a subjective strategy based solely on her ability to detect sobriety and her assumption that inebriated patrons pose the greatest risk, an approach that may be quite limited in practice.

In The Lion's Den, strippers exercised some control over their work by determining for whom they performed, what kind of performance they gave, and how long it would last. In other ways, their influence was limited: strippers did not choose their own music, nor, since they shared the stage with several other dancers, did they choreograph elaborate stage performances. Given potential competition over earnings, strippers oversaw and informally regulated each other to curb unwanted behavior or exact revenge.[15] When a new dancer arrived, long-term "house girls" (more experienced dancers) watched and conferred about the newcomer's stage and VIP Room activities.

On a number of occasions, strippers suspected of indiscretions, such as allowing patrons to touch their bodies or touching patrons' bodies, were the subject of much fervor. One young dancer never returned to work after a rumor that she had sex with a patron in a car parked behind the club. Even unfounded allegations had dramatic affects. Amelia, a twenty-one-year-old Russian dancer, explained that she was the target of baseless claims of sexual contact with patrons: "One dancer did a very bad thing to me. . . . She came out [of the VIP Room], and she was almost screaming, 'She's almost doing a blow job over there!' . . . It was horrible, and I was crying . . . because I didn't know what to do." Strippers did not limit reprimands to other dancers accused of doing "too much." Destiny, one of the few African American dancers, refused to remove her bottoms onstage for the customary $1 tip. As she explained: "Here they want you to do too much for too little. . . . You shouldn't even get to see me for a dollar down south; you have to drop at least five." Other dancers responded that Destiny was "too good for the club" and "destined to make no money."

Unlike other workers, strippers did not officially oversee anyone else's work. Rather, formal authority was concentrated into the hands of management, bartenders, bouncers, and deejays. This particular organization of work roles and routine interactions in the club formed processes "that enact dominance and submission" between workers.[16] Alongside gendered processes, coworkers' expectations around gender and sexuality fostered particular stereotypes regarding strippers. These facets of work in the club created a steep social hierarchy that mitigated collegial ties between coworkers.[17]

Gender and Sexuality as Organizational Resources in The Lion's Den

Strip clubs are products of their local and broader cultures; they reproduce and extend normative understandings of gender and sexuality found in particular clubs and the contemporary United States. As such, The Lion's Den acted as a masculine institution—a context in which both the positions and the processes were produced through gender inequalities and characterized by men's dominance.[18] Thus, performances of masculinity are not simply the product of particular groups of men or of an undifferentiated culture. Though the performances of masculinity in The Lion's Den can be found in the broader culture, the club was also unique. In the club, the rules of engagement were firmly set to women's individual and collective disadvantage through the social organization of work. In this sense, the club was a site where coworkers could engage in degrading remarks toward strippers, free from many of the social constraints that in other settings might limit them. Moreover, women internalize these stereotypes and reproduce them. These stereotypes enabled men and women to use gender and sexuality as organizational resources that fostered a culture of men's superiority and women's inferiority in the club.[19]

Stripper Stereotypes

Expressing a common sentiment in The Lion's Den, Frank, the doorman, argued that strippers were "showing all they've got for a buck." Frank's remark is telling; the assumption is that women with anything else to offer will not become strippers. That point aside, Frank emphasized the centrality of nudity to women's performances. Strippers are reduced to their genitalia, particularly in The Lion's Den, where the stage provided an eye-level view of women's bodies. While vaginas are often considered "private parts," something that women do not share publicly,[20] in fully nude strip clubs they become a main focus.

Discounting the physical and emotional skill stripping involves, both men and women in the club devalued stripping work. Twenty-one-year-old Vivian put it succinctly: "It's not easy, but what prerequisites do you have to have to become a stripper? Granted, if I lose my job as a stripper, what am I going to do? Oh, 'Would you like spicy or mild sauce with that?' [*laughs*]." Strippers and other club workers frequently described strippers as heavy drinkers, spendthrifts, whiners, slobs, and unreliable workers. One worker, Marissa, a twenty-year-old stripper, idealized the dancer stereotype: "[She] is a partier, a druggie, she's untrustworthy, she'll steal your stuff, stays out all night partying, sleeps all day." Roxanne, a thirty-three-year-old cocktail waitress and stripper, explained: "Even the guys that work here think the [strippers] are stupid and obnoxious and hard to deal with." Evangelina, a twenty-two-year-old cocktail waitress, added: "I feel like the guys that work in here treat [strippers] nicely but behind their backs talk a whole lot of shit about them. . . . It's because . . . there've been so many days . . . [with] no dancers. . . . Everyone just takes this place as a joke, so there are no-shows all the time, and I think the guys are mean."

Perhaps it is not surprising that strippers and their male coworkers undermine stripping labor, given normative stereotypes about women generally. The primary work of stripping—taking off one's clothing and developing emotions for others—involves acts women are supposed to accomplish *natu-rally,* as opposed to jobs that require *work.* Similar to the expectations around motherhood, women are presumed to have a natural ability to nurture.[21] In the case of strippers, in addition to the stigma of the sex work industry, they are devalued through a broader set of expectations for how females "do gender."[22]

Many male coworkers stigmatized stripping because it contradicts the values they associate with femininity. Drawing on their beliefs about gender, men located stripping in opposition to the roles women occupy as moth-ers and "good girls." James, a twenty-three-year-old bartender and bouncer, drew a distinction between mothers and other women working in the indus-try: "If you're just a girl going to college who needs extra money, it's not as bad. But if you've got a family, do you really want your kids growing up say-ing, 'Oh yeah, my mommy's a stripper!'" When asked if he would want his kids to work in the industry, Travis, a fifty-three-year-old deejay, replied: "A young child, eighteen to nineteen years old, no. No way. Not old enough. I wouldn't feel comfortable with that; [there are] too many temptations. Take off with a customer, God only knows. It happens. I've seen it happen. No." As he began talking, Travis remembered that his son once worked as a deejay in a strip club. While he "didn't have a problem" with his son's work, he felt differently about his daughters: "You get the sex problems to worry about, you've got guys bringing them home to worry about, you get the drugs—I don't want my daughters working in this business. I think [they] should go work in McDonald's [*laughs*]."

The question of dating or marrying strippers also raised issues for cowork-ers. Leo asserted that negative cultural assumptions about stripping would keep him from dating strippers: "I'm . . . not going to feel comfortable when I'm bringing her to a business dinner with a client, and I'm like, 'This is my girlfriend, she's a stripper.'" Frank put things more bluntly: "If I've got steak at home, why am I going to look at hamburger? I don't need it!" Characteriza-tions like those of James, Travis, Frank, and Leo echo prevailing sentiments about strippers: although they are appropriate outlets for men's desires, they carry stigma when placed alongside feminine ideal types, like mothers, wives, girlfriends, daughters, and sisters.

Patrons' accounts also echoed these refrains. Charlie, a thirty-eight-year-old single man, offered a cautionary tale about a relationship between a dancer and a regular patron who showers her with tips. After some time, they fall in love, they get married, and he whisks her "away from this place." Later, after their kids are old enough to ask, "Johnny comes over and says [*in a high-pitched voice*], 'Daddy where did you meet mommy?'" Laughing, Charlie continued, "'Oh, *she* was a stripper! I used to blow singles on her like there was no tomorrow!' Come on, it's just tough to believe that true love can come from lust." As Charlie illustrates, the presumed effects of strippers' work on their children loomed large in men's narratives.

Tales of distress are not uncommon among strippers, lending some truth to pessimistic perceptions of strippers' lives. At only twenty-five years old, Tess had a story that provides an example: "I went to being jobless, home-less, no car, two children with no way to pay for it. That's why I started doing this. . . . If it weren't for the situation I'm in, I would have never been a stripper." Dawn, a nineteen-year-old stripper, described the common back-grounds she saw among strippers: "All dancers, they grew up with almost the same history. They grew up hard, or they've been on their own for a long time." Winston, a fifty-four-year-old regular patron, linked strippers' problems to abuse, poverty, and running away from home. Over the years, Winston hired strippers from the club to work for his construction business. The women he employed came from similar backgrounds: "No money, no nothing, no place to live." He described young women who were "seduced by the money" in strip clubs. In his words, to "a fifteen- or sixteen-year-old girl . . . that's abused . . . sexually and mentally . . . the money looks big when . . . [they] quit school." Rather than provoking sympathy, histories of abuse and assumptions of poor mental health, coupled with negative percep-tions of stripping work, contributed toward coworkers' abilities to discredit strippers.

Stripper stereotypes served an organizational purpose; they reinforced the gender hierarchy within the club by reasserting "appropriate" ways of "doing gender."[23] In other workplaces, this process might involve demeaning humor about women, feminism, or sexuality.[24] Indeed, some coworkers may have had negative preconceptions about women before they began working in The Lion's Den. Regardless, however, all workers were socialized to understand that strippers were unreliable, untrustworthy, and immature. The language these workers used and the descriptions they gave for their work underscore these beliefs. Since management and the broader club culture understood strippers as expendable, they left strippers vulnerable to abuses from both coworkers and patrons.

Female workers were not the only ones who feared social stigma, or shame in the eyes of others, associated with strip club work. For example, Leo also worried about how the industry might affect him. On the positive side, his current employer "love[d] the fact" that he was a deejay at The Lion's Den.

Leo explained: "He's been a customer here. We can share stories. It's kind of almost, like, regular-feeling to him." On the flip side, "people might look down upon the fact that you've been working in a strip club for a long time. Like what if I go to get a job at some corporation? Would a person hire me, [like] a feminist activist . . . who hasn't [seen] what the place is really like and just doesn't condone places like this?" Though male workers also had reason to fear the stigma associated with stripping work, they did not often mention their fears, and, as in the case with Leo, they recognized the benefits as well as the costs.

The Gendered Substructure of The Lion's Den

The gendered substructure of an organization includes its formal work rules. These rules set the stage for gendered processes and the mobilization of gender and sexuality as organizational resources. To delineate this structure, organizations often rely on texts. In The Lion's Den, the *Employee/Entertainer Handbook* outlined the roles and responsibilities for workers. Documenting the voice of management, it demonstrated how "symbols and images . . . explain, express, [and] reinforce . . . [gender] divisions" of labor.[25]

The perspective of those who set "the rules prescribing workplace behavior" was palpable in The Lion's Den.[26] "I'm a professional babysitter is what I am," Steve, the owner-manager, remarked. Later in the same interview, he explained that "babysitting" referred not to everyone in the club but to the strippers: "My least favorite part of the job is dealing with dancers, basically, because they're mostly unreliable, and they'll lie to you constantly. They actually think I believe all of their stories, which is ridiculous, and I really hate being held hostage by a bunch of eighteen-year-olds." Calling strippers "a bunch of eighteen-year-olds" when they're actually, on average, twenty-three years old (with a range from eighteen to thirty-seven), diminishes strippers' life experiences and potential authority.

What is more, club policy institutionalized Steve's overt resentment of strippers through his *Employee/Entertainer Handbook*:

The Dancers: exactly who do you people think you are?!? . . . Do you want to work here or not? . . . Do you realize that the customers really don't care about any personal problem you may have? . . . Do you realize that brown paper towels will not flush down a toilet? Do you realize that walking around with a beer bottle swigging it down looks absolutely classless? Do you realize that chewing gum on stage is tacky? . . . Do you realize that

I don't really believe your excuses? . . . Do you realize that [The Lion's Den] as opposed to ANY other club around will treat you like a human being, rather than a piece of meat? . . . DO YOU ACTUALLY BELIEVE THAT I NEED YOU MORE THAN YOU NEED ME? (emphasis in original)[27]

This paragraph with its repetitive phrasing was the only passage like it in the entire text. The sheer volume of words devoted to strippers illustrated management's perspective. Strippers had almost two and half pages plus an eleven-page appendix on the detrimental effects of recreational drug use devoted to them.

Strippers had a reputation for being heavy drinkers and drug users, and management believed their alcohol and drug use fostered liabilities such as increased physical contact with patrons. The *Employee/Entertainer Handbook* stated that bartenders should "try to the best of your ability to keep track of the alcohol consumption by the dancers."[28] Underscoring the club's assumption of widespread drug use, Steve offered this admonishment:

If . . . you . . . have an expensive "habit" that you're trying to support . . . that is the wrong path. . . . We have all seen the girls on the wrong path; they are the ones with no money, phone, car or even a place to live. They are always tired, have medical issues, lie to themselves and me constantly and are about as useful as tits on a bull. . . . Now if you're one of those girls on the "wrong" path, my goal is to weed you out.[29]

Steve clearly expected bartenders to serve as foot soldiers in his war on drugs. In contrast, bartenders received a simple list of tasks in eleven lines, bouncers and cocktail waitresses had one and a half pages each, and deejays got two pages. The differences in wording for these sections were noteworthy. The *Employee/Entertainer Handbook* provided readers with a clear indication of the organizational logic of The Lion's Den. Each job was associated with a particular set of expectations that not only delineated the organizational hierarchy but also reinforced the devaluation of strippers.[30] Knowing the gender processes within this context allows us to see how management handed down power asymmetries that were reproduced between workers.

Gendered Organizational Context

A gendered organizations approach enhances our understanding of the ways strip clubs operate. Using this framework, I supplement interaction-based perspectives (microlevel analyses that focus on how power is negotiated between strippers and patrons) by situating strippers and patrons within the club context; exploring the perspectives of owners, management, and coworkers; and analyzing the club's organization. Drawing on the work of Joan Acker, we see how gendered processes, the mobilization of stereotypes, and a gendered substructure produced a clear social and organizational pecking order in The Lion's Den.[31] The club's gendered processes fostered a hierarchy that empowered management and male coworkers to exercise authority over strippers. Underscoring this hierarchy was a gendered division of labor that segregated women and men into different jobs. Male coworkers further perpetuated inequalities by stereotyping strippers. Female coworkers also stigmatized strippers, albeit with less formal influence. Finally, an explicit club policy of stripper surveillance and disparagement skewed the balance of power toward management's agenda.

Applying a gendered organizations approach to a strip club, an overtly gendered setting, contributes to gendered organizational theory. As Acker points out, many workplaces create a gendered substructure that is formally neutral.[32] Day-to-day practices coupled with an explicit policy of gender neutrality make organizations "inaccessible to change."[33] In effect, concealing the gendered dynamics of work further entrenches the status quo. Given how well-established gendered hierarchies are in the sex work industry, gender neutrality in work roles would be difficult to sustain. Some jobs are gendered in their titles, like "doorman" and "cocktail waitress." Moreover, the very premise of most strip clubs is gendered from the start, providing "adult entertainment" for men seeking women's performances.

The Lion's Den's gendered substructure could assume gender neutrality for certain jobs—namely, bartenders and deejays. Indeed, other clubs hire both men and women into these positions. Bouncers, by contrast, are normatively assumed to be "younger, muscular, aggressive, and potentially violent men."[34] Presumably, such stereotypical notions underlie the hiring of men as bouncers. While not an explicit rule within this club, women were not employed as bartenders, deejays, or bouncers. In addition to normative expectations, another explanation rests inside the club context. Given the climate of informality, overlapping work roles, and unfilled shifts, male workers often wore multiple hats. Since any of the bartenders, doormen, or deejays might have been called on to act as bouncers or as managers when the owner was away, this association implicitly gendered these jobs.

Context matters. The realities of particular club settings produce their own gendered outcomes. Rather than emphasizing the role of gender neutrality, this research suggests that gendered organization coupled with worker collusion and a gendered substructure may produce intractable organizational norms and practices, or gendered organizational jeopardy. This gendered organizational jeopardy rests on several key facts: (1) the owner-manager enjoyed almost complete control over club operations; (2) though informal, the owner-manager's hiring practices entrenched gendered job segregation; (3) broader cultural and industry-based club norms fostered men's dominance and their maltreatment of strippers; and (4) a lax and often-cynical environment perpetuated worker discontent. Taken together, this evidence from the club suggests continued inequalities for women, most notably strippers.

Localizing power into the hands of men enables men to act on feelings they may have going into their jobs or come to subscribe to over the course of their work. Men who might have resisted the mistreatment of women in The Lion's Den would have faced an uphill battle. Strip clubs, however, cannot be understood in isolation. They are products of their local culture. Other sex-related businesses that follow a gender-segregated organizational formula have similar results. For example, the soft-core pornography film company for *Girls Gone Wild* hires attractive male employees in the hope of recruiting women who strip for "free" in their films.[35] *Guys Gone Wild* productions likewise feature attractive female camera crews to recruit male performers.[36] Despite the ease with which late-night infomercials portray women's participation in these films, Mantra, the parent organization for these productions, reportedly has a more complicated side. The *Girls Gone Wild* enterprise has been peppered with allegations ranging from luring underage girls and using their images without permission to harassment and sexual assault; these are substantiated and unsubstantiated charges.[37] While an organizational analysis would be necessary to outline the dynamics of this relationship, the connection between gender segregation and women's oppression is strongly implied. These examples suggest that the broader sex work industry reproduces and extends gender inequalities found in contemporary American society. As such, The Lion's Den and *Girls Gone Wild* productions act as masculine institutions—contexts in which both the positions and the processes are produced through gender inequalities and characterized by male dominance that yields hostility toward women.[38] Despite these similarities, it is more culturally acceptable for women to strip for a t-shirt in a *Girls Gone Wild* video than to make a living stripping. Reflected in this flawed distinction is an uneasy mix of American titillation with and loathing of women and sex.

Even given the inequalities faced by women working in The Lion's Den, it would be a mistake to conclude that women's low status in the chain of command necessarily translated into low income. In spite of their position at the bottom of the authority and status hierarchies, strippers often made considerably higher incomes than their male coworkers. The contradiction of greater earnings combined with less prestige is part of a larger paradox of gender. On the one hand, in the broader social context of gender inequality and negative attitudes toward female sexuality, the earnings of strippers are both compensation for stigmatized work and evidence that their physical and emotional labor (tailored to men's needs) is worthy of a high return. On the other hand, the devaluation of strippers by their male coworkers levels the social playing field, enabling men to save face despite their lower earnings. This restores a gender hierarchy in which men turn inequality to their own advantage. Though strippers in The Lion's Den outnumbered and outearned male workers, the club's gender rules disempowered and degraded them at an organizational level. Male workers' jealousy over strippers' earnings and ability to make money with little to no previous experience underwrote their poor treatment of strippers. This resulted in strippers enduring the disrespect and scorn of male club workers while simultaneously suffering verbal and physical abuse at the hands of patrons. The connection between strippers' poor treatment and lack of protection creates a dangerous mix when one considers the content of patrons' expectations and demands.

"It's a Nice Place to Hide, and It's Safe"

The Making of Masculinities in The Lion's Den

After working for several days in the club, I realized patrons requested more than drink orders and conversation from cocktail waitresses. On one particular night, a white plumber in his mid-fifties named Glen approached me. Glen was an infrequent customer in the club, but he knew how the place worked. Men made requests, and, most often, women obliged. That is why my interaction with Glen was puzzling and finally frustrating to him. After ordering his drink, Glen asked me how much I charged to flash my breasts. I replied, "I don't flash." He smirked: "Everyone has her price." I smiled and walked away to fill his drink order. When I returned, Glen modified his request: "Twenty to see your tits." When I said "Nope," he replied, "Okay, just show me your feet; I'll give you 5 bucks." When I declined both requests, Glen pursued my feet saying, "They're only your feet!" Each time I neared his side of the room, he shouted out a new figure, raising the dollar amount in increments of five. He pointed to my feet and said, "Ten dollars" all the way up to fifty. Each time I smiled and shook my head no. Finally he stopped me. He began by telling me that he was divorced and had a sexy lover. He wanted me to know that he did not have any problems hooking up with women. Then he asked, "I gotta know, what's your price?" I told him, "I don't have a price, but I'm very curious how high you'll go!" Glen figured if he offered me enough money I would acquiesce. When I did not give in, he gave up and, to save face, walked away saying, "Forget it!"

Strip clubs are places where men like Glen face little fear of rejection. Glen's frustrated attempts to purchase a glimpse of my body ran contrary to his expectations of strip clubs, where seemingly everyone has her price. In this line of work, patrons seemed to think that no request was out of bounds. Though strip clubs socialize patrons to their particular boundaries by post-

ing signs, having deejays make announcements, and instructing club personnel on enforcement, the rules vary widely. In addition, since the stripping
industry, as a whole, reproduces spaces in which seemingly anything is possible, contradictory messages are sent. Thomas Beller, in a recent article for
Men's Health magazine, describes strip clubs as places that foster men's sexual
aggression.[1] Strip clubs, like the one he studied, make it okay for a patron to
be a "man's man," filled with sexual bravado, alcohol, tobacco, and sports:

> The moment you enter [a strip club], you're awakened from your civilized
> slumber and reminded of the style in which you want to f——, and what
> a gross pig you can be. All the dormant, free-floating sexual aggression
> that's been hovering in the back of your mind all day, making little cameo
> appearances in your imagination at staggeringly inappropriate moments,
> now springs into action and takes over your whole brain. It's a release—
> and a relief.[2]

Beller's patron does not represent every man's experience or behavior, but
nevertheless the club context fosters the possibility that every man can be
awakened from his civilized slumber into a state of sexual aggression. Indeed,
since Beller's article appeared in one of the most widely circulated men's
magazines, its publication reinforces the image of a stereotypical patron.[3] It
is both particular clubs and the broader industry, coupled with men's normative, or conventionally and culturally shared, expectations, that create (and
re-create) strip clubs as spaces in which all men can experience themselves as
desirable, connected, and powerful.

An Introduction to Club Patrons

There are many reasons that men visited The Lion's Den. Some patrons
sought to experience their sexuality in supplementary forms or in ways that
might not have been available in their intimate lives. Men may have been in
search of the limited (primarily visual and verbal) experience of imagining
multiple partners. Viewing and interacting with strippers might have offered
a fantasy that patrons used for masturbation or with sexual partners. Alternatively, patrons might have attended the club to see nude female bodies—an
experience that may have been minimal or absent due to youth, old age, dis-
ability, or insecurity. Other patrons might have sought to experience sexuality with an emphasis on fostering bonds between men. Still others were looking to experience male heterosexual dominance.

Anthropologist Katherine Frank characterizes men's strip club patronage as "touristic practices," based around entertainment and leisure within a context that promotes their dominance.[4] The combinations of products—nude women's erotic performances, alcohol, sports broadcasts, and music—are not found everywhere; they are specialized to these particular locales. As such, strip clubs are bounded by norms and expectations of their own that are different from other recreational outlets and workplaces. At the same time, as products of our culture, strip clubs reproduce broader gender, race, sexual, and economic inequalities. This intersection of club- and culture-based norms produces spaces that are at the same time familiar and distinctive.

The range of masculinities performed by male patrons was not just expected but enabled by the gendered organization of work in The Lion's Den that empowered male workers and disempowered strippers. As mentioned in chapter 2, club management expected female workers to be congenial. Patrons' descriptions underscored female workers' friendliness. Jeff called the club "homey." In his words:

[The Lion's Den] is more relaxed. You can come in and . . . there will be one or two of the girls here you know, even if you're coming by yourself or if you're coming with someone else. And the big deal is the girls are nice, as opposed to being commercial somewhere else. The girls are nice.

Craig explained that experienced strippers can evaluate what men want and modify their performances accordingly:

A girl can go to one guy and be the trashiest dirtiest whore, and . . . for [the next] guy's thirty to ninety seconds that girl's in love with him. I've had girls do it, and I get flustered, I get red, and I get butterflies. . . . It's like being in love . . . [briefly], and it goes away. It's very comfortable.

Rather than being "hectic" like other clubs, Jeff explained, The Lion's Den maintained a leisurely pace. Men did not need to feel obligated to sit at the stage; they could sit in the back of the club, watch the game on television, and be served by waitresses who knew them, understood their tastes, and catered to their needs, like a local pub.

The Lion's Den provided men with the opportunity to act out the same or different performances of masculinity in interactions with a variety of women. The masculinities I documented most often were (1) those seeking affirmation, such as desirability and individual worthiness of attention and affection; (2) those of group connectedness or enactments of male bonding and identification; and (3) those of aggression or acts of verbal and physical force toward female workers. These are masculinities institutionalized by patterns within the sex industry and its norms, as well as those produced by the gendered organization of work and men's performances in the club. Such behaviors were not fixed in particular men; rather, some men exhibited more than one of these forms of masculinity during a visit to The Lion's Den. I focus on these performances because they are common forms of masculinity shaped by interactions and the club's gendered organization of work.

Men Seeking Affirmation

Some men placed strippers at the center of their strip club experience. They sought companionship, conversation, and the fruits of emotional labor during their visits to The Lion's Den, a finding that is supported by previous interview and observation-based research.[5] These patrons focused on the strippers; they described being intensely drawn in or emotionally in need of attention from female workers. Some of these men described feeling individually vulnerable outside of the club; they felt isolated and lonely and lacked self-esteem. However, in the club, they experienced themselves as affirmed, connected, and desired. While some men sought a sense of desirability through conversation about their virility,[6] more often men in The Lion's Den sought affirmation of their comprehensive sense of self rather than solely their sexual potency. David John Erickson and Richard Tewksbury conducted research in two Midwestern strip clubs and found similar behaviors among men they identify as lonely and socially impotent.[7] In The Lion's Den, men fitting those descriptions were united through their common desire for affirmation. Craig, a thirty-two-year-old patron, explained:

> This might be a little revealing, but I'll shoot anyway. Women are incredible. Women are wonderful to look at, but women are very scary. You know, the worst a guy is going to do to you is just shoot you—worst-case scenario, you die. Women will do things to you that can make you want to die for years.

For Craig, the club provided a space where exchanges with women were predictable. He knew the women would "be sweet," and he could "do whatever" he wants. Describing his interactions in more detail, he mused: "If I want to sit there for ninety seconds staring straight into [a stripper's] crotch,

I can do that. And if I don't want to deal with it, I'll just start a conversation while she's dancing because, where is she going to go?"

In addition to providing a predictable environment, the club enabled "safe" interactions. Craig continued:

> It's nice and safe. I can't get in any trouble. Nobody's breaking my heart in here. Nobody's getting pregnant in here. Nobody's giving me any diseases in here. Just by the nature of the way it works, no one's really going to be rude to me in here. . . . It's safe. It's a nice place to hide, and it's safe.

Strip clubs provide a space in which men may have little fear of rejection. Indeed, sociologist Elizabeth Wood points out, "rejection almost always happens in one direction—he refuses her dance."[8] Men's advantages in strip clubs are reflected across the broader sex industry, where men are presented with women who are ever eager to please them. Pornography perpetuates this storyline in films where women continually crave sex anywhere, anytime, with anyone. These pornographic images are reproduced in mainstream music videos. Media scholar Sut Jhally's documentary *Dreamworlds 3* vividly portrays women's objectification for men, arguing that "it is this male heterosexual commercial pornographic imagination based on the degradation and control of women that has colonized commercial culture in general."[9] Both in pornography and in the broader culture, these performances and the images therein reflect men's desires, as well as their fears. Indeed, Katherine Liepe-Levinson argues that in these portrayals of women as sex partners "skulks the male fear of female rejection."[10]

Charlie believed that strip clubs provide an "escape" for men from "the stresses of their own lives." Drawing from his experience as a patron, he thought men came to the club "because they're lonely, and it's a cheap form of interaction." He offered that he visited the club because his "home life isn't very good": "I'm the primary caretaker to my mother, so between work and taking care of her, I can usually zip in here for about an hour . . . and it gives me a little bit of escapism." Echoing Craig's remarks, Charlie emphasized that, in the club, no one troubles him: "I can go in a corner and do nothing. I have nobody yelling at me. I have no stresses, no nothing. And it's nice. I need that for about an hour. I could probably find better challenging ways like taking a walk, but it's nice for an hour." Though Charlie's comments may highlight his vulnerability, he and other men were expressing their need for a sense of affirmation in a space that is structured to their individual and collective advantage. Craig and Charlie typify men's descriptions of a desire for relief from the pressures of life, as well as the knowledge that interactions with female workers will be pressure-free.

Stuart, a regular patron who referred to himself as a "dwarf, or more accurately, a small person," provides an example of a vulnerable man who sought affirmation in the club. Drawing on my field notes, the following is a story from one exchange with Stuart. On this particular evening, the club was empty. Stuart approached me while I was serving another regular patron, Joe. He told Joe and me that he was "going on ten years of unwanted celibacy." Soon he asked if I would speak with him alone. As we moved away from Joe, Stuart leaned close to me and asked if I would ever be interested in someone like him. After some back peddling that he was "just wondering" and not "trying to pick me up," I had a chance to respond. Strippers and cocktail waitresses find such questions easy to manage since patrons pose them frequently. Boilerplate responses included not being allowed by the club to date patrons or having a significant other. In this case, I opted for the latter response, and Stuart switched from pursuant to paternalistic, asking, "Are you happy with him; does he treat you right?" Our conversation ended with Stuart instructing me to "tell my boyfriend how lucky he is."

Stuart's interaction with me was typical of his behavior in The Lion's Den. There were countless strippers and waitresses who shared similar stories regarding interactions with him. He repeatedly exposed his loneliness and search for affirmation. Prejudice impacted Stuart's interactions with average-sized women in the broader society and influenced the form and regularity of his visits. In the club, he faced little fear of rejection in his face-to-face interactions with women, though behind his back female workers ridiculed him. Some strippers rolled their eyes when he entered the club, and some complained that he had bad breath and spat when he talked. In part, female workers' scorn may have been a form of blowing off steam at a patron who was not known for tipping well. However, in this case, they were choosing a particularly vulnerable target.

On the simplest level, most men, like Stuart, were paying for interactions structured to their advantage, at least in a short-term sense. Ted described what he thought men got from strip clubs. He believed that The Lion's Den provided something lacking in men's lives—an interaction with a girl and relief from loneliness: "Men can go [to the club] without fear of rejection or reprisal." Though he acknowledged that women paid attention to him and other patrons because of the cash provided, he reasoned that being treated "nicely" by women could be a "boost to your ego," even within the boundaries of the club. In addition, there was always the allure of having a relationship with a woman extend beyond the club: "You could be naive and think the girl's going to have sex with you because you've got $200 in your pocket. . . . I know for a fact that there are guys that . . . do get lucky. . . . But for the most part, you're a fool if you think you're getting anything else," he reasoned.

The search for companionship and escape from loneliness drew Ted and many other patrons to the club. Candidly, he continued: "If I was dating someone, I don't think I'd feel the need to have to go there because I'd have somebody in my life and I wouldn't have to get [companionship] other ways." When I asked Steve, the club's owner-manager, why men came to the club, he argued there were many different reasons but emphasized men's need for attention and affirmation:

> You have the lonely man whose wife died . . . [who wants] . . . somebody to pay attention to him. . . . You've got the guys . . . that went to the top 40 or rock and roll club, got shot down by every girl there, and need to boost their ego back up and have someone make them feel special again—that's the after-midnight crowd.

Similarly, Frank, a doorman at the club, also raised loneliness as an important explanation for why men attend strip clubs: "A lot of them are lonely. I think 50 percent of them are very lonely guys; they think they can pick somebody up here. They haven't had relations with a girl in while."

Some of the patrons turned to male workers for attention and affirmation. Steve, describing one of the regular patrons, explained, "You've got Jerry. . . . I don't think he has any other friends that would give him the time of day, so he comes in here for the friendship thing." Similarly, Frank argued, "That's why they come in here—to try and get rid of their problems. . . . I talk to a lot of guys, and a lot of guys are coming in here 'cause they've broken up with their wives or they had a fight with them. They're just not happy people." Though male workers in The Lion's Den also provided emotional support to patrons, women more frequently performed this work. Frank was particularly unique in this regard; the majority of men in The Lion's Den did not perform the amount of outreach he offered regularly. Aside from one other bartender, most of the male workers socialized primarily with regular customers rather than with all patrons, as strippers and cocktail waitresses did.

Patrons relied heavily on emotional support from female club workers. In The Lion's Den, management required that female workers treat the club as their "living room" and the patrons as their "best friends." The *Employee/ Entertainer Handbook* reads, "Talk to and get to know the customer . . . basically make these people believe that they are your best friend."[11] Management expected women to make men feel that they were intimate friends, lovers, or whatever the men demanded. It is not surprising that during our interview Steve invoked Wal-Mart as his inspiration for worker and patron (read: guest) relations in the club. He explained that cocktail waitresses should act as the club's greeters—the individuals one meets upon entering the doors of a Wal-Mart. As corporatizations homogenize many commercial relationships between individuals, these models are reproduced again and again in various locations. No doubt Sam Walton did not envision his model for customer care being taken up by strip clubs. Meika Loe found similar patterns in her research at Bazooms, a themed restaurant chain featuring women in midriff-baring shirts and short shorts.[12] In this corporate chain, waitresses were issued clear guidelines about their presentation of self that required "always smiling" and "appear[ing] to have a great time" for customers.[13]

Alongside management's expectations, the pressures for women to conform were significant. To be sure, their livelihoods depended on their ability to attract and maintain men's attention and the associated cash tips. Amelia discussed the huge amount of emotional labor she performed for men and the toll it took on her:

> I would say there are so many emotionally sick people. . . . I have to listen, to be his friend, [and] understand him, to participate in his situation. Sometimes they even wait for me for advice. . . . They all need a good psychologist—they need medical treatment because they're miserable [*laughing*].

Strippers echoed the description of patrons as lonely and needing to be desired. Tamara stressed loneliness as the reason men attend strip clubs: "I think a lot of men are just lonely, and they're looking for a quick lay." Similarly, Tess emphasized both loneliness and affirmation when she explained that older men came into The Lion's Den to talk: "It's not the young guys that we make our money off of—it's the older guys who have nobody at home, who are lonely . . . or even the young guys who are . . . the ones who spend the most money [who] don't want you to dance. They want you to talk [with them]." Stella also felt that many men came to the club for "conversation":

> They want to feel wanted. Like cute girls want them. Like they actually have a chance with us. Even for that half-hour—that hour that they're here— they want to feel like they can have any pretty woman in here that they want come sit next to them—even just to talk to them. To be listened to.

The emotional labor performed by strippers was often effective. Larry described his relationship with Angela, a stripper he visited regularly. Angela was twenty-one years old and petite, with tanned skin and long dark hair. Larry was short and much older, with a receding hairline, a large potbelly, and huge, round glasses. He explained that most people would not understand their relationship: "Most people would think we are friends only because of her work, but we are friends because we have a good time laughing together." He continued: "Most people would be surprised to see Angela with someone like me. But we love to hang out, and she always laughs at my jokes. We are playful together, and that's why we make sense." In this exchange, Larry emphasized the authenticity of his relationship with Angela. Conspicuously absent was any mention of the enormous sums of money he paid to her on a regular basis. By emphasizing the genuineness of his interaction, rather than the money he spent buying Angela drinks or paying for private dances, he reinforced this impression for himself. Men like Larry were displaying their need for affirmation rather than affirming their prowess.

All types of men who are seeking companionship from women in strip clubs are doing so in a space where women must comply or risk their livelihoods. While strippers and cocktail waitresses are receiving at least economic compensation from their work in a club, and for some (particularly new workers) the pleasure that may come with frequent compliments from men, women report that these rewards diminish over time.[14] In addition, these gains are overshadowed by a context and work organization that contribute to women's collective subordination.

Men seeking affirmation often emphasized the "genuineness" in their interactions with strippers by minimizing the role money played in the exchange. As Katherine Frank points out, "The payment of money . . . has the potential to unsettle an interaction because its symbolic value is one·that is ideologically incommensurable with romantic love or true friendship."[15] In her work at high-end gentleman's clubs, Frank observed that some of the men were able to escape the potential disconnect by demonstrating that "money was irrelevant to them" through the purchase of expensive gifts and dinners and buying time off the schedule at $100 an hour.[16] Men in The Lion's Den, by contrast, did not often have the means to accomplish such sizeable financial displays and, instead, adopted a variety of informal strategies to mask their payments. Men seeking a sense of desirability tipped more sporadically in large amounts. For example, rather than simply paying for each $20 dance individually, some patrons paid $60 in advance for multiple dances, as well as providing a tip. They also referred to the money given as a "gift" rather than a payment. Alternatively, rather than buying a dance, they might have bought a stripper a drink in order to spend time with her. In this way, less-affluent patrons were able to save face without going above the typical payment for a stripper's time and performance. While the exchange was still present, it was somewhat masked. In a sense, the patron's money was buying him the denial of the role of money.

In The Lion's Den there was a tension between the impersonal and the personal in exchanges between patrons and women. Women most often emphasized the impersonal quality of their exchanges with men as a means of coping with their work. Stella explained that men want strippers to reduce the role money plays in these transactions: "They know that you're here for the money, but then again they don't want to see it. 'Oh, she's not really interested in me. She was just talking to me because she wanted a dance.'" Stella devised a strategy to address these concerns: "I'll sit and talk with a guy for a couple of minutes, and if he seems really interested, and if we're having good conversation, I'll throw it in there—I'll be, like, 'So do you want a dance?'" Sometimes men responded to her by asking, "That's the only reason you're sitting with me?" In response, she explained, "I'll be like, 'No, if that's the reason I would have asked you a long time ago. I'm sitting here for five or ten minutes talking to you. I could have asked like three other guys for a dance.'" As this example points out, Stella provided emotional support to maintain the charade that she was genuinely interested in a patron and not there just to earn money. Similarly, Tess argued, "They don't want to know that you're here for the money. Men want to feel like you want to talk with them. Even though they know it's your job, they don't want to feel that." Echoing these sentiments, Elisabeth Eaves, a former stripper and author of *Bare*, describes it in her autobiographical account of strip club work:

> It was working the floor of a club and providing all the false kindness that the customers expected in exchange for cash. Flattering a man with looks and words while I calculated what I could make off him had made me palpably more cynical. Even more sinister, however, was the way the customers treated these exchanges as normal. They wanted fawning, illusive female charm, and they knew it was for sale along with everything else.[17]

The patrons had a fantasy of a loyalty that cannot be present if strippers are to make money. Rather than being disconnected from these exchanges, Robin illustrated the way patrons at The Lion's Den became proprietary over the strippers they tipped:

Some guys get weird about it if you . . . talk with them for a little while and then move on and talk with someone else. . . . They'll give you a lot of money, and then they'll see you talking to someone else, and when you get onstage, they'll ignore you, like, what are you doing talking to other people?

Robin relayed a story of her experience with Kevin, a patron she knew from another strip club. He visited the club regularly to chat with her but rarely received dances. Nevertheless, he gave her cash tips. She explained, "We'd just sit there talking, and every couple of minutes he'd throw a twenty at me, because he was taking up my time. He said I'm here to make money, and because I'm sitting there with him I wasn't making money. So Kevin used to pay me to talk with him." Kevin maintained the illusion that he was helping Robin by giving her money, not for her services but because he was "taking up her time" and therefore she was "not making money." Clearly, Robin was making money from Kevin, though he successfully deceived himself that she was with him for conversation. Kevin was so convinced by Robin's performance that when he gave her his number and she did not call, he came into the club and confronted her. As Robin retold the story, Kevin approached her angrily and said, "You gave me hope, and then you take it away like that." Robin continued, "Well, that night when he came in here we got into an argument. He was telling me I was a phony and this and that. He said I was just out for myself. I was like, what did I get from taking two hours out of my time?" Robin's story involved issues of performance and authenticity. It epitomizes the struggle that engaged men and women in strip clubs— the men were seeking, and, in this case, demanding, more intimacy, while women were struggling with the demands of performing emotional support. Kevin, who wanted to view their interaction as more genuine, expressed his frustration when he said Robin was a phony and just out for herself.

Ted demonstrated the difficulty men have with issues of authenticity through his relationship with Jane, a dancer he used to visit frequently in the club. Ted and Jane's connection typified that of a regular patron and stripper. For months, Ted visited the club during Jane's shifts, provided her with tips onstage, bought her drinks, and paid for private dances offstage. At one point in their relationship, Ted claimed that Jane had asked for his phone number. Later, when Jane explained that she had broken up with her boyfriend, Ted invited her to give him a call since she already had his number. To that, Jane replied that she "threw [his phone number] away as soon as [he] gave it to [her]." When Ted learned that Jane had tossed his number, he was furious: "I think [dancers] can be fair to a customer, giving them what they expect without making any innuendos of other things that may be possible, which you know are not. I don't think that's right." Ted's overt disappointment was palpable in his voice, which shook with the strain of mounting anger as he recalled this story: "The girl shouldn't be asking—making promises that she knows she's never going to keep. . . . [She should be] morally honest in a way that the guy's not going to expect something that you're never going to give."

What Ted so aptly described is the tightrope that strippers walk: cultivating interest while fending off fixation. They run the risk that men will misinterpret these exchanges as genuine. Those men, like Ted, who fell for strippers' acts often responded harshly when they realized that what they got in the club was paid labor, not "free expression." Jane's reaction was in keeping with the behavior of most strippers, who threw away many patrons' telephone numbers each night. Though it is possible that Jane asked or perhaps simply agreed to receive Ted's phone number in order to foster his interest or increase her tips, it is unlikely that she planned to call him. This event provided a turning point for Ted: while he remained friendly with Jane, he no longer visited her as a regular patron. Instead, Ted became an employee of the club. Given the strain and anger still expressed in his voice as he told this story, the experience may very well have influenced his treatment of other patrons and dancers in similar situations.

The search for intimacy and authenticity by patrons in The Lion's Den runs counter to normative assumptions about why individuals seek the services of sex workers—namely, to gain a sexual experience that lacks ties or attachment. Earlier arguments about sex work and money, like those made by Georg Simmel, emphasized this claim. Simmel and Donald Levine argued that the "nature of money resembles the nature of prostitution" because of "the indifference with which it lends itself to any use, the infidelity with which it leaves everyone, its lack of ties to anyone, its complete objectification that excludes any attachment."[18] This assumption that prostitute-client relations lack attachment reflects a false distinction drawn between sex workers and non-sex workers. As legal scholars David Selfe and Vincent Burke argue, "prostitutes are distinguished from non-prostitutes because of the ephemeral nature of their associations and converse lack of long term relationships[;] . . . [however,] it is clear that many prostitutes do have regular customers."[19] Given the variation in the kinds of work performed, context provides the key to understanding the content of relationships between sex workers and clients. Wendy Chapkis explains:

Sex workers all perform erotic labor, but their accounts of that experience vary dramatically from the "happy hooker" to the "sex work survivor." The source of those differences may be less in the "nature" of erotic labor than in the social location of the worker performing it and the conditions under which the work takes place.[20]

The emphasis on fleeting prostitute-client ties may also stem from the fact that much of the research on prostitution focuses on street workers, despite their relatively small numbers and disproportionally difficult working conditions.[21]

What the narratives and observations from The Lion's Den indicate is that some men seek just the opposite—not an impersonal encounter but a personal tie and a sense of attachment. Studies of strippers and regular patrons have found similar results.[22] Dancer-researcher Danielle Egan found that regular strip club patrons "fall in love in exotic dance clubs" and "blurred the lines between affect and consumption."[23] Egan's argument is that regular patrons sought emotional consumption of uncomplicated relationships. In her words, "regulars did not want wives, girlfriends, or mistresses—they wanted dancers" who could provide "connection and love without responsibility."[24] Similarly, Katherine Frank, who also worked as a stripper while researching regular patrons, concluded that men focused on the authenticity of their interactions with strippers to understand and negotiate their sense of self, as well as their club relationships.[25] In both cases, male patrons were not seeking an alternative to strip club interactions but a meaningful understanding of how their own identities and relationships made sense, given the context.

Focusing on the perspective of workers, Elizabeth Bernstein, a sociologist and feminist activist, contends that "sex workers advertise themselves as 'girlfriends for hire' and describe the ways in which they offer not merely eroticism but authentic intimate connection for sale in the marketplace."[26] Here again the emphasis is on contextualizing meaning and setting to fully understand sex work and its implications for workers and consumers. Rather than either providing intimacy or not, contemporary sex work is best understood as part of a larger trend of the late twentieth century that saw service work, carework, and emotional labor increasingly supplied in the marketplace.[27] Today paid workers, including sex workers, satisfy diverse familial and household needs.

Performances of Group Connectedness

In contrast to the men who sought affirmation, some men focused on other men—friends they attended with, regular patrons, or club workers. These men's primary interest was with one another and their group affiliation. While they also sought affirmation or desirability, for them, female club workers formed a backdrop that facilitated relations with other men. They had identifiable, interdependent, and previously established identities put on display through their interactions and conversations in the club. Other groups were loosely identified, such as groups of friends bonding around ritualized events like birthdays, bachelor parties, or fraternity outings, where the event became the focus. What sets group attendance apart is that, in these cases, men were attending to interact with strippers and cocktail waitresses in the presence of specific other men.

The connection social actors experience between their sense of self and collective dynamics is explored in Erving Goffman's 1959 classic sociological study, *The Presentation of Self in Everyday Life*. Drawing on stage acting as a metaphor and guiding principle, Goffman considered social interactions to be performances (just as actors perform on a stage). He was concerned with how social actors create meanings and understandings in these performances for themselves and others. On the group level, Goffman drew an analogy between collections of individuals and teams. To create collective meanings, teams work together in their performance. Consider supporters of sports teams, who reaffirm their group membership by attending games together, talking about their teams, learning and reciting chants, and wearing team garb. Groups of men who visited the The Lion's Den typified Goffman's groups by cooperating to perform their connectedness. As such, groups of patrons often consisted of men with "bonds of reciprocal dependence and reciprocal familiarity" as employer and employee, family members, or coworkers.[28] Far from being inconsequential, Goffman argued, perceptions of self are built during such occasions that facilitate group performance.

When Ted began thinking about why men go to strip clubs, he immediately raised the issue of groups:

> There are the groups who just come to hang out, and they seek a good time being with friends. Having entertainment there probably solidifies things that they can do together. . . . The guys who come in large groups might be showing off or proving you're a man.

Through conspicuous consumption of drinks and interactions with numerous women, adult men can live the fantasy of the ultimate playboy. As rites of passage, strip clubs usher young men into a space for adult masculinity and sexual fantasy. Taken collectively, strip clubs reproduce this process on a massive scale through thousands of clubs nationwide. Similarly, Playboy

Corporation and its empire have "collectivized" mass standards for masculinity through multiple media outlets. Raewyn Connell elaborates:

> The readership of this magazine was positioned as a corporate sexual hero, consuming an endless supply of desirable "girls." The Playboy Corporation managed a double commercialization of this fantasy in 1960 with the opening of the Playboy Clubs. A readership was converted into a membership, with women employees grotesquely subordinated as "Bunnies." The growth of the video pornography industry suggests this collectivization is still going on.[29]

Strip clubs continue Hugh Hefner's work, collectivizing the sex industry's vision of the consummate male "playboy" performance. It is this collective experience that allows men to perform masculinity for other men in a safe space with no real fears of rejection and the presence of women to mitigate homophobia.

Leo identified men who attended in groups as a distinct category. In his opinion, group strip club attendance had more to do with group unification than it did with a sexual experience:

> There's a lot of guys who come in here—it's something to do with guys— like you get a bunch of guys and instead of drinking in a bar, you come in and drink in a place like this, which is cool. . . . Take your friends out for their birthdays and get them onstage and embarrass the hell out of them.

For Leo, groups centered on the "unsexual side" of strip club attendance. While there may have been sexual components to group attendance, Leo's emphasis on the interactions within the group demonstrates that "masculinity is a homosocial enactment": men perform their manhood for other men's appreciation.[30] The meanings generated by these groups' performances varied. In some cases, "participants co-operated together as a team or were in a position where they were dependent upon this co-operation in order to maintain a particular definition of the situation."[31] There was also, in one of the cases presented below, both cooperation and resistance to a particular performance of masculinity. The key here is that masculinity is a performance that, especially if it is to be successful, requires an audience. All three of the stories that follow are drawn from my field notes.

The first group included three coworkers. All dark-haired, white men, in their mid fifties, this group arrived dressed in blue jeans and t-shirts. Sitting at the stage, the men ordered two rounds of Heinekens and filled their ash-tray to overflowing before engaging me in conversation. One by one, the men introduced themselves, asked my name, offered theirs, and complimented my skills as a waitress. Throughout the night they called "Kim!" across the club to beckon me to the stage to take their drink orders. Rather than purchasing private dances, the men stuck together in the same seats all night, provid-ing $1 tips to the dancers performing onstage. All the while, they traded off paying for three additional rounds of identical drinks. As each took his turn picking up the tab, he asked loudly if his friends had been tipping me well. The eavesdropping friends both protested and laughed at this gesture. Every time, I smiled and said, "Yes, they are being quite generous."

Later in the evening, two of the men explained that they were celebrat-ing for the third friend, who was leaving on vacation. The vacationer, they explained, had worked long hours at a large retail food company's corpo-rate headquarters, where they were all employed, presumably in white-collar jobs. Initially, they praised the vacationer's hard work and long hours on the job. Later, they ribbed him for vacationing without them, asking if I agreed that it is wrong to leave one's friends behind. Responding to this teasing, the vacationer asked me to join him on his upcoming travels. As I thanked him for his offer, his friends feigned disappointment through groans and sighs. Our pattern of interaction continued until the three men were almost out the door. At the end of the night, they called out to me as I hurriedly cleared drinks. They asked if I could remember their names. I remembered and called out two but forgot the third. This led them to single out and heckle the forgotten man with laughter. They then made a point for me to remember his name: "It's a classic Italian name—you must know it!" So, I called out, "Tony?" They responded with cheers and patted their friend on the back as they left, saying, "You're not a total loser—she didn't forget you after all."

As coworkers, this group acted out its connectedness through discus-sions of themselves with me. Their displays focused less on any hierarchy that may have been present and more on demonstrating their mutual friend-ship through jokes about tipping and whether I remembered their names. Rather than opting for conspicuous consumption in which some men might tip from 50 to more than 100 percent of the tab, these men opted for more routine displays. All of the men watched as each tipped between $2 and $3, depending on the size of the bills they used, or nearly 20 percent every round. Demonstrating their financial resources for each other was less a rivalry than a routine since they were all in cahoots and followed the same patterns. Simi-larly, sharing their names was part of sharing their interactions with me in a more personal way. By using my name, the men may have appeared to be regulars to other outsiders in the club, though they had never visited The Lion's Den before this occasion and, to my knowledge, did not return.

Relationships among patrons were not always this egalitarian, as illustrated by a narrative about a group of four Korean American businessmen. During a Thursday shift, I approached the men seated in club chairs near the center of the room and offered to bring them drinks. One man in the group, dressed in a white button-down shirt and dark wool trousers, took charge and ordered a round for the others, handing me a $100 bill and requesting his change from the drinks in twenties. His companions were more casually dressed in khakis and white, short-sleeved t-shirts. When I returned to the bar to fill their order, the bartender explained to me that the patron who placed the order was an out-of-town businessman who came in periodically with different groups of workers. After delivering four Heinekens, I approached the boss to return his change. He handed me the remaining singles and turned to his companions and asked, "Isn't she beautiful?" He then turned to me and said, "You are beautiful." I thanked him and asked, "What brings you to town?" The boss explained, "We're in the area on business." As I walked away, a stripper between her stage sets pulled up another large club chair and joined them. From the service bar, I could see lots of smiles, laughter, and drinking among the group.

Later in the evening, the boss requested another round from across the room by raising a bottle and holding up four fingers. When I returned with the second round of drinks, the boss made an even bigger fuss over me, repeating again and again how beautiful I was and asking his companions, as well as the stripper, to agree. He waved around a $20 bill to coax me closer and to amplify the visibility of his tip. I thanked him and politely declined his offer to place the tip down my shirt by instead reaching my hand out and taking the offered bill. He then waved me away. While it was somewhat uncommon to receive such a high tip for a single round of drinks, it was common for businessmen with their clients or coworkers to tip visibly well. Over the course of the evening, I returned to this group four or five more times with rounds of beers ordered by the boss, while half-full beers sat on the table.

Later, when I filled in behind the bar so the bartender could take a bathroom break, the boss joined me and began again to tell me how beautiful I was. Before his arrival, I had talked with a stripper whose cat just had kittens. By way of introduction, I mentioned this to the patron as he approached and I introduced him to the stripper I had been talking to. He latched on to the kitten idea and began repeating that he wanted to be my cat. He described how he could crawl around my feet while I was naked. I laughed at the direction our conversation was taking as he moved it toward such sexual talk. Each time I served a drink to the few patrons who approached the bar, the boss tried to touch me. I was relieved to have the bar between us. His companions looked on from across the room and whispered to each other while we talked. When I noticed his friends leaving, I asked him if he should join them. He replied that they would just have to wait for him, reminding me again that he wanted to be my cat. In all, he had them wait for about fifteen minutes while he talked with me at the bar. He asked to join me in whatever I was drinking, so I offered him a Coke. He drank with me, asking if it was okay for him to stay and chat. I replied, "Of course," and tried to turn the conversation toward him by asking him questions about himself—where he grew up, where he currently lived, if he liked his job—but each time he returned to his line about being my cat. After approximately ten minutes, he moved to leave, telling me that he would be back to see me after his vacation.

In this group, the boss demonstrated his power over his employees in many ways: by paying for round after round of unfinished drinks, providing extravagant and highly visible tips, orchestrating the groups' conversations about me, leaving the group so they could watch him interact with me, and, finally, by making them wait, presumably out in the car, while he talked with me. Since, as the bartender informed me, the boss attended the club regularly with different groups of workers, we can say that he ritualized these events. Through these performances in The Lion's Den, the boss habitually displayed his place in the hierarchy. The employees resigned themselves to his agenda by whispering and eventually leaving before he did.

The third narrative example focuses on a group consisting of a white professional father and his two sons. Dressed casually in t-shirts and blue jeans, the two young men sat to one side of their father, who was wearing khakis and a polo shirt. The three men were positioned so that the eldest man was sitting just outside of the sandbox in the over-twenty-one section, while the two younger men were confined to the sandbox's seats for eighteen- to twenty-year-olds. As I approached the trio, the older son asked me to guess their ages. I told him I was not good at guessing ages. Then he asked if I could tell who was the father and who were the sons. Though I could clearly pick out the father as well as the order of their ages, I played along, to their delight. I feigned contemplation for a few moments and then smiled, pointing to the youngest, and said, "You must be the father." With this, the older son leaned back in his chair, laughing. I paused a few moments, pointed to the father, and said, "You are clearly the youngest." With this, the father motioned me closer and whispered, "You really can't tell these are my sons?" I smiled again, moving away, and told him that he must be kidding, or he must just age well. He smiled widely and mouthed, "Thank you." When I came back with their drinks, a beer and two Cokes, the younger son said, "Isn't our dad cool? He's always taken us out with him!" I replied by acknowledging the family: "Yes, it's great when family members enjoy each other's company so much." The father then leaned toward me and told me that he'd always taken his sons out: "I'd rather have them experiment with me than with their numbskull friends who will get them into trouble."

The third group played out their bond through their roles as father and sons. By playing the age game with me, the sons sought to praise their father. The game was somewhat ridiculous, since the young men were seated in a section designated by age, providing evidence that this might have been their first trip to The Lion's Den. Still, the young men showed a familiarity with tipping at the stage, an activity that usually comes with some experience, perhaps from other clubs. The family's display of their connectedness was central to their interactions with me. There was agreement within the group as to their performance: the sons drew attention to their connection with their father and his role in their upbringing. They sought my appreciation, recognition, and approval to underscore the appropriateness of their performance. In so doing, the father expressed a coming-of-age motif that is reflected in the gender literature. As Michael Kimmel explains, "Pornography occupies a special place in the development of men's sexuality. Nearly all men confess to having some exposure to pornography, at least as adolescents; indeed, for many men the first naked women they see are in pornographic magazines or videos."[32] Similarly, by bringing his sons to the strip club, the father demonstrated the normative role the sex industry plays in constructing adolescent men's sexuality.

While these groups differed in both their interactions and their makeup, their relationship to the cocktail waitress played out in similar ways. They each sought to establish particular bonds within the group through their interactions with me, the cocktail waitress. Anthropologist Anne Allison, in her book *Nightwork,* examined Tokyo hostess clubs—establishments that offer alcohol and entertainment (female hostesses and karaoke) to groups of Japanese businessmen at the expense of their companies.[33] While there are many differences between hostess clubs and strip clubs, the similarities are striking. Describing a series of interactions among groups of patrons, Allison writes, "The planners selected the same format—alcohol, women, and sexual play. This format was chosen for its assumed appeal to the male participants and to encourage a heightened sense of maleness that would link them together. That is, maleness was made to be ritualistic and symbolic."[34]

For the women performing the work of cocktail waitresses and strippers in The Lion's Den, interactions with patrons also became scripted encounters, with similar expectations of attention, kindness, and flirtation.

In addition to the groups of patrons who attended the club occasionally, a core group of men frequented the club many days each week. For such regulars, The Lion's Den was a home away from home. While at times regular patrons sought out a specific dancer and fostered a routine relationship with her, their principal allegiance was to The Lion's Den more generally. By contrast, other men identified more with a particular dancer, following her to her appearances at other clubs. The regulars were known by the club's workers and provided a reliable source of income. Club regulars became part of the friendships and community associated with The Lion's Den. Often these men performed favors like going to the store, or they might be given a formal job within the club. Brad was one such patron who visited The Lion's Den many nights each week, helping to clear glasses and stock beer after closing. He began frequenting the club after he turned twenty-one, when a friend "dragged" him to visit. Living nearby, Brad's visits became routine; he saw The Lion's Den as his "neighborhood bar." He became friends with strippers, as well as the bartenders and bouncers. Rolling his eyes toward the strippers performing on the stage, he said to me, "You know, I don't come here for that. This place is like *Cheers* for me: you come in and everyone knows your name."

Conventionally, strip clubs are considered places where men come to interact with women; however, this was not the only motivation for many of the club regulars. Club regulars usually sat together with other men watching the strippers or stood at the bar talking with the bartender and other employees. Roxanne explained that nearly all of the regulars visited the club because of friendships they had developed with workers or strippers: "Ninety percent of the regulars are friends of the doorman [Frank]. I have a couple of regulars who come in . . . that I consider friends. That's why they come in—we hang out and have a couple drinks and talk and stuff." Rather than emphasizing the fantasy or erotic content of the club, Roxanne believed these men visited "just to hang out." She described the difference between regular patrons and everyone else who visited the club this way:

> They know us better. Like Vince is a prime example. He comes in all the time. He'll give you 50 bucks to do a table dance. You do your dance, but 90 percent of the time he's talking during it. He just knows us so he comes in and hangs out and says, "Here's some money."

Club regulars often sought to normalize the goings-on in The Lion's Den and, consequently, to normalize their frequent attendance. However, they seemed acutely aware of the associated stigma. Thirty-three-year-old patron Jack had this to say when I asked what drew him to The Lion's Den: "A healthy dose of testosterone and sports, that's what I'm looking for when I come here, and there's nothing wrong with that, right?" Jack, however, rarely paid much attention to the television sets or the dancers' stage performances, despite his emphasis on their importance in The Lion's Den. He was most often found around the bar talking with workers or seated at a table talking with other club regulars. Ned, thirty-six years old and a veteran club bartender of thirteen years, offered this description of the club's regular patrons: "Some [patrons] come in to shoot the shit. Some of them come in here to ease their way into diddlin' [female workers]. You know my lingo." Rather than emphasizing a difference between men who want to talk and those who want to touch the dancers, he concluded, "Ultimately, they're both here for the chicks. The ultimate goal is to diddle, for them all. You can talk sports anywhere—men come here to diddle."

The difference between regular patrons and other patrons more generally was that most patrons sought out company with strippers and cocktail waitresses, not employees or other patrons, aside from those they arrived with. Instead, the regular patrons preferred talking about sports with Ned the bartender or Frank the doorman. Perhaps the conversation with the other men drew regular patrons. It is also possible that conversation made the regulars more relaxed before they interacted with the dancers. Alternatively, the regulars may have regarded their connections with club workers as a segue to meeting and gaining the trust of the dancers. Regular patrons may have also seen their connections to other workers as a ticket toward free entry into The Lion's Den or free drinks. The benefit of free entry and drinks may have been crucial to patrons attending The Lion's Den several nights each week, since the $5 door fee and one-drink minimum (beginning at $3) quickly adds up. For others, regular patronage and club connections led to fill-in or permanent job offers. Marcus explained: "My girlfriend was actually a dancer at the time, and they needed somebody to fill in. . . . The following week [it was] the same thing. . . . The manager walks up and goes, 'I'm just going to leave you on from now on.' . . . Four years later . . . [laughs]." Similarly, Ned described the many friends he hired into club work: "I've had so many friends. If they're really hurting, numerous times I've hired friends of mine, numerous times. . . . I just hired a guy; he only worked for a few days, but he called me up out of nowhere."

Though regular patronage and connections may have made a worker seem easier to hire or more desirable to the club, turning patrons into workers could have had problematic consequences. Take, for example, the previous discussion of Ted's relationship with Jane. Ted's continued anger, still apparent many months after Jane discarded his phone number, suggests that he may not have always been a neutral figure in his roles as bartender, bouncer, and doorman. In particular, his role as bartender necessitated that he serve as manager in charge when the owner-manager was away. As such, he could have been called to protect women like Jane. Moreover, since Jane still performed in the club from time to time, he oversaw her work. The potential for men like Ted to project frustration onto one particular dancer or another could result in biased judgments and abuse of authority, both of which could spell problems for dancers.

Performances of Aggression

Alongside patrons seeking affirmation and group affiliation were performances of aggression in The Lion's Den. As Connell reminds us, "in adult sexuality, a predatory heterosexuality may co-exist with desire to be nurtured."[35] Nowhere is this more evident than within the environment of a strip club, where norms around perceptions of what counts as "aggressive" or "predatory" are context-bound. For example, strip clubs permit a range of sexually explicit talk that might be considered offensive elsewhere. Add to this Erickson and Tewksbury's assertion that "opportunities for men to be stereotypical men are diminishing; strip clubs provide this opportunity."[36] Some of the men's requests were commonplace—patrons expressed interest in viewing certain body parts, hearing certain stories, or having no conversation at all. Steve explained to me that female workers knew what to expect with strip club work. Nevertheless, he said, "I ask them all in their interviews if they have a problem with the nudity and if they have a problem with guys making rude comments, 'cause we are serving alcohol, and the guys are going to tell you things that they aren't going to tell you in church on Sunday." More specifically, Tamara argued: "A lot of men like to degrade women; they have anger issues toward women." When I asked her if she would recommend stripping to her friends, she explained her hesitation:

> Depends on what they look like. . . . Guys are mean. Guys can be really mean. Especially if you're a little bit overweight or anything like that, the guys will come down on you, and they'll make rude comments. I've seen girls get so crushed from it, so I would try to protect my friends from that.

While strippers expect sexually explicit verbal exchanges with men, female workers recognize a boundary between acceptable and unacceptable talk. As Mindy explained, there is some variation from night to night:

Like, if it's a slower night, and the guys are nicer, and they're not saying rude things to you, it's easier to come to work and be happy and to not get upset. But there's nights when there's guys in there that'll say things, or they're just rude in general, and it puts a mental strain on you. It's kind of harder to deal with.

Although the range of acceptable behaviors may be broader than in many work contexts, female workers in the club considered some comments to be outside the scope of acceptable behavior. Unacceptable talk included verbal aggression in the form of conversations about forceful sex acts, put-downs, or negative comments about strippers' bodies or minds. Summer explained:

This guy told me I had saggy boobs. He's like, "Your boobs are saggy." I'm like, "What are you talking about?" Fucking men. They get off on shitting on people, I guess. I see it all the time. They shit on the dancers, the waitresses. . . . It's a power trip to make themselves feel better.

Attributing men's behavior to the club context, Roxanne said, "They want . . . to touch you or grope you or do whatever . . . and say whatever they want to me, stuff that they wouldn't do or say to their girlfriends or wives. . . . I think 90 percent of why [men] come in here [is that] they can disrespect us." In addition to aggressive talk, patrons used offers of money to control or humiliate strippers. Stella relayed the following story: "There was this one guy who was in here one night that offered every girl $20 to hop down the bunny trail—down one end of the stage, hopping like a bunny."

Many of the aggressive comments made by patrons toward women in the club were not precipitated by any outward hostility on the part of the targeted women. For example, Chris was a familiar patron from his many nights in the club. A quiet and apparently mild-tempered man, Chris would often ask me how my research was coming. Although he typically sat in the back of the room near the television and chain-smoked as he downed beers, on this particular night he was seated at the stage. When he motioned to place a drink order, I approached while Rebecca performed for him. Chris asked for a shot, and Rebecca leaned over to request that he purchase one for her, too. He replied, "Shut up, you cunt. I just want to see your cunt, not hear you." In these comments, patrons normalized aggression and violence toward women by reproducing it and giving it an accepted and unchallenged space. The following event from my field notes took place on a Saturday night after the funeral of a longtime patron named John:

> Kent, dressed all in black with a large gold cross around his neck (and positioned over his shirt like a clergyman), made a toast to John, a deceased friend and regular patron. After bellowing to the deejay to turn up the Led Zeppelin song he'd requested in John's memory, Kent raised his shot glass to the two bartenders on staff and said, "Here's to a man who could drink, fight, go home and beat his wife . . ."

Kent's comments were met with bowed heads, heavy nods, and raised glasses. To thrive, violence needs an accepted space where it can be discussed and enacted without hesitation or disruption.[37] The Lion's Den provided this space. Even when violence was not committed, the space for it was reaffirmed.

Patrons' aggressive talk took a variety of forms. Regular patrons often played up their identity as "men" by speaking about physical bar fights and heavy drinking. Regulars and male employees emphasized physical aggression and toughness in their exchanges with one another. Most of the club regulars were white and engaged in racist dialogue with the white workers about Latino and African American men. Their racism toward Latina and African American female workers was present, albeit less consistent. Hank, a white male patron who wore leather and rode a Harley Davidson motorcycle, provided an example in a story he told to his white male friend, Ned the bartender, and me. Hank's tone of voice was harsh, and his eyes narrowed as he described a recent surprise he had planned for his girlfriend. She had two jobs and was working consecutive shifts on Valentine's Day. Hank met her at the bar for her early shift with a dozen red roses and twin lobster tails. He parked his pickup truck outside her workplace, thinking he would return soon. He ended up having a drink and staying longer than he had planned, and when he returned to the lot he found his window smashed, all of his CDs gone, and his phone removed. Red-faced, he spat, "I'm not racist; I like black and Puerto Rican people." He turned and gestured out toward the rest of The Lion's Den, presumably to indicate that any African Americans or Puerto Ricans present were exempt:

> It was a fucking nigger or a spic . . . a fucking nigger or a spic! Goddamn bastards! Oh, do I want to find that guy. I'd like to pump a few rounds into

him. It was my fucking entire CD collection, and I'd just replaced it for over $375. And my phone was another $200. I'd like to get my hands on that bastard.

Ned just shook his head at Hank and said, "That's too bad, my man."

Hank's performance was racist and violent. He spouted race prejudice with only one hesitation: his racism excluded those African Americans and Puerto Ricans who might happen to be in The Lion's Den. Here the "talk is of differences in culture, class, values and life-styles" in addition to race.[38] This was the form most of the racist talk took in the club: men denied being racist and indicated that they had friends who were of the targeted racial or ethnic minority. Once this disclaimer was made, the racist dialogue that followed was not interrupted. This racism seemed to rest on economic issues—African Americans and Puerto Ricans were scapegoats for an economy that left many of the white, predominantly working-class males in the club behind. Like the working-class men in Lillian Rubin's *Families on the Fault Line*, men in The Lion's Den "[came] together, bound by their whiteness, to protect their turf."[39] Most regular patrons sought to escape their own lives, even if only temporarily, through visits to The Lion's Den. Racist conversation provided a way to blow off steam at the same time. Men's storytelling about other men also allowed men to construct boundaries around whiteness (and in previous examples, around heterosexuality and masculinity). This kind of indirect policing allowed storytellers to present themselves as robust without any follow-through. The Lion's Den was a haven for such simulated realities that were fitting for the context. Alongside the ability to feel desired, connected, and powerful, men got to experience themselves as tough without *actually* having to fight other men. They got to assert racial boundaries while simultaneously disavowing them in a context where they were the clear majority.

While men's physical aggression toward women was less common in the club than verbal aggression, it remained an ever-present threat. Two of the women interviewed described being cornered and assaulted by patrons during the fourteen-month period I worked in the club. Women in The Lion's Den were not alone in their experiences with aggression and violence; other recent studies of stripping have also found violent behavior from patrons.[40]

Strippers chose pseudonyms and fabricated backgrounds for the express purpose of fending off men who might seek to harm them. Tamara explained: "I have known dancers that have gotten attacked or chased or stalked by customers before. Or customers would come and find them at their other workplaces and harass them." Her strategy was to "give them a fake identity and residence." When they pressed for too much detail, she would say, "I'm really not comfortable telling you." Such precautions were not always successful. For example, an entire team of local hockey players followed Robin (a twenty-three-year-old stripper) home from a club where she worked before working at The Lion's Den. She immediately called the police, who responded quickly, but her concerns led her to leave that club and work farther from home.

In another story, Shane, a twenty-nine-year-old regular patron, confirmed, "some guys have stalked girls out of the club." His ex-girlfriend was a stripper who was followed to his home one night after her shift. When she pulled into his driveway at 3:00 AM, another car turned in, too. Initially irritated because he thought she was bringing home a friend, Shane emerged from his house and approached her car to ask who was behind her. When she replied that she did not know, he told her to stay in the car. He continued, "I go over, and it's some Puerto Rican guy. He's talking to me in Spanish, so I'm like, 'What are you doing here? What's going on?' He's like, 'I think I must be wrong.' I'm like, 'Yeah, you're off, get out of here!'" Shane's real worry was what could have happened if his girlfriend had gone to her own house instead of his. Attributing the stalking to a desire for a more enduring relationship with a stripper, Shane explained, "I don't trust half the guys that come here. They all think that they're going to get something from the girls, and they're not. . . . I think it's a bad thing for a lot of guys, because . . . it gives them false hope in the sense that these girls are really, really nice to them." This push and pull that patrons feel is a job-related risk for strippers, who must attract patrons to increase earnings.

In The Lion's Den, minor offenses, such as displays of verbal aggression, did not often result in intervention. Patrons frequently dismissed indiscretions as "boys being boys," as Fiona's story illustrates: "Amateur night, I was standing in the middle of a group of guys talking to this one guy, trying to get him to buy a VIP. Another guy comes up behind me, grabs me by my hips, and puts his hard-on right up against my ass! He's like, 'You like that, don't you?' I'm like, 'No! If I want to do that, I go talk to my boyfriend at home!'"

Ostensibly, the club's central responsibility was to provide patrons access to strippers' performances while preventing physical contact between the two groups. In part, conformity was the product of sex work laws that regulate and define a club's rules regarding performance content and contact between strippers and patrons. These laws are determined on both federal and local levels, as discussed in chapter 1. Through a series of Supreme Court cases including *Barnes v. Glen Theatre* (1991) and *City of Erie v. Pap's A.M.* (2000), the high court has upheld that while nude dance is permissible under the

First Amendment, local laws may regulate so-called secondary effects associated with sex-oriented businesses on a case-by-case basis. Secondary effects include criminal activity like prostitution and the reduced property values of nearby homes and businesses. In addition to federal law, local municipalities (partially as a result of the *Barnes* decision) can regulate other aspects of nude dance, like physical proximity between strippers and patrons, as well as amounts of nudity, consumption of alcohol, and zoning. From the club's perspective, clearly some adherence to state and federal laws was based on the perceived consequences of violating those mandates. Violation of legal regulations could result in the clubs being cited or shut down by local authorities. As a result, The Lion's Den worked hard to maintain good relations with the local police department by contributing generously to their organizations.

Assuring patrons' compliance with club rules was difficult; the club had less control over male patrons than it did over its female workers. Since the club was geared toward meeting patrons' needs, male patrons generally felt entitled to whatever services they desired. In particular, male patrons who had few personal ties to the club demonstrated little attachment to a particular club's policies. In addition, if the club were to heavily regulate men's behaviors, this might decrease their satisfaction with the club. As a result, The Lion's Den maintained an explicit policy that patrons were innocent until proven guilty, as outlined in the *Employee/Entertainer Handbook*:

> Unless the customer is being a blatant asshole (continuing to break the laws after them being explained to him), I see no reason to kick anybody out. What I do see is kicking the dancer out after being completely assured that you know she knows the laws and [is] allowing the customer to continue to break them without seeking assistance.[41]

In the absence of formally recognized authority in the club, strippers became the workers who *needed* regulation and oversight but provided none themselves. The Lion's Den was not alone in encouraging this system of oversight. Lisa Sanchez, in her study of sex workers in the northwestern United States, found that "the local liquor control commission and, to a lesser degree, the police kept dancers under surveillance, but overlooked the indiscretions of customers."[42]

Worker and management cynicism put strippers in jeopardy and made them vulnerable to harassment and assault by patrons. Though violent acts were not a regular occurrence, every woman I met in the club either had her own story or the story of another dancer who had been attacked by a patron.

As Tamara described, "I have known dancers that have gotten attacked, or chased, or stalked by customers before. Or customers would come and find them at their other work places and harass them." Stories ranged from women having their breasts or genitals groped during private performances to more violent assaults, including rape. Marissa implied that being touched is just part of the job:

> You'll see a girl get touched . . . and the girl doesn't want it to happen, and [bouncers may] catch the guy after and tell him no, but it happens; you can't stop it from happening. Shit, if I wasn't even in this business, no guy would have touched me where I didn't want him to touch me. There are things you just can't control.

In fourteen months of my participant observation, I witnessed the club eject only one patron. The incident occurred late on a Thursday night when an inebriated patron did not refrain from touching a dancer during a private performance in the VIP Room. After repeatedly requesting the patron to stop touching her, the dancer called a bouncer into the room. After a short conversation, the patron and bouncer emerged from the room together. The patron broadcasted slurred protests that he was "just having a good time" and "didn't mean to do anything." The bouncer responded with only one phrase, repeated twice, "It's time to go buddy; it's time to go," as he led the patron to the door.

Because the gendered organization of work in The Lion's Den marginalized and devalued female workers, strippers were often harmed before they were "protected," as the following story from nineteen-year-old Mindy illustrates:

> Saturday night was the worst night I've ever had dancing in my entire life, because I was onstage, and some guy decided he wanted to stick his finger up my crotch while I was onstage. It was awful. It's the worst thing that's ever happened to me. It was disgusting, and it's like as soon as he did that I just immediately felt my chest get real heavy. I couldn't breathe. I just started shaking, and I didn't know what to do. I just backed away and told him, "You can't do that." I was like, "No, don't do that." And I turn around, and I just got offstage, and it bothered me. It really did. I couldn't stop shaking, and I started crying, and I was just very, very upset that someone did that.

When asked how the bouncer reacted, Mindy explained, "He grabbed and yanked him and threw him out and told him to never come back." Nearly in tears, she said that due to bills and rent she had "no choice" but to strip, despite her desire to quit on the night she was assaulted.

Though rape laws are determined by each state independently, there is considerable overlap in statutes.[43] Most rape laws include the language of nonconsent to the sexual act in question that may involve force or coercion. While rape "had been defined as sexual intercourse," the law now includes insertion of other parts of the body or anything else into the vagina or rectum.[44] While Mindy did not describe it as such, the assault clearly met the legal definition of rape set by the state, yet no one called the police or encouraged her to press charges. The rape was seen as "inappropriate" by the club; the only consequence for the patron was being asked to leave. The club's norms around violence superseded those of the state. The decision not to pursue charges against the patron let him and other men know that they could get away with violating strippers.

Faith, a traveling dancer, based her fear of men in the club on not knowing what they might do. Dangerous interactions were often unexpected and happened quickly, despite the common understanding by most patrons that strippers were not to be touched. Faith described how a patron trapped her in the corner during a private dance: "A guy had me pinned right between his legs, and I had the bottom of my heel right on his balls. . . . He didn't budge, he didn't blink, he didn't turn red—nothing. He was on something. . . . That got scary. You know, guys going to clubs on drugs." Without a firm code of conduct and discipline for employees to enforce, patrons in The Lion's Den could (and did) inflict serious physical and emotional harm on strippers with few, if any, repercussions. In addition, since boundaries around physical contact between patrons and strippers vary from place to place, patrons may arrive with expectations that are incongruent with a particular club's practices. Roxanne argued that patrons believe that strip clubs entitle them to treat women with a range of behaviors that would not be tolerated elsewhere. "Dancing and strip clubs are kind of prehistoric," she said. Furthermore, she explained, most women would say stripping is "degrading" and would not tolerate the things that happened in The Lion's Den. By contrast, she stated, "*Here,* it's okay to be degraded, and we've got girls that walk around here with dog collars on. Would you do that out in the real world? Hell no! We used to have a girl who wore a dog collar with a leash. No one in the real world would do that—at least no one with half a brain!"

Research over the past several decades suggests that strip clubs accommodate men's abuse of women. As Chris Bruckert explained in her study of Canadian strip clubs, "dancers labour in a highly volatile environment where the potential for verbal and physical aggression is continually present."[45] Jacqueline Boles and A. P. Garbin, in their study of a strip club in the southeastern United States several decades ago, found that "male customers are frequently abusive to strippers. They curse them, grab at their legs, burn them with cigarettes and tear their costumes."[46] Recent scholarly research echoes these findings, arguing that the major costs of stripping include various forms of ill treatment.[47] In an Associated Press article from 2006, Megan Scott argues that stripping is a job "that isn't in the Labor Department's list of the 10 most dangerous professions in America" but should be.[48] Quoting Mary Ann Layden, a psychotherapist who counsels strippers, Scott writes: "How many women do you know who are willing to work in jobs where they are slapped, bitten, called 'cunt' and 'whore'? Think about it."[49] Women's experiences with violence are also found at the hands of management,[50] as reflected in the numerous experiences with bullying and violence encountered by Olivia, the title subject of Jody Raphael's study of a former drug addict, stripper, and prostitute.[51]

The social norms around women's collective liability and rape myths regarding sex workers help explain why men's abuse of strippers persists. Using the concept of "collective liability,"[52] Diana Scully argues that women, in general, are surrogate targets. She points out that rapists may not target women they know but other women who take the place of significant others who have done them wrong.[53] Jody Miller and Martin D. Schwartz combine the concept of collective liability and rape myths, "cultural assumptions that support and promote rape," to argue that prostitutes are at greater risk because they constitute a category of women deemed "unrapeable," by being public sexual property or deserving of violence.[54] Similar norms operate in strip clubs that foster a space for verbal and physical aggression toward women.

Roxanne and Faith pointed out that strippers recognized the dangers of their work, as well as the expectation on the part of patrons and the club that they will tolerate a range of behaviors that would not be tolerated by women elsewhere. As Lisa Sanchez argues in her study of sex workers, "violence needs a space," and "for customers and perpetrators of violence, the local sex trade is a space where they feel entitled to take what they wish with or without consent, and they suffer little, if any, consequences for their behavior."[55] What facilitates this space for aggression and violence toward strippers was the gendered organization of work that devalued and demeaned strippers and instilled norms that reinforce men's dominance over women.

Outliers and Exceptions

Not all forms of masculinity were encouraged or even tolerated in The Lion's Den. Reflecting a larger cultural pattern in the United States, normative sexual hierarchies, or social rankings for what is acceptable and unacceptable, operated inside the club that marginalized male homosexual identities.[56] While there was tolerance of strippers who were bisexual or lesbian—especially since sex acts between women may serve as sexual fantasies for men—such tolerance was not extended to bisexual or homosexual men. Homophobic jokes were sometimes shared between male employees and between male employees and regular patrons.

Stated as put-downs, male workers referred to each other as "fags" or remarked that so-and-so had, or wanted to have, sex with another man, often a man present for the conversation. The term "fag" was used in similar ways among the high school boys in sociologist C. J. Pascoe's study of adolescent masculinity: "The fag epithet, when hurled at other boys, may or may not have explicit sexual meanings, but it always has gendered meanings."[57] In other words, when boys use the term "fag" they are calling a boy's manhood but not necessarily his heterosexuality into question.[58] While infrequent, during my research "fag" comments happened half a dozen times; they defined the boundaries of appropriate talk and behavior. To the extent that groups of patrons frequented the club together and sought joint or collective sexual experiences, elements of homoeroticism were present, but they were not framed as such, except perhaps in men's unspoken or subconscious desires. The club did embrace, at least in their fantasy forms, heterosexual nonmonogamy and promiscuity. Indeed, these were part of the context of conspicuous heterosexuality in The Lion's Den.

Precisely because the club culture catered to men's needs, it also tolerated less-threatening diversions from typical masculine performances. Though men's behaviors were largely patterned, there were also occasions in which men's behaviors stood out. Two such examples come from Craig and Shane, who shielded themselves from strippers. Craig described his "routine" this way:

> If a girl comes over to dance, I don't like to be touched. I'm very uncomfortable with too much intimacy with a stranger. So I immediately throw up warning signs—my ashtray goes right in front of me, my beer, my drink, or whatever, goes right in front of me. I light a cigarette as a literal smokescreen. They're [the] sort of things that you do that say things to other people—that say "stay back."

Craig's ambivalence about The Lion's Den stemmed from a combination of cynicism and faith—in religion, fraternal organization, and traditional women's roles. As an active Freemason and Christian, Craig distanced himself from those who were not part of his community. His general curmudgeonliness moderated what could be seen as a pious reaction. He did not want women too close, and he used an icy stare and physical distance to demonstrate that. His behavior was hardly a threat to other men in the club; he could easily be interpreted as a loner, someone who was disinterested in the women in the club, or a cheapskate who did not want to tip. Though a lack of tips affected all workers, these characterizations were generally more important to strippers in search of income than they were to the other men (both coworkers and patrons) in the club.

Like most of the regular patrons, Shane did not sit at the stage or purchase private dances. When he visited the club, he chose a seat near a back corner. Shane premised his decision on being well-mannered and not behaving like the typical "drooling" patron seated at the stage: "I think it's more respectful. . . . I don't like sitting at the stage and being an idiot like the rest of the guys. If I want to give [strippers] money, I'll do it discreetly on the side and be like, 'Thanks.'" Shane stood out from other patrons because he was actively trying to get his life in order. A former drug trafficker and avid strip club patron, Shane was trying to embrace a new self-image as a loyal father and boyfriend. Self-conscious of his "hypocritical" stance, he rationalized his frequent club attendance as a remnant of his past that he maintained due to habit and friendships. Though unique and against the grain of club culture, both Craig's and Shane's active distancing was supported by the club. In short, when men's behavior conformed enough to club culture (i.e., the patron paid his door fee and continued to buy drinks), they found the club to be a safe haven. Similarly, men on the other end of the spectrum—those who sought more attention from strippers—also found the club to be a hospitable place.

The Consequences of Men's Behaviors

The Lion's Den made possible performances of a variety of forms of masculinity—affirmation, group connectedness, and aggression—by many different men in a context designed for their pleasure. Although these performances are, of course, also present outside the club, the gendered organization of the club and its culture encouraged these behaviors by making it far easier for men to "pull them off" successfully there than in other public spaces. Thus, performances of masculinity are not simply the product of particular groups of men or of an undifferentiated culture. Performances of masculinity are also products of particular situations and specific arrangements of power. Research on other clubs' gendered organization is needed to unravel how different arrangements may reproduce or mitigate performances of masculinity.

Though the performances of masculinity in The Lion's Den can be found in the broader culture, the club was also unique. In this club, the rules of engagement were firmly set to women's individual and collective disadvantage through the social organization of work, as well as club and patron expectations for what constituted reasonable behaviors. In this sense, The Lion's Den was a site where men could perform aggressive masculinity free from many of the social constraints that in other settings might have limited them. The club provided a space where performances of masculinity, though constrained in particular ways (i.e., at the intersections of sexuality and race), were at the same time lax, permitting aggression and violence with little challenge or resistance.

The expression of gender relations within the club had consequences for men's and women's lives outside the club. For the patrons, gender relations in The Lion's Den were set up to distance men from conventional obligations in their exchanges with women that may serve or frustrate them. The Lion's Den addressed a temporary desire for interaction with women and gave men a temporary sense of power. However, these exchanges may also be dissatisfying to men. Men who are seeking more than just a fleeting encounter or a limited exchange are bound to be let down by their experiences in strip clubs. Moreover, men who cannot be dominant outside of the strip club context are bound to experience frustration and inadequacy, which might have negative consequences for the women in their lives.

While the ethnographic data presented here are from one particular site and can, as a result, provide detail and thick description, generalizations outside of the club context must be made with great care. That said, it is important to consider what the study of masculinity in strip clubs has to say about constructions of masculinity more generally and what the club's relationship was to the outside world. The question here is, did The Lion's Den challenge, reproduce, or extend gender relations in the broader culture?

Due to the social organization of work and the norms around men's and women's roles in the club, The Lion's Den did not present a challenge to current normative conceptions of male dominance and female subordination. Rather, the club was a space for masculinity that reproduced or extended gender relations in the broader culture. On the one hand, the club represented a manifestation of gender relations in the broader society—patterns of male domination, female subordination, women's performance of emotional labor, the collective liability of women, and normative rape myths. The club acted, in this sense, as an extension of the world outside the club. On the other hand, the club acted as compensation for men frustrated with typical boundaries around masculinity in the outside world. In this sense, the club became a particular space in which men could act out and try on different performances of masculinity that are not available in other public spaces.

The club provided a unique space that both reproduced and extended the broader patterns of gender relations in our culture because the club's structural logic put women in gendered organizational jeopardy. For strippers, their economic need to strip was exacerbated by almost total exclusion from organizational authority over their work, as described in chapter 2. Simultaneously, workers in the club stereotyped and belittled strippers; even the strippers themselves engaged in this behavior. Since management and club rules institutionalized these practices, the club exhibited an explicit form of gendered organization in which men dominate women. In effect, the club intentionally fostered the circumstances under which all, but especially male patrons and coworkers, could engage in various forms of aggression toward strippers. The resulting gendered organizational jeopardy created tremendous burdens for strippers, who negotiated the concurrent demands of emotional, physical, and erotic labor, as well as the risks of verbal harassment and physical assault.

Tradeoffs and Troubles

Managing Stripping Labor

Before studying The Lion's Den, I interviewed dozens of strippers about their work. Without exception, all of them worked under difficult conditions. Rundown clubs are commonplace in the stripping industry.[1] Erin, a stripper in her mid twenties, described developing a red rash on her knees while working in one such club. The rash, she later learned, was ringworm that she and other dancers contracted from the club's carpet. Disgusted, a group of dancers got together and collectively demanded the owner clean or pull up the carpet. In response, the club asked the entire group of dancers to leave. The club's position, Erin explained, was that it could hire new strippers at a moment's notice. Although The Lion's Den faced chronic stripper shortages, it adopted a similar perspective on repairs. The club never faced the kind of organized resistance described by Erin, and complaints (even those made in unison) were simply not addressed.

A club that devalues strippers puts them at risk of physical and emotional harm. In The Lion's Den, dressing rooms and stages were in disrepair, flooring throughout the club was old and dirty, and the bathroom toilets were often clogged. The stage itself was both symptom and symbol of the club's lack of regard for strippers' safety. The physical condition of the stage was a near-constant source of strife between strippers and management. Strippers made repeated requests to fix the stage flooring that splintered and cut the dancers' bodies. One year after the strippers insisted the stage be cleaned and repaired, management had yet to meet their demands. While the stage dance poles were repaired, this work was clearly more for the benefit of the patrons than the dancers. Tamara described the stage:

> The stage is never clean. . . . There's been dirt piles on the stage. . . . I've gotten up there and had sticky spots where people have spilled drinks or something else [laughs]. There are these huge gouges on the floor where

you can cut yourself. There are loose panels; there are pieces of metal. . . . The poles used to always be broken, and when [the poles] weren't screwed into the floor, there'd be a hole in the floor with a rag stuck into it.

Strippers felt devalued in this dirty and dangerous environment. Tamara continued: "They don't care about the dancers; they don't care how much money the dancers make onstage or what happens as long as they're selling their alcohol." In effect, strippers experience on multiple levels the consequences of being devalued, fueled in part by negative assumptions about stripping that operate concurrently within club texts, policy, and characterizations produced by management and workers.

The stripping industry considers most women expendable. To be sure, elite porn stars or other celebrity entertainers are the exception to this rule, since securing big-revenue entertainment necessitates meeting star performers' needs. By contrast, local dancers, working in middle- and lower-tier clubs, tread a different terrain. Often there are enough new recruits entering the industry that clubs need not cater to the average dancer's demands, particularly if those demands are going to tap off owners' profits. Indeed, there is little incentive for owners and managers to secure a low turnover in dancers since a steady stream of new dancers can actually be a draw for patrons. The Lion's Den, however, faced chronic dancer shortages and empty shifts—factors that certainly affected the owner's bottom line. Roxanne explained: "Here [strippers] don't show up to work. There's nobody here. The doorman and I were talking today, five guys came in, and there were no girls." Even under economic pressures, the club simply ignored strippers' demands.

Under the best conditions, stripping entails often-intense emotional, embodied, and erotic performance. These performances are not unique to The Lion's Den; strippers in most clubs provide some combination of these skills that each contains its own occupational hazards. In their intimacy with patrons, strippers perform emotional and physical labor, practices they act out in particular ways under pressure from industry and club norms. Strippers' erotic and embodied performances are particularly affected by the club's gendered organization and culture; its established pecking order; the types of performance (partial or fully nude); and age-, size-, and race-based standards of beauty. While it might be tempting to see these issues as just part of strippers' work, they clearly spill over into dancers' private lives. Indeed, it becomes less clear, looking at strippers' narratives, where the boundaries lay between their work-related practices and their sense of self or identity away from the club.

Under hostile conditions, any kind of work (regardless of ease or complexity) becomes more difficult. Given strippers' consumption of alcohol and other drugs, which they used to enhance their abilities to perform emotional labor, strippers at The Lion's Den experienced increased risks, especially given the tendency for bartenders and bouncers to treat dancers with suspicion when providing protection. It was common for strippers to consume several alcoholic drinks a shift. Often my first task as a cocktail waitress was to deliver drinks to the dancers' dressing room. Illicit drug use was commonly hidden, though everyone knew how, when, and where it probably took place. Strippers used marijuana, cocaine, and other drugs outside of plain sight, either before work or in the dressing rooms' bathrooms. Their use of various substances also provided a way of distancing themselves from their work, as the strippers' narratives illustrate.

These characterizations had material consequences. Unsafe working conditions and an environment of hostility within the club made strippers vulnerable to physical and emotional harm, substance abuse, and patrons' harassment and assault. Together with The Lion's Den's workplace organization, resulting dangers created not just accumulated risks but gendered organizational jeopardy. With gendered organizational jeopardy, the logic behind the dangers women face is institutionalized and systemic rather than idiosyncratic. Here inequality is woven into the fabric of workplace rules and culture.

Emotional Labor

Since the early 1980s, a number of feminist writers have argued that emotional labor is deeply gendered and most often performed by women, both inside and outside of families.[2] In the realm of paid work, emotional labor has been linked to a variety of jobs in the service sector, such as retail and beauty industries, as well as occupations like nursing.[3] Strippers also perform emotional labor for pay that has much in common with these other jobs. As Lynn Sharon Chancer explains, "To somehow differentiate sex-economic from other economic strategies for 'getting paid' . . . is to obfuscate the fact that most of us transact some form of sale-of-self on a routinized daily or near-daily basis."[4] Moreover, making connections between emotional labor and constructions of femininity across multiple forms of women's work is critical, because it underscores the vast numbers of women performing this work inside and outside of the household, paid and unpaid.

The Lion's Den expected the performance of emotional labor. The *Employee/Entertainer Handbook* reads, "I expect that you as the entertainment will also give the club a more upscale look, not only with your choice of outfits but also your attitude."[5] Here the club explicitly demanded that strippers perform with a particular "attitude" toward patrons. The emotional labor performed by strippers often entailed masking their own feelings, a process Hochschild describes as "emotion management": "Surface and deep acting in a commercial setting, unlike acting in a dramatic, private, or therapeutic context, make one's face and one's feelings take on the properties of a resource. . . . It is a resource to be used to make money."[6] Strippers make money by representing a sexual fantasy—flirting with patrons, acting coy, and developing sultry stares. As part of this labor, strippers must make their performances seem like something else—not work, but something they appear to genuinely feel.

Stripping is in many ways unique from other forms of sex work such as pornography and prostitution. Because strippers are performing live, they "lose their status as unique people to become the fulfillment of male fantasies, while generally withholding the actual fulfillment of those fantasies."[7] Stripping differs from film and magazine pornography, in which women provide fantasies but are not immediately present. It is also different from prostitution since, in prostitution, women are present and go beyond simulation to actually carry out the fantasies. While there are some similarities between stripping and Internet pornography, the actors and audience are not physically present in Internet pornography as they are in club stripping.

While strippers may or may not be unique to the men for whom they perform (i.e., for some men, strippers may be interchangeable, while other men may seek a more long-term relationship with one dancer in particular), they face a qualitatively different set of risks than women who participate in print pornography. The proximity of the stripper's performance and the active participation of the patrons necessitates that dancers manage not only their presentation of self but also their interactions. This work requires that strippers evoke in themselves and in their customers an inventory of emotions: desire, trust, romance, companionship, intimacy, and lust. They use both surface and deep acting to generate and exhibit these expressions. As Hochschild explains, surface acting involves "body language, the put-on sneer, the posed shrug, the controlled sigh."[8] By contrast, deep acting "is a natural result of working on feeling; the actor does not try to *seem* happy or sad but rather expresses spontaneously . . . a real feeling that has been self induced."[9] For example, when Tamara explained her preparation for work, she alternated between descriptions of surface and deep acting:

There's a long drive out [to work] when I'll go into the mindset of the character that I portray [in The Lion's Den], where I leave myself behind. It's a very lonely drive. I've been having my boyfriend take me lately, and I feel like I do better, because I'm more connected with myself when I get there, and I'm not just part of a person. I'm bringing some more of me there. . . . But it's sometimes hard to get myself to work because it's so hard to get back into that mindset of [*raises her voice an octave and with a mocking tone*], "Hi! How'ya doin'? Oh, you're hot. Oh, would you like a dance?" You know [*laughing*] . . . a lot of what I say as Tamara is fake or is designed to please or impress a stranger and is very superficial—it's very witty and on the ball, but it's not genuine. But *she* does have sensuality that is part of me that I have as a dancer outside of the club. (emphasis added)

In this last line, Tamara demonstrated her alienation as she stood apart from herself and said "she." The concerted efforts Tamara went through to generate her dancer persona included elements of surface acting: changing her voice, using stereotypical language, and being fake or superficial. In addition, Tamara demonstrated her use of deep acting: crafting a persona that was "more connected" to herself and that had "sensuality that is part of" her. Tamara also revealed the risk that deep acting will result in alienation when she described that she did not want to be "just part of a person." Just thinking about generating her sense of self at work prompted her to describe her preparation as a moment when she will "leave [herself] behind" on "a very lonely drive."

Other dancers echoed Tamara's comments. Fiona, a nineteen-year-old stripper, explained that she felt like a "different person," like she's "acting" when she's at work:

This is pretty much like acting. Like you put on a different face. You come to the club, and you put on the fancy clothes, you put on the makeup, you do your hair nice, you paint your nails or get your nails done. . . . You're like a different person. And you've got to feel it like a different person.

Consider the following description of deep acting from Roxanne, who had danced for more than a decade:

You have to not think about the person that you're dancing for. You have to make believe. You have to make believe that you're in love with everybody that you dance for. And you have to make them believe that you're going home with them tonight.

Roxanne explained that accomplishing this task involves "the way you look at them. The way you act around them. Dancing slowly. Making eye contact. Talking to them. Sometimes it's impossible to do."

Strippers have to master the precarious balance between encouraging desire and fending off men's advances: "You have to make them believe that you're going home with them tonight." While strippers in The Lion's Den rarely went home with patrons, men who wanted to believe the performance was real sometimes misinterpreted strippers' attempts to cultivate desire. Since the exchange was explicitly designed around the striptease performance, the conversations that occurred beyond sexual innuendo were, at times, misunderstood as constituting a different sort of connection between strippers and patrons. Marissa explained this dilemma:

> If [a patron] thinks you're a little more comfortable with him, he'll try and touch you or something. And you've got to be like, "Whoa, buddy, back up. You were nice like five minutes ago, and now you're trying to get in my pants! Why did it change, because you got a little more comfortable with me or something?" You've got to put up a shield and not let people get in real quick. Don't let them know too much about you because then they're going to come back and be your regular customer. If you don't like the guy, don't tell him [you do], or he's going to be here all the time on your schedule and want to take you home and want your number all the time.

The potential for multiple interpretations loomed large since the only sign that the exchange was economic as well as interpersonal, other than payment for the stripper's job, was the club context itself. This was particularly the case for men seeking a sense of desirability and connectedness, who sought connections that seemed freely given and genuine in character. The patron-turned-bartender, Ted, is a case in point. His interactions with Jane epitomized these issues—when he realized Jane threw away his phone number, he felt betrayed. His feelings of betrayal stemmed from a belief that her interactions with him were real.

The emotional and physical components to deep acting include an emphasis on eye contact. Many dancers stated that eye contact was important in delivering a convincing performance for patrons. However, this visual connection was also a source of fear. Robin provided this example:

> I [can't] do eye contact when I first get here, but after I have like two drinks I do eye contact. And when you make the eye contact . . . it makes them

feel, like, real personal, and they give you more money. Like, the more eye contact you make, [the more] they trust you—like you're not fake.

Robin's explanation demonstrates how doing eye contact is designed to generate the appearance of being "real personal," "trust" worthy, and "not fake" for patrons.

The use of alcohol and other drugs was a common method of generating strippers' comfort with eye contact. Many of those I interviewed consumed at least four mixed drinks a night (the bar's limit for dancers). Since the alcohol did more than reduce their inhibitions—it also hindered their perception, reflexes, coordination, and potentially their judgment—it put strippers at risk. It made strippers vulnerable to patrons who might prey on them.

In some cases, alcohol was described as crucial to strippers' confidence. Tess explained why she did not go onstage without drinking first: "For me, I absolutely have to be buzzed to get onstage. I did it straight, and I hated it. I was so scared, I was so shaky, I was so nervous, and the people were so mean to me." Similarly, Stella explained that drinking became part of her stripper persona:

So, if I go up there for my first set—I hate my first set at night because I'm dead sober. I haven't had one drink yet, and I don't like it because I feel like Susan [a pseudonym for her real name] when I'm sober; when I'm buzzed, I feel like Stella. I can get more into it; it's like acting, pretty much.

For these women, the risk was not just being harmed at work but suffering from alcohol abuse and addiction over time.

In contrast, those strippers who did not drink to get into character had other strategies for developing their sense of self at work. Destiny described the challenges she faced by stripping without use of alcohol or other drugs:

The mental thing is just the absolute hardest. It might take me forever to get ready. Some girls drink, some girls smoke, and that's how they block out their mental [issues with the work]. Instead of looking at people's faces, they're just there [on alcohol or other drugs, so] it doesn't faze them. But with me, I don't drink and I don't smoke. So my whole thing is mental. I just have to sit up there and think to myself. I'm like, "Okay, as soon as I step in the door, I'm Destiny." I say, "That's it—that whole school thing, that whole church thing, the whole homework thing—that's all behind me." I just sit there, and I'll be there for—it takes me about a half hour to get ready because when I'm putting my makeup on and I'm doing my hair or whatever else I have to do, I'm like, okay, "I'm Destiny, I'm Destiny . . ."

For Destiny, putting on makeup and doing her hair was supplemented by repetition of her goal: "I'm Destiny." The problem was that sometimes these personas were difficult to maintain. As Tamara described, "I like to separate Tamara and who I really am. I don't take anything home from work with me. As soon as I get home and shower, it all goes away, which is nice." Though this goal of separating work and home was something many strippers strove for, it was not always easy to accomplish. As Fiona, a traveling stripper, explained: "It's hard to go from being Anita at home, having my life here, coming down to Railton and playing somebody totally different." Jen had only recently been successful at keeping her home life separate from work:

I don't take my job home with me. . . . I guess I keep doing it, so I want to leave it there. And [at] one point in my life, I was very involved in the scene. That's all I hung around with were people from work. People that are generally involved in [the stripping industry], they need drama and a lot of it. It just gets to a point where you grow out of it, and I decided I wasn't happy with how I was leading my life, so I quit doing drugs and I quit the drama.

Similarly, upon getting home, Mindy continued to think about work, wondering if the costs outweighed the rewards:

It's hard, because you go home, and you think of everything that went on during the night, and it runs through your head. There's been times when I've gone home, and I've asked myself, "Why am I even doing this? Is it really worth me doing this, after all I have to put up with and the things I have to go through?"

Likewise, Vivian emphasized how replaying a night's work tormented her:

When I first started . . . I came home and I'm exhausted, beat to hell. I'd be awake just replaying my whole night in my head. And, ya know, I don't want to think about what these guys are thinking about me. I just want to know that they gave me their money, and now I'm home with my family. That's the hardest part, really. I don't mind physically being beaten. I don't mind it because I really firmed up from just the first couple weeks of working. They put you in it, and you're ripping and pulling [your muscles] in heels, but you know you're [physically fit and] better for it.

While bartenders and cocktail waitresses also performed emotional labor in the form of companionship and intimacy, their performances differed from that of strippers. Robin Leidner's work is helpful in illustrating this difference.[10] In her study of workers at McDonald's and agents at Combined Insurance, she argued that there are three types of emotional labor in service work: when personality is inseparable from the product (e.g., teachers), when personality is provided in conjunction with the product (e.g., flight attendants), and when personality facilitates purchase of the product (e.g., salespeople).[11] Bartenders and cocktail waitresses resemble Leidner's description of flight attendants in that they provide emotional labor with another product: drinks. Doormen and bouncers, since they are often the first people to meet the customers, act most like salespeople—encouraging and making entry into the club possible. The contrasts Leidner makes fall short when we think about what strippers produce. Since strippers are simultaneously inseparable from their product, providing personality, and facilitating purchases, they begin to look like hyper service workers. What is more, strippers' service work includes an added dimension, erotic labor. Erotic labor performed in the nude is the central product of strip clubs, shaped by broader cultural, industry, and club-based norms.

Erotic Nude Performance

Setting the scene for erotic performance, the club was saturated with sexual symbolism, including music with suggestive lyrics, nude pictures of adult film stars, and erotic art. Because few other venues feature live nude shows, strip clubs provide a unique offering. Increasingly outside of the sex industry, however, sex work is ubiquitous in popular culture. Big-box retailers market graphic t-shirts boasting Playboy bunnies, the brand "Porn Star," and suggestive phrases like "I may be cute but I still bite" to adolescents through their juniors' departments. Video games like *Grand Theft Auto* feature strippers as "prizes" for successfully completed missions.[12] These kinds of mainstream representations of striptease result in what media scholar Brian McNair calls "the sexualization of the public sphere," in which celebrities, as well as the person next door, produce a "striptease culture."[13] Music videos have capitalized on this message, emphasizing stripper chic. Communications scholar Sut Jhally explains: "Music videos are all about the girls, and indeed, the presence of sexualized female bodies is so prevalent that the major conventions for achieving this goal are relatively easy to identify."[14]

Ideas from the broader culture are also reproduced in strip clubs. Within this setting, women's performances mimic typical constructions of female roles and jobs found outside the sex industry. Tamara provided this description:

> The guys want to see different things. They'd like to see a nurse and a maid and a schoolgirl and, you know, a superhero or something onstage. They like to see the varieties. That's why not everybody who works there's blonde [*laughs*], although I think management would like that.

The characters Tamara mentioned typically engage in caregiving, cleanup and service, or naive adoration. As such, strip club performances draw on conventional images of male fantasy: women as sex objects, nurturers, youthful, and vixens. Club performances amalgamate the archetypal roles and dress of many adult films featuring the "candy striper," "maid," "teacher," "seductress," "schoolgirl," or "Lolita." The trope of women as sex objects emphasizes the male gaze and spotlights women's desire to be watched. Similar to fashion models, the female body is clearly a spectacle in strip clubs, elevated to runway status. Showcasing the roles of nurses, teachers, and maids highlights women's caring and instrumental labor. As The Lion's Den's strippers described so vividly, much of their labor involves making conversation and providing emotional outreach, caring for patrons. The seductress reflects women as sexually ravenous. Two versions of this include the innocent but experienced young girl, or "Lolita," and the woman (perhaps a teacher or librarian) in conservative clothes, eyeglasses, and bun who is really a porn star. The message in both is the same—girls and women are insatiable; they want sex anywhere and all the time.

Tamara's reference to a superhero reflects an actual Wonder Woman costume worn by one of the club's strippers. Though Wonder Woman's strength and power provides some contrast with the other examples, her scant clothing fits in inside the club. While strippers crafted their appearances for what the "guys want to see," they also followed management's rules and the norms of the sex industry. Management required dancers to come to work with multiple costumes, so strippers could change their clothing for each stage set. Many new dancers had to borrow clothing from other dancers when they first began working. As such, strip club performances involve women putting on gender quite literally in the form of costumes, various see-through garments, short skirts or long gowns, high-heeled shoes, makeup, and styled hair. Though there were other costumes worn by dancers in The Lion's Den, such as an ice hockey team cheerleader, most women opted for simple costumes that cost little money—cutoff jean shorts and a bikini top, lingerie, and string bikinis.

The irony about elaborate superhero or eveningwear-type costuming in The Lion's Den was that, despite the club's emphasis on changing clothes between sets and the notion of a striptease performance that eroticizes bodies in various stages of undress, dancers did not wear their costumes for long onstage. In fact, beyond their first stage performance for a patron, many strippers remained fully nude for the rest of their set. Mostly, this was because the patrons were often seated nearby, and dancers found it foolish and a waste of time to re-dress. As a result, many dancers insisted their performances were not striptease at all but, rather, nude dance. To be sure, strip clubs are known for their featured nudity, but in The Lion's Den the central aspect of strippers' performances was popularly known as a "spread show." More cynically, one respondent termed it the "gynecological exam." The result was that strippers often simply posed or gyrated their genitals in assembly-line fashion for one patron and the next. This kind of performance made women's vaginas central over the rest of their bodies or their ability as dancers.

As a fully nude strip club, The Lion's Den placed particular burdens on women who provided nude performances. Nude performances are conventionally deemed outside the scope of mainstream culture, television, and film, despite increasing amounts of skin and sexual activity on network television, on pay cable channels, and in both PG-13- and R-rated films. In a society that continues to place value on women's innocence and chastity, the stigma associated with women who perform in the nude for many men comes as little surprise. Barbara Risman and Pepper Schwartz suggest that girls in general continue to be stigmatized by engaging in sexual encounters with multiple partners outside of a relationship:

> A remnant of the sexual double standard is alive and well. . . . Girls today may be able to have sex without stigma, but only with a steady boyfriend. For girls, love justifies desire. A young woman still cannot be respected if she admits an appetite-driven sexuality.[15]

While the sexual double standard may be waning, it has not disappeared. Women working in strip clubs challenge dominant constructions of femininity, as discussed by Risman and Schwartz, through unattached performances of sexually explicit acts for many different men.

Nude performances heighten differences between the work roles of strippers and cocktail waitresses. Though the two jobs were most often kept separate during a single shift—a waitress who was also a stripper would rarely get onstage to dance, and strippers seldom waited on customers—many cocktail waitresses were current or former strippers. Given the considerable overlap, one might expect few differences in their treatment in the club; nevertheless, the "good girl" and "bad girl" components to these work roles persisted. Indeed, they were mutually dependent. Cocktail waitresses served as strippers' alter egos, or the good girls of the club, because they were clothed. But these waitresses remained bad girls in the broader culture from guilt by association with the adult entertainment industry. Though both strippers and cocktail waitresses experienced the sexism that was pervasive in The Lion's Den, the distinctions between strippers and cocktail waitresses also translated into different levels of control and authority: more for cocktail waitresses and less for strippers.

In U.S. culture, most women fall somewhere between good girl and bad girl. Sex workers, though, epitomize the bad girl. Learning to be a bad girl is an important aspect of being a stripper, as Destiny explained: "You have to learn how to cuss, you have to learn how to talk—stripping is a whole hustle; you just can't go to prison for it." For her, strippers are "hustlers" like drug dealers or illegal gamblers. The club's purpose was to foster and legitimize this work: "Stripping, as long as you're doing what you're supposed to do and following the rules, and the club is following the rules, there's no chance of you going to jail."

One major reason behind the stigma associated with stripping is women's nudity. Participating in nude performance holds a mixture of excitement, routine, and stigma for strippers. Some dancers argued that they enjoyed the risks of breaking societal taboos and presented themselves as sexual renegades. While strippers maintained this persona in the club or in the presence of other strippers, they did not emphasize it in interviews. According to their explanations, the bad-girl act was more connected to strippers' work performances than to a sense of self or a coping mechanism. Other strippers described that being nude became normalized over time and that they became used to their own bodies, as well as the bodies of other women. As one stripper remarked, "It becomes like wallpaper after a while." Still others indicated their concern over the social stigma attached to nude performance, especially when people they knew saw them in the club.

While vaginas are often considered "private parts," something that women do not share publicly,[16] in fully nude strip clubs they become the main focus.

Workers' assessments underscored the role of nudity in the contrast between female workers, depending on whether they are clothed or nude, good girls or bad girls, and cocktail waitresses or strippers. Roxanne's comments illustrate how strippers were treated based on working in the nude: "The Lion's Den thinks that because you get naked for money that you're stupid, so that's how they treat you." She also questioned whether such negative perceptions were really off base, given the low pay for onstage performances: "I'm getting naked for you for a dollar. I can't even buy a pack of cigarettes for a dollar; I can barely buy a pack of gum with a dollar. And I'm taking my clothes off for a dollar?" Given how little monetary value is assigned to stripping stage performances, it comes as little surprise that Roxanne questioned whether the work was worth the paltry compensation. In addition to nude performance, stripping entails substantial physical strength, flexibility, and endurance. However, normative expectations on strippers' bodies do not end there. Like women in the broader culture, strippers are subject to beauty expectations that deem certain physical proportions, features, skin tones, and hair either beautiful and acceptable or ugly and offensive.

Bodies at Work

Being a stripper is a socially created activity, a performance that women have to learn, even as it is presented as something entirely rooted in women's physical attributes. Like breastfeeding, stripping is portrayed as something women *should* know how to do. Male patrons often remarked that women in The Lion's Den were doing what they were "born to do," using their "God-given" talents. Oddly, these words emphasize effortlessness, while strippers talked continually about struggles and learning curves. The men's words stand in contrast to those of Simone de Beauvoir in *The Second Sex*: "One is not born, but rather becomes, a woman. . . . It is civilization as a whole that produces this creature . . . which is described as feminine."[17] Similarly, women *become* strippers; strippers are produced by their experiences, strip clubs, and broader cultural understandings of stripping. Far from being easy, stripping work is often fraught with uneasiness and entails physical as well as mental difficulties. Embodying the role of "the stripper" means confronting ageism, racism, and sizeism, in addition to sexism. These forms of discrimination pit real women against idealized concepts of female good looks, or what Naomi Wolf called "beauty myths" that emphasize a need for female perfection.[18]

Social norms around age, race, physical body types, and standards of beauty were reflected by The Lion's Den's employment of mostly young, white, thin women. While not all workers fit this ideal, it remains the industry standard. The pressures on strippers to conform by looking physically fit, flexible, and young is something shared by women in the broader culture. Susan Bordo argues:

> When we look at the pursuit of beauty as a normalizing discipline, it becomes clear that not all body transformations are the same. The general tyranny of fashion—perpetual, elusive, and instructing the female body in a pedagogy of personal inadequacy and lack—is a powerful discipline of the normalization of *all* women in this culture. But even as we are all normalized to the requirements of appropriate feminine insecurity and preoccupation with appearance, more specific requirements emerge in different cultural and historical contexts, and for different groups.[19]

As Bordo contends, there are "specific requirements" for particular settings and groups. Strippers keenly feel the pressures to cope or conform to ideal types in strip clubs. For example, strippers are expected to have large breasts; tanned skin; shaved legs, underarms, and pubic hair; painted nails; and well-groomed, preferably long, blonde hair.

Patrons' demands for particular bodies—especially young, white bodies—has consequences for female workers. To be sure, many interviewees referenced this ideal type, with only slight variations. Destiny explained what she has learned about ideal body types for dancers:

> I learned some girls are not big enough, and some girls are too big. Some guys are just so picky about anything. A handful is enough, and those are too big, those are too small, and your butt's too big. Especially in here, they're like, "Oh my god, your butt is so big!" Actually, it's shrunk some, so how do you like that?

Despite her sense of humor, Destiny struggled with stripping. She coped by "[learning] to toughen up" and argued, based on her experience, that women who "get hurt easily" should not work in strip clubs.

While most women undergo body work to achieve normative standards of beauty,[20] those standards exact a particular price on strippers. The collective financial cost of maintaining the above-described look was high, involving visits to salons offering tanning, manicures, haircuts, and coloring. Dancers pay for changes that are not only self-motivated but, in the case of The Lion's

Den, demanded by management. The pressures of an industry that privileges youth, beauty, tanned whiteness, and thinness exacts tyranny on women's bodies, encouraging them to diet, shave, pluck, and tan. Often these transformations are potentially dangerous. Four strippers at The Lion's Den underwent breast augmentation surgery during my participant observation. Of course, this number does not take into consideration those who completed surgeries prior to or since my participant observation. The use of tanning beds was also common. As Tamara described, tanned skin was particularly valued in the club:

> They've told other dancers that they need to get a tan because tan lines are what should be on a dancer. I think people get in their minds what they think of as *stripper* and what they think of as *erotic* and think that everyone else will then think that same way [*laughs*].

As Tamara's comments illustrate, the normative assumptions about how strippers should look were made known to strippers in the club.

Such body transformations are part of a "larger cultural matrix of power relations."[21] Women are not making limitless choices about which body modifications to choose; rather, women's modifications are in line with narrow expectations for how their bodies *should* look. While not all changes are equally invasive (e.g., nail application/painting, hair dying, and tanning versus a surgical procedure like breast augmentation), they impose and reinforce similar norms on strippers' bodies that encourage a continuum of practices from minimal salon-type procedures to outpatient surgery. Those who resist such presentations are often met with scorn. When I asked about women who did not "follow the rules" and refrained from shaving their pubic hair, for instance, strippers and patrons described such dancers being met with ridicule. As one patron remarked, "No one wants to see some chick's hairy bush!"

To be sure, women are not only subject to certain body norms found in the broader culture, sex industry, and strip clubs but are themselves active agents in perpetuating them. Roxanne described the things she had done to stay in the industry:

> Because of dancing, I've had an eating disorder to the point where I would eat and throw up so that I wouldn't gain weight or get fat. I've gone into debt to get my boobs done. I mean, just the stupid things that you do to be here are not worth it.

The reproduction of these norms was made most visible when strippers resisted or failed to meet patrons' assumptions of stripper embodiment. Although strippers' bodies are on open display in full nudity, they are also tightly controlled. For example, men have the expectation that menstruation will not be visible. Fiona complained that "the hardest thing about dancing is having your period and trying to hide your tampon string":

> Cut them, tuck them. How else are you going to dance for them without them knowing you're ragging it? Can't leave it hanging out [*laughs*]! We don't get time off. It's always there stuck in your head: "Can they see it?" I make myself paranoid when I am onstage. They get these looks on their faces sometimes. Is something hanging out? A piece of fuzz? I'll look over at them: "You got something to say?" It makes me nervous. "What are you laughing about?" I'm like, "No, I'm serious! I want to know!" I'm like, "I'm here, and you're making me nervous!" That's one of the things that I'm most commonly worried about.

Embodiment means exposing certain aspects of oneself while vigilantly concealing others—disciplining one's body to "look the part."

In strip clubs, perhaps more so than in the broader culture, beauty is equated with youth. Writing about strippers' management of age, Carol Rambo Ronai provides this description:

> The aging experience is socially constructed by individuals and through contexts that assign meaning to the physical body.... Appearing and acting like an old dancer breaks the tacit rule that women who sell their bodies in one form or another should be selling young, attractive, and cooperative commodities."[22]

Indeed, these bodily requirements exert the greatest pressures on women who either do not possess these ideal traits or cannot alter themselves to do so. Not surprisingly, strippers at The Lion's Den frequently discussed stripping as a temporary job, not something they could do for the rest of their lives. Robin asserted: "I don't want to be doing this when I'm thirty." Roxanne, who was awaiting callbacks from a number of different waitressing jobs, had worked into her early thirties and could not wait to finish stripping:

> It's just the emotional crap that you go through, and the baggage that this job gives you is not worth it, no. Not to mention there's girls in here that

are eighteen years old that look forty! I mean, everybody tells me that I look young, and I'm thirty-three, but that's from years of being very careful, taking care of yourself.

Joking about the aging stripper, Vivian laughed and said:

You can't retire at fifty-five from being a stripper! Unless there's some club in southern Florida where the old guys are all hooked up to their catheters and IVs and oxygen tanks. Really, do you want to be dancing for that anyway? "Oops, sorry, I unplugged ya!" Guy's heart line goes flat! I would be so embarrassed. At least then, if you're knocking over their drinks, you'd be like, "Oh wait—you get a free one!" Reach around a little arm in front of him and plug it back in! "Let me get you a new orange juice and some loving!" I don't think I want to do this forever.

Given the parameters of stripping work, women cannot continue stripping in clubs over the course of a lifetime—their careers are necessarily limited. In addition to being rule breakers, however, older dancers who do not conform to the expectations of eager youthfulness may be viewed as less genuine in their performance, as Ronai explains:

As chronologically young as [a stripper] may be, she can be old. Her body is not as supple and her dance not as animated as it once was. Her gestures toward customers are construed to be abrupt, demanding, nagging, less patient than before. A dancer's sexual utility and the sincerity of her presentation come into question.[23]

In addition to age norms, there is particular potency in the norms around weight. The variety in body types found in The Lion's Den arose more from a need for dancers to fill shifts than a desire for diversity. While strippers of various sizes could be seen onstage, heavier dancers were disproportionately found working the weekdays with the fewest patrons. Eighteen-year-old Nina was approximately five foot seven inches, and her weight was about 150–160 pounds. Though ordinary people might not think of her as overweight, those in the club considered her fat. She explained how difficult it was to be considered an overweight stripper:

Sometimes it can be really degrading, and it can make you feel awful. When I first started, I was beaten on to lose weight all the time. It really picks apart your self-esteem. That part's hard to get through. They're still telling me to lose more weight, and it's frustrating at the club, too, because you have men and other people picking me apart.

As Nina's remarks demonstrate, strippers who fall at one end of the spectrum—being seen by management, club workers, other strippers, and patrons as too heavy—were subject to scorn.

Like older and larger women, women of color confronted a hostile environment in The Lion's Den. There were two African American bouncers (one of whom was fired after a few months), one Hawaiian part-time bartender, three African American strippers, and three Latina strippers out of approximately fifty workers at any given time. Given the palpable racism in the club, it was not surprising that few African American and Latina dancers worked in The Lion's Den, and those who were hired did not stay long. As Tamara explained, there were "not a lot of ethnic girls at our club." Her explanation was that "the manager won't hire them" because "he's very prejudiced." She explained that women of color did not "fit [the manager's] ideal. They're not blonde, big breasted, with tan lines and tall." As a result of the small number, Tamara was able to list off all of the strippers of color she had seen in the club, including one Asian and one Indian dancer, in addition to a few African American and Latina strippers. She described a few days in which the club had a diverse group of women working in the club: "One weekend, it was just beautiful; we had an Asian girl and an Indian girl, and we had a black girl, and we had a Spanish girl, and I'm like 'This diversity is beautiful.'" In support of more diversity she argued:

They're so cute, and they're exotic, and they're different.... But there are not a whole lot of girls that are like that, and that's a shame.... I really like to see diversity, and I've been really excited when we have.... But ... the club doesn't hire those kinds of people usually.

In Tamara's estimation, women of color "did well," meaning they made good tips and "the customers liked them." However, her positive attitude seemed more the result of her desire for diversity than knowledge of women of color's experience.

In transactions with primarily white men, women of color had qualitatively different experiences than did white women, though there was some disagreement in my interviews as to how these interactions played out. Like

Tamara's comment that "customers like" women of color, another white woman, Roxanne, argued that racial lines were often crossed in the club in ways that they would not be elsewhere:

There aren't a lot of black or Puerto Rican guys that come in here, but [those who do] like white women. You very seldom see a Puerto Rican girl dancing for Puerto Rican customers, 'cause they realize that Puerto Rican guys don't want to see them. But you will always see, if you have a decent-looking black girl, white guys will put down crazy money for them. You will never see a black girl go up onstage and not make money. Something about it being different, I guess. . . . And I think guys come in here because they might not do that outside of here. . . . "Oh my god, I wouldn't date a black girl out there" or "I wouldn't sleep with a black girl out there, but I can come in here and I can look at it, and I can fantasize about going with it, and being there with it and doing it."

Roxanne's emphasis on African American women's financial triumphs was connected to the competition between women in the club. Often strippers assumed that if they were not making money, someone else must be. Since African American strippers were alienated from other strippers, they were not in a position to discuss their earnings, leading other strippers to assume they were a threat.

Despite the assumptions of white women in the club, the experiences of women of color indicated patterns of racism. Rather than crossing racial boundaries, interactions in the club were often segregated. In spite of Roxanne's observations, many of the other dancers (regardless of their race) said that white patrons pulled their dollar bills off the stage when African American or Latina dancers appeared. While any dancer may have experienced such a gesture from a patron, discussions of this practice were most often linked to race and prejudice. Jade, a Latina dancer, raised the issue of racism: "I'm not going to say racism, but it's a preference. A lot of the guys in here are white, and most of them prefer white women." Describing specific events onstage, she put a visual image with her comments:

Sometimes . . . there's a white guy sitting there, and he's got a dollar up, and there's another girl dancing, and she's white, and he's looking at her, and I'm walking by, and he takes the dollar away. Obviously he doesn't want to see me; he wants to see her.

Similarly, Destiny compared her experience making the transition from being in an all-black club to this predominantly white club:

This [place] is very white. It's so white that I think some of these people have never seen black people live. I even asked a white guy one day, and I felt embarrassed when he was, like [in a very sarcastic tone], "Of course I have!" But I'm like, "You don't act like it."

She has also had men take their money off the stage during her shift: "I would go onstage, everyone would take their money off. And then a white girl would come onstage, and they'd just, like, put all their money back onstage." When asked why, Destiny explained:

It's the whole white-standard-of-beauty type thing, but I can't help that. I'll go over to a tanning salon, and I'll work there, and I'll be, like [in a sarcastic, high-pitched voice], "See, this is what you're going to come out like. You're going to look like this after a while, you keep coming here everyday [laughing], and it's going to stay! Ha ha!"

Destiny's critique of the white standard of beauty transcended the strip club, as her tanning salon example illustrates. The difficulties faced by African American and Latina women in The Lion's Den constituted a double burden. They coped with the demands of nude performance, as well as emotional and erotic labor, but they also faced the simultaneous burdens of sexism and racism.[24]

How Women Manage Stripping Labor

While women of color face particular burdens, all women have to develop a consistent set of strategies to navigate in an industry that is predicated on their subordination. The overarching patterns among strippers at The Lion's Den included identification, denial, cynicism, transformation, and separation. Women who identified with being a stripper bought into the compliments and attention, often relying on the self-esteem generated from patrons' goodwill to counteract the negative aspects of the work. Denial involved concealing stripping work from family and friends. Cynicism was a distancing technique that involved focusing on money as compensation for their labor. Transformation was used to rationalize the work by comparing it to other, more "legitimate" forms of employment. Separation involved the compartmentalization of work and home; some strippers selectively protected certain parts of themselves as "off limits" to preserve their sense of control, while others separated from work through personal de-eroticization and bathing rituals. Identification, cynicism, and separation are categories used by Hochschild in her analysis of emotional labor at work.[25] While the use of these terms here is somewhat different, the general meanings are quite similar. These techniques were not mutually exclusive, and strippers often described using more than one.

"Buying into It": Identifying as an Object of Desire

While every Lion's Den stripper interviewed told stories of patrons' criticisms, some strippers emphasized their positive experiences and the boost dancing gave to their self-esteem. Laurie Lewin captures the importance of these informal rewards in her autobiography, *Naked Is the Best Disguise*:

> Outside of work, I became the stripper. I must be attractive if men would pay to look at me. I must possess the secret charm every woman yearned for. Outside of work, I could allow the illusions to filter back into my mind. Forgetting the smoke, catcalls, and groping fingers. (emphasis in original)[26]

Those strippers who emphasized the extrinsic benefits closely resemble Hochschild's discussion of workers who "[identify] too wholeheartedly with the job."[27] Strippers drew on such associations to feel good about themselves and their work. For example, twenty-two-year-old Stella commented that what she liked best about her job was the way stripping made her feel better about herself:

> [I like] the attention—definitely. Because out of here I don't like my body. I think I'm too thin, and I don't like it. But in here, I feel comfortable with myself. I love all the compliments I get. And things I didn't even know about myself like [customers saying], "Oh you have beautiful eyes" or "You have pretty hair," and I just feed off of that.

She believed that the work had changed her for the better in at least one way: "I have more self-esteem about myself, I think. But that's about the only thing." Angela was also drawn in by compliments: "I always had a very low self-esteem. That's one of the reasons I never even thought about dancing. I didn't think I was pretty enough to dance or good enough." With some coaxing from others in the club (strippers, male workers, and patrons), Angela was encouraged to see herself as attractive. As she explained, "Now, like, even the guys [are] complimenting me, and even the girls, too, will sit there and say, 'You're beautiful,' and this and this and this." Robin described how stripping had made her more comfortable with her body both inside and outside the club: "I was wickedly shy about my body [and] conservative until I got drunk one night and got naked." Robin had a boyfriend for five years, and during most of their relationship, she would not let him see her naked. She made him turn the lights off and always wore conservative pajamas to bed. After a few weeks of stripping, she transformed into someone who "[walked] around naked all the time. It didn't faze me at all." Along with this dramatic shift in Robin's comfort with nudity came better self-esteem about her body:

> I used to think I had small boobs, and I hated my boobs, and I thought, "No one wants to see me naked." Then I started waitressing, and guys started offering me—one guy offered me 500 bucks for a private dance, and I was like, "You know what? My boobs are small, but there can't be anything that wrong with my body if people are offering all this money to see it."

Strippers often emphasize the positive aspects of their work in order to rationalize the hardships they face. Stacey, a participant from my previous research, explained: "I was such a wallflower before this; I really didn't think very highly of myself. . . . The attention's really great."[28] The attention and the compliments become an unexpected bonus; however, comments from patrons can be a double-edged sword, as Jen described:

> Patrons will pick out any flaw that [you] maybe even possibly have, and it doesn't matter how minor or how major, or even if it is a flaw or not. They're just brutal sometimes, and it doesn't matter; you could be perfect, and they can find something. And they'll make it a point to make sure that you notice it because it makes them feel better to bring you down, and that's because of their insecurity, or just because they're a jerk, or because they have a dissatisfaction with women in general. They're like, "I'm paying you, so you're going to have to put up with what I choose to tell you."

Mindy described the ups and downs strippers experience night to night. When she was not bringing in patrons or money, she began to ask herself,

"What's the matter with me? Why aren't the guys liking me?" Sometimes she turned to comparisons with other dancers: "Why am I not making money, and she's making $600 when I have $50?" On the flip side, she explained that, at times, stripping can be an "ego trip. You'll get guys in here that'll be like, 'You're so beautiful. You're the most beautiful girl in here. You should be a model.' It kind of balances itself out." However, when they rely on the rewards from men's attentions, strippers run the risk that men will also deny them this source of self-esteem. As Mindy said, "Some nights you walk out of here, and your head's so big you can barely fit through the fucking door; other nights you want to cry." These night-to-night and even minute-to-minute changes in working conditions make stripping an often-discordant experience. Sociologist Bernadette Barton argues in her research on stripping that these kinds of ups and downs constitute "a Möbius strip of rapidly changing feelings and events that wear on women the longer they dance."[29] Drawing insightful distinctions between early- and late-career dancers, Barton argues that when strippers are relatively new to their work they emphasize the positive aspects—the money, flexible hours, and their enjoyment of performing. Beyond three years of employment, strippers emphasize the costs of their work, such as the longer-term effects of substance use and abuse, bodily strain, and aggressive and abusive patrons.

Denying Involvement: Keeping Stripping a Secret

Strippers often attempt to compartmentalize their "stripper" role and their sense of self outside of work by keeping stripping a secret from friends and family. This strategy, in effect, aligns strippers more with strangers than with their close companions. In part, strippers' secrecy is due to the stigma attached to their work. Within sociology, the definition of stigma emphasizes a dynamic process that gives rise to "spoiled identities."[30] For example, Erving Goffman explored in his famous study *Stigma: Notes on the Management of Spoiled Identity* how "spoiled identities" are formed not a priori but through interactions between individuals and social groups that produce shared and contested meanings.[31] Drawing on case studies, Goffman identified stigma as a facet of social life that leads one person to devalue another based on perceived characteristics.[32] Stigmatized individuals respond by trying to manage their presentation of self and their stigmatized identities for others.[33] Goffman argues: "A very widely employed strategy of the discreditable person is to handle his risks by dividing the world into a large group to whom he tells nothing, and a small group to whom he tells all and upon whose help he then relies; he co-opts for his masquerade just those individuals who would ordinarily constitute the greatest danger."[34] This compartmentalization is precisely what strippers do. Strippers, however, go beyond concealing their stripping work from family and friends.

Strippers have the added burden of concealing themselves twice—rather than "telling all" to patrons and coworkers, they create a fictive self. Virtually all of the women in The Lion's Den used stage names and created alternative identities (e.g., made-up jobs and home towns) to protect themselves from patrons who might try to find out where they lived or worked outside of the strip club. This was of great concern to many of the strippers, especially those who kept their work a secret from people in their lives. The patrons knew and often understood this practice, as Charlie so aptly explained:

> Ninety-nine percent of these girls don't even want you to know their real names; they've got dance names. And I don't blame them—there's a lot of weirdos. How would you feel if you had to change your name to do what you wanted to do? How would you feel if you had to travel sixty, eighty miles from where you live because you're afraid that somebody you know in your family is going to walk in and see you naked on the stage? That's got to be terrible for these kids.

Though fake names and jobs were supposed to protect strippers from exposure and put their minds at ease, many strippers faced great fears over being discovered.

The effect of emotional and psychological stress was perhaps most apparent for those strippers who actively concealed their work from family and friends. Tamara's description of her drive home provides one such example:

> I have a hard time getting home because I usually drive the speed limit. I don't want to get pulled over. I have this terrible fear that I'm going to get in a horrendous accident, and my parents will find out that I was dancing. And, it will be like [gestures with her hands in the air], "Stripper caught in fiery blaze" or something [laughs]! Yeah, the newspaper would like to print things like that. Call it an irrational fear, but my parents would be disappointed, especially since they paid for me to go school, and I should be doing something with that [laughs]. I am, but slowly.

Later in the same interview Tamara explained that, coming from a conservative family, she chose not to tell her parents about her work: "When I started taking ballet dance lessons, my mother was livid [*laughs*]. She was like, 'As long as you're not stripping, I guess it's all right' [*laughs*]. So I didn't start dancing until a few years after that." Her primary concern was over telling her mother: "My mother is very against anything sexual or erotic in a woman. [Sex] can happen maybe in the bedroom with the lights off with your husband after about five years of marriage [*laughs*]." Similarly, Jade's brothers did not know about her work, and she was constantly worried that they would enter the club: "I think about it a lot, and sometimes it bothers me because I feel like I'm doing something wrong. But then again, I think that I need money. I need to make money somehow." Her brothers often went to strip clubs, so she envisioned how their presence in The Lion's Den might play out:

They would probably drag me off the stage and whatnot. . . . I'm just hoping they don't come in one day 'cause I wouldn't want to dance. . . . I'd probably just talk to Steve and say, "I can't dance. My brothers are out there, [and] they don't know I'm dancing." I don't know if he would understand or not, but that's what I'd do [*laughs*].

Destiny, who also concealed her stripping from most of her family and friends, had this to say about how stripping fit in with the rest of her life:

I wouldn't recommend it. If you don't have to dance, don't. It's too much work . . . mental and physical stress. I kind of think it's more physical than mental, but your mental catches up. It's just a whole totally different mentality that you have to have working here.

Since Destiny kept her work a secret, she, in effect, led two different lives. For example, if she saw someone from work in another setting, sometimes she would pretend she did not know that person. In her words:

School, family, and friends, that's right here [*taps her chest*]. Destiny, booty, breasts, naked, men, cigarettes, that's all over here [*gestures away from her body*]. . . . [At work] I look totally different, act totally different. . . . This is where you're a bitch. And when you get out, you can be nice if you want to; you can keep the bitch mode on if you want to.

Though Vivian was open with many of her friends and family about stripping, concealing her work from a few family members was difficult. In particular, keeping her work from her mom made conversations stressful. Since she was a traveling stripper, she could not discuss any aspect of her life in another state, where she traveled over the weekends to strip at The Lion's Den. She explained:

> I can't comment to my mom on how the weather was down here this weekend. "Oh, you were in another state? What? What were you doing there?" Even if I buy something down here, you know, "Where did you get that?" Oh, quick, think of something, someplace where they couldn't find it again. "I found it at Goodwill, brand-spanking new."

Keeping club work a secret also extended to cocktail waitresses. Evangelina hid her job from her family because she envisioned a harsh reaction: "Because they would probably kick my ass. I come from a strict family background. I'm 100 percent Greek, and my mom and dad don't speak English. . . . We're very Greek, so they're pretty strict with me." Imagining what would happen if her family found out, she said that her mother would "probably yell . . . and say, 'What are you doing? Why do you have to work there?'" She did not, however, think her mother would tell anyone else in her family, because of all the trouble it would cause for Evangelina. In particular, she believed she would get a lecture from her uncle, the patriarch, "who can be really strict. He would probably not go for it at all." Maintaining the separation of home and work was a problem faced by all the female workers at the club, but those whose work was kept secret from family and friends felt it most acutely.

Cynicism and Alienation

Many strippers adopt a cynical attitude toward their work. Recognizing the societal stigma, these women emphasize lucrative rewards as adequate compensation for the job. Fast, easy money—that is the veiled promise that strip club work conventionally holds for many women. On the surface, this may seem to be true. While stripping and cocktail waitressing are skilled jobs, they require little experience, education, or formal training. They provide employment that can be part-time, and often lucrative, especially when compared with other part-time jobs that do not require previous experience or training. Behind the normative assumptions that stress the relatively high income of strip club work rests the often contradictory relationship women have with erotic labor. While strippers frequently cite economic need and the promise of lucrative returns on their labor as their reason for entry, there are other factors at work.

What is missing from the economic explanations is that women may use these rationales as a means of coping with stigmatized and emotionally demanding work, basically arguing that the ends justify the means. If women are entering the stripping industry out of economic desperation, they might reconcile a whole range of costs based on the promise of economic rewards. Moreover, if the economic rationale seems plausible—this job pays disproportionately more than other available employment options—strippers may further justify the tradeoffs of stigma, physical strain, and emotional stress for pay. For example, Tamara explained that stripping allowed her to work one day a week: "It's very tiring, but I do like the money when I come home. I only have to go in once a week. I guess I could be making a lot of money if I worked more shifts, but it drains so much out of me."

Many of the women I interviewed found that their work was lucrative, though earnings were inconsistent—typically between $150 and $300 on an average weekday shift and more on weekends. Since strip clubs have seasonal attendance swings, with high attendance during "stag season," when bachelor parties dominate the club, and just before the winter holidays, workers who rely mainly on tips for their income can expect considerable ups and downs. Strip clubs, like other businesses, are subject to ups and downs in the broader economy. The region in which the club is located also affects tips. The Lion's Den was near a small city, so it could not attract the quantity of business one might find in a major metropolitan area. Not surprisingly, strippers report greater earnings in larger cities. Earnings also vary from stripper to stripper. One stripper may have a particularly charismatic personality and attract a greater number of patrons, or a stripper may be the only one of a particular physical type—such as the only brunette—and corner the market in that category, or a stripper may move more quickly than the others from one patron to the next. Simply asserting that strip club work is lucrative without analyzing the worker, club, and region leaves much to be explained.

In an attempt to reconcile the costs and rewards of stripping work, Scott A. Reid, Jonathan S. Epstein, and D. E. Benson argue:

> Dancers only "play at" the deviant role without letting the unsavory characteristics of the role "contaminate" their true sense of self. The dancers can avoid the contamination, they assert, because they seek external rewards (primarily money) rather than internal rewards (personal satisfaction) from the deviant occupation.[35]

Adopting this approach, Destiny singled out the role of money in her coping strategy. She explained feeling "drained" after work and being very thankful once her shift was finished. It was primarily the money that kept her going: "Once you count your money, it's all, you know, it's all differ-ent. . . . The best thing is the money." Describing a slow shift, she said, "Like today, I've made, like, $5 in like two hours, and I'm like, 'What's the point of me coming all the way out here?'" Demonstrating that things can often change in an instant, she said:

> I walked by, and this guy was like, "You wanna dance?" And, it's like, boom, here's $20, and I was like, "Oh, that's cool." It gives me a chance to laugh because I'm looking at them like, "You're so slow—I'm just going to get your money and go." You just learn to play with it. You have to see where they are, where their minds are. That's how you make your money.

For Mindy, money enabled her to rationalize the ups and downs of the work:

> It's not bad. Mostly I don't have any problems with what I do for a living. I'm okay with it as long as I make money, and I usually do pretty well. If I'm making money, I can put everything aside and say, "No, fuck you, I just made 500 bucks." It's a lot easier when you're making money.

However, Mindy's perspective depended on having more lucrative nights than not. In her words:

> Because I'll tell you what, there's nights I've left here and literally went home and cried because I have like $50 or $60, and I was here for seven hours getting naked all night for guys, being tired because my feet hurt, my back hurts, and for what? I can be a waitress and make that.

Quickly shifting back to better times, she countered: "But like last night, I had an awesome night. It wasn't that busy, there weren't really that many girls in here, but I walked out of here with $385 on a Monday night, so it's nights like that that make it worth it." Similarly, eighteen-year-old Daria explained that she thought stripping was degrading at first, until she rea-soned through the situation:

I'm like, "This is so degrading, this is so degrading." And then I was like, "Well, they're the ones that are giving me the money to take off my clothes. So who's the smarter sex? Who's the one that's benefiting from this? Not them."

In some cases, money also became a means of dealing with problematic patrons. As Robin argued, "I don't care how big of an asshole they are, as long as they're still throwing money at me." Money and the right outlook enabled her to cope with the work and distance herself from the toll it might take:

I have the right attitude for it. Whatever someone dishes out, I'll give right back. As long as they're giving me money, I won't take offense. . . . If they're going to throw fifties at me then, hey, do whatever you want, baby. Do whatever you like.

Likewise, Stella emphasized that strippers cannot let difficult interactions with customers get in the way of making money. Stella expected only a small minority of men to be problematic: "Like one out of fifty guys insulting me, [while] the others just tell me how beautiful I am, so I just shrug it off, and I don't let it bother me." Distancing herself from being distressed by men's negative comments was important:

Because if you let it bother you, then you'll be in a bad mood for the rest of the night, and you'll make no money, and I don't give them the satisfaction. . . . To me, they all look the same; they all look like one big money sign. That's all they look like to me.

Given that men attended the club to perform aggressive masculinity and that women were given little organizational support or protection, using money as a means of coping only compounded the problems faced by strippers in The Lion's Den. While money in the abstract may lead strippers to justify their work, the preceding examples demonstrate the ways in which a focus on money can put strippers at risk of verbal or physical aggression from patrons.

Strippers recognized troubles as a result of their earnings. Though not reflected in other strippers' narratives, Layla's story is a case in point. While Layla's family had been supportive, her relationships with friends were strained. She explained that she had many friends before she started stripping. Since then, she felt like she had only one friend, and even that friend was problematic:

> My best friend, she's the only one who stood by me since, and even her, she don't hang out with me as much. She likes to hang out with me because of the fact that I have money. We can go shopping and go do all kinds of stuff.

Other friends she used to spend time with "[thought] of old debts" and asked her for money. She also had friends who asked too much of her, in her eyes. Once, when she was homeless, Layla stayed with a friend and her child for a week in exchange for babysitting. Given the money Layla made, her friend concluded that childcare was not enough and asked for half the rent, which was over $600. She summed up her losses this way:

> [Friends are] the only thing I've lost by taking this job. I've got money. I've gotten everything I've wanted for a long time. I picked up my whole house. I've got really nice furniture and stuff like that from doing this, but it's just the friends. Yeah, my house looks nice, but I don't have anyone to come over and see it.

The isolation and loneliness Layla experienced, as a result of her friends' reactions to her work, was an unexpected cost associated with stripping.

Transforming the Work

Tamara had a different and noteworthy approach for coping with stripping work. While she recognized the costs of emotional labor, this aspect of her job also provided a means for her to legitimate her trade as "healing work," comparable with that of therapists or counselors. Tamara provided this description:

> Basically I try to make a connection with each person I dance for. My goal is to make everybody smile or to bring some kind of beauty to them. I don't know, I've been told that I do healing work through my dancing. I try to reach out to people and understand that they're lonely or they're just there to have fun. I keep it very separated. I am very professional, but at the same time we can make a connection, and for that five minutes I can make that person feel very special, and that's important to me. I also like to show them the human body in motion and how beautiful that can be. I like to hear the words, "you're mesmerizing" [laughs].

Tamara's entire persona in the club was crafted through her belief that she healed men. She adopted a New Age presentation of self, speaking to patrons in soft tones and often wearing costumes resembling those of a belly dancer.

Carol Rambo Ronai and Rebecca Cross argue that strippers employ "narrative resistance" to construct a positive sense of self in spite of a stigmatized job.[36] While Tamara claimed "separation and professionalism," she did not maintain this position throughout her interview. Instead, this position appeared more as rationalization or justification to make stripping seem more legitimate and positive. While other women hinted at sentiments like this about the work, they were only mentioned at the beginning of the interviews and quickly faded away as they responded to more specific questions about interactions with patrons. Tamara's sustained discussion may stem from her other job as a massage therapist, work that employs a healing framework.

Another example involved Faith, who, after working in the industry for countless years, planned to quit dancing when she turned thirty-seven. While she commented throughout her interview about how much she wanted to "get done," she also echoed her love for the dancing component of her work:

I like to dance. I love the dance. I love the aerobics. I love the gymnastics part of it. . . . I adore it. If I could keep my clothes on, I'd probably do this the rest of my life until I drop. It doesn't matter what kind of money I made [laughs].

For Faith, the transformative possibilities of dancing were strongly linked to physical fitness: "It's taught me a lot. I'm basically a quiet, shy person, and it's helped me to come out of that a little bit. I mean it has done some good, kept me in great shape for a lot longer. It kind of gives girls the incentive to [stay in shape]."

Creating Personal Boundaries, Selectivity, and Acts of Opposition

Sex workers separate part of their sense of self as "off limits" to patrons as both a coping mechanism and a form of resistance. In the film *Pretty Woman,* the lead character, Vivian, would have sex with customers but drew her boundary around kissing. By doing this, she secured her perception of *real* intimacy that she would not share with johns. She becomes confused and dismayed when she kisses her john and future romantic partner, Edward Lewis, and violates this rule. Some strippers use a similar tactic, compartmentalizing their work and home lives. As Heidi Mattson asserts in her autobiography, *Ivy League Stripper*:

At the club, you can "buy me" (that is, unless you're a grabby, offensive jerk), but run into me at the grocery store, like Manny, a customer did once, and your money is no good. You're not a patron anymore, you're a stranger.[37]

Mindy expressed hostility at men's demands for emotional labor from strippers; for while she was willing to show her naked body, she was not willing to listen to patrons' problems. She described emotional support for patrons as "the most aggravating part" of her job. Placing boundaries around providing such labor for men, she explained:

> I hate guys that just come in here and think they can tell you their whole life's problems, just sob on your shoulder. And you sit there, and you're like, "Why are you telling me this? I am a complete fucking stranger. Do you think I care? I'm not here to listen to you. I'm here to show you my pussy, my ass, my tits, and you pay me."

Daria asserted boundaries around intimacy: "I remember the first time I ever got up onstage, I was, like, so scared. So they get to look at my crotch; they'll never get to look at it again in any other way." Tamara also created boundaries, but hers were focused around physical contact and intercourse. She explained she would never have sex for money since she needed "to be in love." For that reason, her job was different from providing the sexual services of a prostitute:

> I don't see my job as prostitution; I see it as a sexual service or kind of like watching porn or watching someone on TV. Even though it's making a connection with somebody, I'm still far away; I'm not really available. I'm just a fantasy. And that's what I like to maintain. "No, you can look, but you cannot have me."

As an act of self-preservation, strippers preserve a part of themselves for outside of work. Mindy explained, "I come to work, I dance, and I leave it at that. I don't involve my work in my normal everyday life. I just kind of separate it—from when I'm here and outside of work." For her, the contrast was between her "normal life" and work within the club:

> When I'm outside of work, I live a normal life. My boyfriend lives with me, so it's like I'm taking care of the house, I'm cleaning, cooking, doing laundry, running errands, and getting stuff that we both need

and just taking care of each other. When I'm at work, I work, I do my job, and then I go home. I don't really talk about it much when I'm not at work.

Tamara emphasized her desire to separate herself from the dirt at work: "The stage is absolutely disgusting. I just feel so grimy and gross when I come home. I don't want to like touch anything in my house. I don't want to bring anything from work in there." Using a physical separation from her stage name, Tamara, as well as the dirt in the club, she explained:

My bag, like, is designated to a certain corner. I don't always remember to wash my clothes as much as I should. Even though I'm only wearing them for like fifteen minutes every night, I should probably wash them just to get the smoke out of it, but when I'm here, I forget so much about Tamara that I don't even think about my bag.

Sometimes these distinctions were made not outside of but during work. Elsie, a stripper I interviewed for an earlier project, explained how she came to view her own sexual arousal as separate from her private dance performances for patrons:

Sometimes I'm dancing, and I've got my legs spread apart. It'll sound strange, but say I've just done a long dance for somebody, and I told him this great fantasy, and I'm getting wet from what I said. It doesn't matter who the guy was because I've got my eyes closed the whole time [*laughing*]. [I was] whispering in his ear, and I didn't care who he was. And I've got to get up onstage as soon as I'm done with that dance, and I spread my legs for somebody, and they see that I'm wet [*laughs*]. It's like they love it. They eat it up, so to speak. And I'm sitting there going, "This is so fucking bizarre that I'm spreading my legs for this person, and he can see that I'm wet, and it's really none of his business." It's weird. What am I doing? It's so weird. If my mother only knew [*laughs*].[38]

Not surprisingly, some strippers are not able to maintain these boundaries, and it affects their relationships with men generally, as Layla explained:

I think [stripping] definitely brings out the worst in people. Once [strippers have] been here a while, they start telling off customers if they're rude, and it just gets worse. People's attitudes get worse towards men in general, not just at work. Out on the street, you can just see a guy, and if he says something to you, usually you'd just be like, "whatever," but you freak out because you're used to telling off your customers! They're a lot of girls here who will tell off their customers if they say something wrong to them.

Problems sometimes spilled over into their intimate relationships. Most of the strippers I spoke with shared stories of strained relationships with their intimate partners. Tess explained that she sometimes had difficulty being intimate with her boyfriend after work: "I hate it because I'm sexual for people all night long, and then I go home to him, and it's hard to be sexual with him. And he doesn't like that." It is difficult, she explained, "because I don't want him to feel like I'm doing for him what I do for other people." Tess struggled with precisely the same aspect of herself that she sought to reserve for her relationship. While she explained her fears in terms of worries over how her boyfriend was feeling, it is also possible that she did not want to feel that she was "doing for him" what she "did for other people" since she had been "sexual all night." Likewise, Tamara did not like to be near her partner until she had showered:

I don't feel clean, and I don't feel like I want to touch him or I want him to touch me. I'm so used to being in the mindset where you cannot touch me, and this is my space. This is as close as you can come to me. It's hard for me to then come home and hug him or kiss him until I've showered.

Sometimes, if her partner wanted to shower with her, she told him to "get out" so she could have the water to herself. Tamara linked distance from her partner with her transition away from strip club performance and toward feelings of cleanliness. Daria also struggled over intimacy with her lover:

I could not get near him. I pictured the guys in the club, and I was like, "If they're like that, he has to be like that, too." It totally played with my head for a while. I wouldn't let him touch me. I didn't like kissing him. It was like I didn't talk to him about it because he was the guy. He was the enemy.

It took time, Daria explained, but "finally I got over my bad self, you know; it's just a job, and you learn to accept it, but at first it was really hard for me." Previous research has detailed connections between stripping and "the negative effects the job can have on women's lives . . . [such as] relationship problems [and] the inhibition of heterosexual desire."[39] Sweet and Tewksbury also found that strippers have difficulty "maintaining an intimate relationship outside of the club" and become "desensitized sexually" over time.[40]

Washing Work Away

The personal strain that spilled over into strippers' lives—their feelings of physical dirtiness, emotional danger, and risks to their sense of sexual self— were palpable in their interviews. When I asked Summer what she thought of men in the club, she offered the following:

Some of them are too drunk to even notice, but some of them get all excited. Some of them, in the VIP Room, you see them touching their balls and their penis. . . . I feel like I'm almost dirty. I wonder sometimes when I'm dancing how many guys out there are pedophiles.

Patrons routinely told strippers that they were too fat, or too thin, or unattractive. Describing verbal aggression from patrons, Vivian seethed, "Guys in here were just mean, rude, obnoxious, vulgar—just assholes all the way around!"

In my previous interviews with strippers, they told stories that indicated a process of de-eroticization.[41] Outside work, the strippers dressed in baggy clothes, wore little or no makeup, and generally sought to avoid attention from men. In short, they separated their sense of self outside of work from feelings or exhibitions of eroticism. This process was their means of coping with the burdens of stripping work—a breakdown in their attempt to selectively reserve a part of themselves for outside of work. Similarly, Lisa Pasko found "considerable social and psychological costs" for strippers that "creates difficulties in their daily lives."[42]

Transitioning to and from work also creates troubles for strippers. Strippers in this study struggled with their transition home; most used a ritualized bathing routine they carried out after each shift. These were not ordinary showers or baths; strippers often shared stories indicating the infliction of pain to cope with their suffering. Ronai described her difficulty transitioning from work to home. Her ritualized washings were critical to this process:

The shower is very important to me. First, I suds up from head to toe and rinse the foreign touches, foul odors, sweat, and grime from my body. After I consider myself squeaky clean, I make the water as hot as I can stand, and rotate slowly under the shower, making the temperature hotter still. The burn is purifying.[43]

While bathing rituals were described as a means of separating or "washing away" work, they also vividly illustrate the costs of stripping and the ways in which this work pervades the bodies and minds of the women who perform it. Tamara explained how important her after-work shower was to reconnecting with her sense of self outside of work. The shower was typically the first place she went:

> I'll get in the shower and turn it up really, really hot, and I'll probably fall asleep in there sitting on the floor [*laughs*]. . . . It would take me like forty-five minutes sometimes just to stand back up because I'm just so tired from working. It's just such a drain on your body. . . . I usually sit in there until I run out of hot water.

In addition to scalding temperatures, some strippers used harsh chemicals in their baths. Robin explained, "My knees, when I get home, I wash my knees with Brillo pads. . . . The dirt gets so ground in there. Like, our stage is filthy." Destiny's bathing routine included the use of bleach. She offered, "I used to take showers in bleach. I have taken baths in bleach to get all the dirt off me." She argued that bleach helps with both the physical and mental "dirt":

> Mentally you feel really dirty—like, oh my god, I'm showing myself to people that I don't even know, and they're going to fantasize about me and this and that. To me, I felt really dirty, and I used to just take and put like this much bleach in [*gestures less than a centimeter*], just enough.

At times she used too much and began to "smell like bleach." Describing her friend's reaction, Destiny raised her voice an octave and sarcastically remarked, "'You better stop doing that. It's going to get in the wrong place one day.' And I used to take showers with it and stuff." However, Destiny found the bleach comforting because she could "see all the dirt that comes off." She did not come up with the use of bleach herself; rather, her boyfriend's grandmother talked of regularly "[taking] baths in bleach with white towels all the time, and [she can] see the dirt that comes off." By contrast, Destiny argued, "I only do it every now and then. I've been trying not to do it because it's so harsh." Roxanne also took different showers after work than she did on other days:

> Oh god, yes, you scrub a little harder when you get out of here. I take showers—the water is so hot, I get out of the shower [and] it looks like I have sunburn. I'm bright red. You can look at me and push down, and I'm blood red. Because I have to have the water so hot just to scrub all the crud off.

She explained this was both for "the physical dirt, and it's the psychological, it's getting this place off you." Getting away from the strip club and its grime was a primary focus for most strippers after work. While the washing process provided some psychological relief by rendering troubles into physical sensations or pain, it was temporary. The problems with the work reappeared during subsequent shifts—the emotional and physical costs, as well as the stigma. Though strippers attempted to transition to home through their bathing rituals, these transitions were fraught with emotional strife that led them to scald, scratch, and harm their bodies with chemicals.

Women in The Lion's Den adopted various strategies to resist having the role of "stripper" spill over into the rest of their lives. In these actions, strippers attempted to deter themselves and others from identifying them too closely, if at all, with their social role.[44] They delimited "front stage" and "back stage," or public and private, in their lives.[45] While their attempts often failed, they are not alone in an experience that faces most, if not all, such workers today. While estrangement can promote cynicism, it can also trap workers in a duality of "manufactured" versus "real" emotions.[46] As the preceding examples illustrate, strippers have difficulty managing various facets of both work and home lives. In effect, strippers are required to perform a particular kind of erotic labor that necessitates they make their "work" seem like something else, something freely given, associated with their sense of self, and generated genuinely. This tension between the demands of their work and their failures at coping make strippers struggle over the relationship between work and home, real and feigned identities, public and private selves.

The flight attendants in Arlie Hochschild's study *The Managed Heart*, who performed a great deal of emotional labor, faced similar tensions. Hochschild explains: "Some workers conclude that only one self (usually the nonwork self) is the 'real' self[;] . . . the majority will decide that each self is meaningful and real in its own different way and time."[47] Looking at the work of prostitutes and other sex workers, Wendy Chapkis builds on Hochschild's analysis, arguing that the major factor affecting sex workers' ability to negotiate these challenges is their working conditions. She writes, "status differences between worker and client, employee/employer relations, and negative cultural attitudes toward the work performed may be at the root of the distress and damage experienced by some workers."[48] The difficult working conditions in The Lion's Den were key to the struggles strippers faced.

Strippers' Resistance

Despite the emotional and physical burdens of their work, many strippers are vibrant and assertive. Whether stripping helps mold them into strong women, or they were strong before they started, strippers are a force to be reckoned with. Consider the following story from my field notes:

> Marcus said that he and a friend were in the deejay booth one night while he was working. Sasha, a dancer at The Lion's Den, was coming in to ask when she was due onstage. Sasha is a particularly outspoken woman, known for her loud voice, who enjoys playing jokes on men in the club. According to Marcus, Sasha walked into the deejay booth, lifted her leg, and asked, "Is my tampon string showing?" Marcus, who was eating his dinner, stopped and stared in shock. Sasha giggled and said, "Oh never mind, that was last week."

Similarly, Fiona described in vivid terms why she liked performing:

> Good college kids, pussy in their face, like this close [*puts a hand in front of her face*], and they don't know what to do with themselves. It's so interesting to watch the reactions and the conversations that go on. To interact with them, to fuck with them, to get inside their head and take their money without them . . . having too much of a problem with it.

Fiona used humor to entertain and resist by maintaining distance from her work:

> I'll get out there, hoot an' holler, stomp around. Insult the guys just to make them laugh. "You must be a cop!" "Yeah, why?" "You've got a big doughnut ass!" And the guys laugh. Shit like that. Clever little ways to separate real world from work world.

For other strippers, like Robin, reactions to men's attention changed over time:

> Before I started dancing, like when I used to go to bars when I grew up, as far as the girls knew, I was one of the guys. I was like a little redneck girl. Like I used to drive a big truck. I was never like, "guys want to look at me," when I was younger because I was like one of them. Going from that to

dancing. Then after dancing, guys were like all over me, and at first it was like, "yea" and then it was like, "you know what, fuck you! Fuck you!" Like guys hitting on you all the time. In general now when guys come up to me I'm like, "You're so original" [*sarcastically*].

Disruptions like Sasha's and empowering sentiments like Robin's and Fiona's provided a means of resisting the burdens of stripping work. In addition to using humor, strippers also vented their frustrations and demonstrated their resistance directly toward patrons. Stella's approach was as follows:

If they insult me about being thin or something, I just insult them right back, or I just laugh at them and walk away. I don't let it get to me. In the beginning I would have let it get to me, but now I figure I'm never going to see—what's the chance of me seeing them again?

Jen also verbally retaliated against those patrons who behaved in mean-spirited or inappropriate ways:

Mentally it's a difficult job. You deal with a lot of crap. You deal with a lot of crudeness. Some nights . . . if you're not in the mood to deal with it, . . . I'll just look at that person and be like, "You're an asshole." The customers, you know, they're married, or it's their bachelor party, and they're all like, "What do you mean I can't touch you?" and "Why aren't you going to grind on me?" And you're like, "Dude, you're married. Go home to your wife if you want that!"

Strippers also actively engaged patrons with verbal reprimands if they were not tipping well. As Robin explained, "If it's some guy who's like a lousy tipper, and he's trying to [be] rude and stuff, I'll be like, 'You know what, you can take your fucking cheap ass and just leave because your dollar ain't worth that much to me!'" Fiona also chastised patrons for failing to tip or sitting apart from the stage and watching television:

It drives me fucking nuts. I go over there and say, "Hey, is that what you guys are here for? You here to watch the game, then why don't you go watch it at home? You know, you're here at our table! Put your hand in your pocket and throw that money up onstage!" I have a big mouth, so I do stuff like that [*laughs*]. "What the hell are you doing, get up there!"

These reprimands are similar to those used by waitresses in Greta Foff Paules's study *Dishing It Out*: "By speaking out, by confronting the customer, [a waitress] demonstrates that she is not subservient or in fear of losing her job; that she is not compelled by financial need or a sense of social hierarchy to accept abuse from customers."[49] In this sense strippers, like waitresses, use reprimands and tips as a means of taking control over a situation.

Nonetheless, women were resisting in a context that was stacked against them, and many opted to leave the club instead of fighting back, resulting in a high turnover rate and low worker solidarity. When asked if she thought it was possible for dancers to work together, Roxanne replied:

> Honestly, no. I've heard that it's been done. Here in this club I know it wouldn't happen, because the girls don't stick together now. We've had girls bleach other girls' clothes, mine included, because they were in the wrong bag at the wrong time. We've had girls fight with other girls, ripping earrings out of ears, ripping eye rings out, yeah, punching people, [and] hitting bottles over their heads. These girls can't even stick together to make a schedule to keep girls working so guys will come in here.

With little possibility of collective action to produce change, strippers were left alone to cope with their work as best they could. Those who failed to manage both their work and home identities risked developing a negative self-image and physically harming themselves.

Stripping Strippers' Power

Stripping in The Lion's Den was, if you will, stripped down. While there was variation in the specific content of stripper-patron interactions, strippers determined whom they would perform for, what kind of performance they gave, and how long it lasted. In addition, strippers informally monitored and trained other strippers in the club. As such, strippers exercised some authority over their work. Still, in most other ways, they remained greatly curtailed. Strippers did not choose their own music, because deejays decided what to play. Nor did they choreograph elaborate stage performances, since they shared the stage with several other dancers. Pressures to conform to narrow ideas regarding femininity, beauty, and sexiness also hemmed in strippers as they struggled to achieve the "right" bodies, good looks, and presentation of self.

While we might lament the difficult working conditions faced by strippers in The Lion's Den and feel disgust over outbreaks of ringworm at other clubs, such conditions are not likely to prompt public outrage. American culture has ambivalence about stripping—simultaneously stigmatizing most club work as sleazy and lowbrow while characterizing some aspects as chic. Although recreational striptease exercise classes and dance poles for in-home use may bring stripping to the mainstream, it is not likely to make strippers themselves seem mainstream. Moreover, facets of stripper chic—clothes, popular media performances, and so forth—are not likely to garner public support for women like those in The Lion's Den who are making ends meet in the least desirable parts of the industry.

By failing to provide clean and safe working conditions, strip clubs like The Lion's Den devalue women and put them in danger. Strippers unhappy with their working conditions face an uphill battle. Collective action is difficult under the best conditions. When you consider that many of these workers at The Lion's Club were transient and sensitive to the stigma attached to stripping, agitating for change became an even greater (and less likely) challenge. Though it might be tempting to separate out and chastise The Lion's Den or the sex industry for the physical and emotional troubles they cause workers, doing so would only deny the broader cultural burden of sexism by scapegoating one club or one industry. It is U.S. culture and the social organization of work that together made The Lion's Den (and many other strip clubs) a harsh work environment for women. Within the broader culture, the sex industry only seems like an outlier that pushes presentations of femininities to their logical end. Though such presentations of femininity may offend mainstream sensibilities, underpinning sex industry norms are broader cultural assumptions about what it means to be a desirable female. Furthermore, the stripping industry's devaluation of particular groups—impoverished, working-class, and racial/ethnic minority women—echoes a common historical refrain.

The consequences of these working conditions are real. Strippers' coping mechanisms, especially their bathing rituals, suggest the intense burden they associate with their work. The women I interviewed were scalding, scouring with Brillo pads, and bathing their bodies in bleach. Not only are these activities beyond the scope of typical hygiene rituals, all of these practices imply distress that a person manifests through pain and self-harm.[50] I am not arguing for medicalized or pathologizing interpretations. The evidence from strippers' narratives suggests that sociological explanations underlie their self-harm practices. As sociologists Patricia Adler and Peter Adler found in their study of self-injurers, all "were troubled in some way. Some were repressed; some were depressed; some used it as a coping strategy."[51] Strippers' narratives and the timing of these events (after leaving work) suggest a close link to their experiences stripping and imply a coping strategy rather than a psychological illness. Adler and Adler suggest that it is important to address how individuals self-injure. Strippers' self-harm behaviors appear to be learned from family members and developed on their own.[52]

While other workers engaged in emotional labor experience alienation with similar costs, the question remains whether work in the sex industry is unique. In Barton's study of stripping in San Francisco, Hawaii, and Kentucky, she found that "50 percent of [her] sample described experiencing an aversive response—fatigue and nausea—to thinking about and preparing to go to work."[53] These feelings mounted over time, and the toll "involved them becoming increasingly cynical, jaded, and ill . . . both with the actual work and with the motivations of men."[54] These reactions suggest sizeable problems for other groups of strippers.

Is it possible that the intersection of emotional, physical, and erotic labor has a greater toll on one's sense of self—asking a person to trade for cash too much of what we conventionally view as private in our lives? Not necessarily. There is nothing inherent about either the emotional, physical, or erotic content or even the buying and selling of sex that renders sex work problematic a priori.[55] In fact, a cynical view is that the sex work industry is just a sign of things to come for other workers, as our culture and our increasingly global economy leads us toward more service work and a greater commodification of self. That said, sexual labor cannot be understood apart from its context, which can vary considerably.[56] Evidence from The Lion's Den suggests that broader gender inequalities can make the organization of stripping work particularly difficult. What makes The Lion's Den (as well as other facets of the sex industry) unusual is that it produces contradictory outcomes or gender paradoxes, like stripping's high pay and low prestige.

5

Dollar Dances and Stage Dances

Strippers and Economic Exploitation

In the spring of 2002, Steve hired traveling strippers through a small company called Vixens to fill empty shifts. Evangelina explained, "I think especially because this club hasn't been doing that well, so they got [the traveling] girls in from [a nearby state], and a lot of the [house] girls got mad." Fiona's frustration, as a traveling stripper, was palpable:

> I don't pay much attention to the club. I'm not there working for the club. I'm working for myself. As far as I'm concerned, the club is privileged to have me here working for them or here entertaining—what their house girls should be out there doing and taking care of, we're here doing. We get trained to do this stuff, and then they get tossed out there in their Payless shoes with their Salvation Army clothes [*laughs*], and they're expected to be an exotic dancer or a stripper, whatever. The expectations in this place—like the club expects you come here and be professional about it when you've got the house girls standing behind us going, "Those girls are skanky." How can we come here and do our jobs and be professional about it when we're competing? When we're getting dirty looks? You know, the atmosphere, the negative energy that just gets pushed at us, especially from being out of state. It's a little overwhelming at times.

Interactions between The Lion's Den's house girls and the traveling strippers were tense, especially in the beginning. House girls saw the traveling dancers as competitors for limited resources and did what they could to discredit them.

The experiences of traveling strippers were different from those of local house performers in numerous ways. Vixens handled everything related to the traveling strippers' performances. The company trained women in striptease, booked their shows, and provided transportation to clubs within two hundred miles of their headquarters. Since The Lion's Den was four hours from the strippers' homes, Vixens provided lodging at a nearby motel. As a consequence of traveling, Faith saw herself as an independent worker who was "not there working for the club" but "working for herself." Nevertheless, as I explore later in this chapter, a stripper's status as either self-employed (an independent contractor) or an employee is in flux. There is little agreement within and among the courts, clubs, and workers as to strippers' status, as fierce industry and legal debates have illustrated.[1] The Vixens strippers provide yet another form of stripping organized by a third party. For these strippers, work was overseen and organized not just by The Lion's Den but also by their corporation, Vixens. Once within The Lion's Den, the relationship between economic and organizational authority had contradictory outcomes for Vixens and local strippers who were simultaneously empowered and disempowered.

In part, what compelled Faith and others to travel with Vixens, rather than become a house girl at a local club, was the promotion of a supportive and "less-aggressive" working environment (at least among the travelers). Faith continued:

> In this kind of business, everybody's out for their own. It's a cutthroat business. You can't really have a lot of friends because you can't give in to one dancer because that's money out of your pocket. . . . It's a cutthroat business. No matter how you try to be nice and polite, but it is. Our company that we work for, it's not a cutthroat business because we all work together. But you don't find a lot of companies that. . . . Honestly, what our company represents are—it backs us up and finds us jobs.

Vixens promoted solidarity that stemmed from strippers' training and traveling together. Though traveling certainly made Vixen's dancers' experiences different, nowhere was the distinction between traveling strippers and house girls more evident than in their economic realities. Faith detailed her expenses to Vixens and The Lion's Den:

> We pay our boss $40 a night, and then we pay the deejay $10–$20. From 4:00 to 7:00 pm we pay $5 to the deejay, and then 7:00 to 2:00 you pay $10 to another deejay. So, on Saturday night, [I paid] $55. You make 100 bucks on a lousy night. For instance, yesterday, it was dead in here, and you tell me if it's worth it! I got one VIP, because there wasn't a lot of guys in here,

and I made $100; 50 of that dollars [was paid out to others]. I made about 30 bucks! I took home about 30 bucks last night. You tell me if that was worth dancing! That was eight hours last night. Now if I didn't work for this company, I don't know what they take out [speculating about house girls' tip outs in The Lion's Den], probably $25. Easy, I'd have gone home with a lot more money.

In a business where the risks of emotional and physical abuse are real, the traveling strippers were willing to sacrifice earnings for solidarity, management, oversight, and protection. When they traveled to clubs, Vixens' owner would stay and monitor their work. Ostensibly, this was to protect his "product," but it also gave strippers the impression that they had extra security. Despite Vixens' owner's watchful eyes, Faith reported being pinned against the VIP Room wall by a patron in The Lion's Den. Even with some social and economic differences between them, both travelers and house girls had the common experience of work in a hazardous space.

Gendered Paradoxes and Organizational Jeopardy

Stripping is a job with contradictions that are part of a larger gender puzzle. The gendered meanings and outcomes produced through and by stripping contradict societal expectations. For example, normatively speaking, we expect workers with more control over their incomes also to have broader organizational power within their workplaces; typically, higher earnings are compensation for greater authority. A case in point involves mid-level and upper-level corporate managers. When compared with general staff, management positions are associated with increased authority and earnings, since managers make decisions and oversee other workers. For independent entrepreneurs or artisans, institutional power hinges on the deals they broker in setting rental fees for space, material provisions, wages, benefits, and scheduling. For example, in some mom-and-pop and high-end hair salons, stylists set their own schedules, fees, techniques, and equipment. In others (think Best Cuts), the salon sets schedules, fees, techniques, and equipment. These relationships did not hold true for strippers in The Lion's Den, who, despite greater earnings, did not hold significant influence over the club or its workers.

Strippers in The Lion's Den lacked both authority and adequate protection, illustrated by management and workers' stereotyping and put-downs and by patrons' verbal and physical aggression. These risks were a product of the gendered arrangements in the club, fostered by industry-wide culturally based norms handed down by the club's owner-manager, reproduced by coworkers, acted out by patrons, and internalized by strippers. Taken together, these risks formed a patchwork of organizational hazards for women. At each level, from the practices of everyday actors to the organizational rules of those at the top, The Lion's Den demonstrated antagonism toward strippers. The dynamics of the entire context enabled patrons' and coworkers' aggression toward strippers. Club turnover did little to promote significant challenges to these circumstances.

Despite strippers' clear organizational disempowerment in The Lion's Den, the relationship between economic and organizational authority was paradoxical because it contained contradictory outcomes like simultaneous empowerment and disempowerment. Specifically, economic arrangements in The Lion's Den produced two sets of practices. Under one set of practices, the club did not economically exploit strippers. The club's economic organization enabled women to retain partial control over their pay; they received money directly from patrons and retained or distributed the profits. Therefore, in a strange twist of fortune, given a lack of organizational authority, self-employed or independent strippers were the only club workers who maintained control over their earnings. Employees, by contrast, relied on club-paid wages or a combination of wages and tips from other workers. At the same time, under the other set of practices, the club exploited strippers not just as women but also as workers. The Lion's Den was a capitalist club. The club's exploitation of strippers most clearly resulted from stage dancing, a dubious but necessary facet of their work, for which the club seized the profits. However, self-employment was also a two-edged sword since it pitted strippers against each other in competition and excluded them from the gains of regular employment—namely, a steady income and benefits.

Looked at this way, the cumulative effects of organizational dynamics made it more than likely that women would experience oppressive working conditions—as the strippers so vividly described. Structurally, these risks were part of their jobs in The Lion's Den, established a priori. Nevertheless, strippers struggled against overwhelming odds to transform, resist, and cope with their work. They also retained some economic advantages over other workers, especially in terms of their control over their earnings. Collectively, despite some benefits to their work, these cumulative realities paint a troubling picture of stripping.

Performances, Power, and Profit

When patrons enter a club, they are purchasing a variety of products. They pay for the ability to sit in the club, to view nude performances and television, to listen to music, and to consume drinks. They make payment for these products and services in various forms—tipping, door fees, and elevated drink prices. What The Lion's Den collected directly through door and drink fees was its own property. The workers assigned to these tasks—collecting door fees, serving drinks, and performing dances—provided the means by which the club was able to charge entrance and high drink prices. In short, this is the process that generated revenue for the club. As is standard in capitalism, the surplus or profit produced through the collective efforts of club workers passed directly into the hands of the owner. Strippers neither appropriated nor distributed the profit collected by the club. The owner did.

Strippers' earnings came from stage, private, and table dances. All performances involved physical and emotional labor. Strippers' physical labor included crouching their bodies low to the stage to show and fondle their breasts, slapping and swaying their butts, and displaying their genitals for patrons. In addition to physical labor, strippers also provided conversation, companionship, support, and erotic storytelling. Though similar in content, stage and private dances had very different economic consequences.

For stage dances, each patron typically gave the stripper $1, hence the term "dollar dance" used to describe these performances. As Frank explained, "Twenty-five years ago they put a dollar up on the stage, and the inflation has gone up and it's still a dollar at the stage." Each dancer determined the length of time for a $1 stage performance, though they typically lasted thirty seconds to one minute. Patrons indicated their desire for a longer performance by placing multiple dollars on the stage. However, the club regulated this by requiring strippers to remain onstage for a particular length of time that increased on nights with fewer performers.

By contrast, VIP (or private dance) performances had a more structured time frame; they lasted typically the length of one song and cost $20. Roxanne explained her understanding of stage and private dance performances: "All you really have to do [onstage] is go, 'Here [are] my boobs, here's my ass, here's my pussy, here you go, see you, bye.' You don't have to carry a tune in a bucket." Private dances involved similar components: "[It's the] same thing [for VIP performances]. I don't understand VIP dances because you're getting exactly what you get out there for $19 more." But some distinctions did exist. Patrons did get more time in private dances, as Roxanne explained: "They get a song, [but] there's really no more intimacy than any-thing else. You get to talk to them a little more, but it's no more than if you talk to them at a table." However, the perception held by both strippers and patrons was that some strippers provided more physical contact during pri-vate dances. Roxanne continued: "Some girls give them more in there. Not being talented [at] dancing . . . they give them contact more and boobs in their face . . . and letting them do stuff more. [However], not everybody or anybody with any morals does." It was this perception of greater intimacy, proximity, and the possibility for touch that allowed private dances to main-tain their allure, despite overwhelming similarities between onstage and off-stage performances.

The three types of dances strippers performed—stage, VIP, and table dances—had unique characteristics, with profits flowing into different hands. Unlike the elective private dances, mandatory stage dances were a necessary condition of the work. The club required strippers to perform onstage for rotations lasting ten to thirty minutes of every hour or so, times that varied, depending on the number of dancers and patrons present. This way of regu-lating the labor process ensured that the club had a constant flow of onstage action and profit. The first type of private dance performance, the VIP, took place in a separate room of the club that was walled off by large glass win-dows (see club diagram). The performances were named for this space: the VIP Room. A separate sound system and four semiprivate booths created a more intimate atmosphere away from the goings-on in the larger main room of the club. At $20 a song, VIP dances were the strippers' most profitable performance. Though patrons could negotiate longer performances, they typically lasted for the duration of one song. The club also introduced a new product: table dances. Before introducing table dances, VIP dances were the only private performances available. Table dances provided an intermediate performance between stage and VIP dances. Costing only $10 a song, table dances were less expensive. Carried out on tables in the center of the club, they offered more privacy than stage performances but less than VIPs. None-theless, in content, table dances reproduced the same offering: a one-on-one (though at times they were performed for more than one patron) nude per-formance. The major differences between private VIP, table, and stage per-formances were that private and table dances were voluntary and generated the bulk of strippers' earnings.

Given the low rate of pay associated with stage dances, strippers some-times tried to get around the rules mandating these performances by arriv-ing late to the stage or skipping stage shifts altogether. In response, Steve devised a strategy to keep strippers performing their scheduled stage shifts: prohibiting VIP Room access if a dancer failed to appear onstage. The club articulated this rule on a dressing-room flier addressed to dancers:

> No one, and I repeat no one, is allowed to come in and just do private dances. If you skip your stage sets to do private dances, then your VIP privileges will be taken away. We understand that if this happens you probably will walk out and the club will suffer, but at least you will suffer also.

The club clearly understood the space was contested, where strippers pursued self-employment and its rewards; the owners of the club wanted their cut.

As the flier implies, stage dancing served an important purpose for the club. The club's ability to charge a premium for entry and drink prices rested on the presence of nude dancers whom patrons may or may not choose to tip. Roxanne described the way the club made its money and her frustration with the impact it had on strippers:

> It really is an exchange. . . . It's four quarters, but I'm listening to your problems, I'm counseling you on your girlfriend, I'm getting naked for you for a dollar. . . . The markup [for alcohol]—you don't even pay that much for gold or jewelry. I could go buy a diamond ring and go and hock the diamond ring, and I couldn't even make close to what I got. Here they're paying pennies and making dollars, and it's all because of us [strippers] being here. Does it irk you? [she asks rhetorically] Immensely! When we complain that we're not making any money, and they say, "Oh it's your own fault." No, it's not our own fault! If The Lion's Den weren't charging inflated drink prices, people might come in here and spend money [on dancers]!

Roxanne's comparison of The Lion's Den's to the jewelry industry—which is known for charging a 100 percent markup—is actually an underestimate. The club's markup was often considerably higher. For example, the club charged $11 for a 40¢ pitcher of beer that would have cost far less elsewhere. The premium price was no doubt dependent on the presence of nude dancers. Indeed, without the nude stage performances, the club would only have been an overpriced bar.

Another strategy employed by strip clubs to increase revenues was to institute shift fees. Shift fees are monetary charges to strippers for each shift's work. Amounts range widely, from $20 a shift in smaller towns and rundown clubs to hundreds of dollars in larger cities and in more elite contexts. Though strippers' employment status is contested terrain, most clubs interpret the monies as payment for the opportunity to be a self-employed worker or an independent contractor.[2] Indeed, the fees differentiate strippers from employees and enable clubs to avoid associated employment benefits and obligations. The Lion's Den always threatened but never set up shift fees. Instead, Steve opted for a complicated and ever-changing set of fines for tardiness and missed shifts. Traveling dancers, in contrast to the house girls, paid shift fees of a sort to their company in exchange for booking them with The Lion's Den and providing striptease training, transportation, and lodging. Shift fees, stage dancing, and fines contribute toward an economically hostile environment for strippers. But does this constitute economic exploitation? Before exploring the economic implications of this term, we need to explore how exploitation, as a concept, has been used in previous sex work research.

Exploitation: Same Term, Different Meanings

The literature on sex work employs multiple meanings of exploitation, usually focusing on inequalities of gender, sexuality, and power. Many theorists, the most prominent being radical feminist and legal scholar Catharine MacKinnon, argue that forms of work in the sex industry are forms of gender exploitation—the exploitation of women's bodies and sexuality as women. This is a theoretical framework necessary to understand the exploitation of sex workers. MacKinnon's writing has raised awareness about how women fall prey to abuse and violence from industry norms, police, courts, pimps, and johns. Her work draws heavily on both Marxist and feminist theory. Perhaps it is because MacKinnon dichotomizes Marxism and feminism, arguing that each is a "total theory," that she cannot see the ways that class and gender intersect. Indeed, MacKinnon argues that women cannot escape the logic of patriarchy. In her view, "subjection itself, with self-determination ecstatically relinquished, is the content of women's sexual desire and desirability."[3] Even when MacKinnon directly addresses the questions of work and exploitation in the Marxist sense, she transforms these questions into essential questions of power. Drawing a loose analogy between Marxism and feminism, she writes:

In my view, sexuality is to feminism what work is to Marxism. . . . Both Marxism and feminism are theories of power and of its unequal distribution. They each provide an account of how a systematically unequal social arrangement . . . is internally coherent and internally rational and pervasive yet unjust.[4]

Because MacKinnon derives her theory and her object of study from a structural understanding of patriarchal power as a pervasive force running through all social institutions, she remains unable to understand sex work and stripping in any other terms: namely, the autonomy or exploitation of sex workers as *workers*. MacKinnon sees labor primarily as a question of essential power, such as men's power over women through authority arrangements. Separating these understandings of power makes it possible to see both exploitative and nonexploitative conditions, as well as the agency of individual workers to challenge conditions they find unjust.

The second prominent notion of exploitation draws on the identities of strippers themselves. Here stripping is understood as a job that attracts women locked in a cycle of emotional, physical, and sexual abuse.[5] This argument rests on an assumption that strip clubs are "no place for any 'self-respecting lady' to work."[6] Strippers reproduce their own gender exploitation as a manifestation of childhoods dominated by neglect, mistreatment, and abuse.[7] As Charles McCaghy and James Skipper describe it, patrons are positioned as exploiters: "The occupational image [of the stripper] served to attract an assortment of persons bent on exploitation: those males who would treat the stripper strictly as a sexual object, those seeking to satisfy unusual sexual proclivities, and those who would become financially dependent on the stripper."[8]

Cycle-of-abuse arguments are problematic for a number of reasons. First, such positions are built on the a priori belief that sex work is a form of coerced labor rather than a legitimate employment option. Certain forms of sex work (maintained by sex trafficking and sexual slavery) are more overt forms of coerced labor. However, this does not preclude the analysis of other forms of sex work in specific contexts where the issues of exploitation may be more complex, nuanced, or almost absent. Second, these arguments rest on an assumption that stripping is inherently deviant and thus negate any reason to investigate the ways in which meanings of stripping and deviance change over time.[9] Third, these analyses are subject to the same critiques as MacKinnon's power analysis; they remain unable to examine and analyze the experiences and autonomy of individual actors. While strange bedfellows, the radical feminists and the advocates of cycle-of-abuse perspectives have in common a definition of exploitation based on men's abusive power over women. In contrast to this approach, recent work by Jennifer Wesley looks at how women struggle to "reclaim power" after sexual abuse, through stripping.[10]

A third understanding of exploitation turns the previous two arguments on their heads. Rather than arguing that strippers are exploited, this libertarian position asserts that strippers, by virtue of payment for what other women do for free, become the exploiters. As Marilyn Salutin explains, "[Strippers] claim that if they didn't exploit the public's need for a sex outlet, that is making a profit on it, men would be making a profit on them— that is, they, as women, would be taken advantage of by men. They would be touched, screwed and not paid."[11] This sentiment is echoed by Camille Paglia, who claims that "the feminist line is strippers and topless dancers are degraded, subordinated, and enslaved; they are victims, turned into objects by the display of their anatomy. But women are far from being victims— women *rule*; they are in total control."[12] These reverse-exploitation positions, asserting strippers' exploitation of others, are problematic because they overstate strippers' power and minimize their vulnerabilities.

Radical feminist, cycle-of-abuse, and libertarian perspectives each offer disparate arguments about strippers' work experiences and identities. Radical feminism confronts the oppressive conditions under which sex workers toil, both within the sex industry and in the broader culture. Deviance perspectives highlight the intense stigma associated with stripping work. Cycle-of-abuse arguments highlight the often-cited abuse that sex workers may experience before or during their work in the industry. Reverse-exploitation arguments assert that sex workers are active agents, not simply passive victims. Each of these perspectives provides useful insights into stripping. At the same time, these explanations present totalizing visions of stripping that rest on assumptions about who is doing the job without regard to the conditions under which the work is performed. As this ethnography of The Lion's Den illustrates, these conditions depend on context. Further, in order to examine the gendered economic organization of labor within various strip clubs, we need to use a framework that examines exploitation in terms of class relationships as they intersect with gendered work.

Stripping and Economic Exploitation

When we view stripping through an economic or class lens, several realities emerge. Strippers labor beyond what they need to live on—to pay bills, secure housing, and purchase food. The work that strippers do brings in more than the strippers earn in tips and wages. In economic terms, their "surplus labor" is treated as profit rather than as compensation for their work.[13] This profit is distributed to the owner (as profit) or to other employees (as wages) rather than to the strippers. By using an economic framework, we centralize the work performed in the club, such as production (stage and private dances), as well as the appropriation and distribution of profits from surplus labor. Although stripping is often described as lucrative, strippers themselves are not always the primary beneficiaries of their own work. In The Lion's Den, the club's owner-manager seized or appropriated and distributed the profits produced through strippers' stage performances. In strict Marxist terms, the club's owner economically exploited the strippers.

For their stage performances, strippers were paid far less than the value of their labor. As Fiona explained:

> In a place like this, a dollar for somebody to look at my pussy—that's not enough. A dollar to see my tits—that's not enough. You know, you go out in public, and you ask any normal chick, "Would you take a dollar and show somebody your pussy?" Hell no! You know, but in a place like this you're expected to be okay with it. Whether or not you like it, it's just one of those things you've got to deal with.

In contrast, the club reaped most of the proceeds of the dollar dance through its door fees—$7 for those ages twenty-one and over and $5 for those ages eighteen to twenty—a one-drink minimum for patrons legal to drink, and premium drink prices. In other words, the price paid for a seat and a drink in the club included a payment for the dollar dance, the drink, and the seat. Tamara vented her frustrations with the club's payment setup:

> If it weren't for the dancers, this club would make no money. You couldn't charge 3 bucks for a soda, $5 to get in the door—for what, for television? Big deal, you can go to a sports bar and get that. But they tend to believe that the girls can't live without the club. The girls can go anywhere—there are clubs everywhere. This place does not respect their girls. It does not treat them well, and it's amazing that they even have girls with some of the shit that they do. . . . It's all about the money.

Later in the interview, Tamara explained further:

> The Lion's Den caters to a clientele that is not going to bring in a lot of money because they don't care. [The club will] allow people to sit in the back and not tip as long as they're making their money off the alcohol, and that bothers me. Because the alcohol is what the club cares about. They

don't care about the dancers; they don't care how much money the dancers make onstage or what happens, as long as they're selling their alcohol. So it's kind of hard for us when there's a lot of guys that are cheap that come in, and they do cater to that. It's not like a gentleman's club—it's a frat-boy-guy/truck-driver club.

The club did not share Tamara's unhappiness about strippers' "free rider" problem—patrons who paid for entry into the club and watched but did not pay for strippers' performances—for a variety of reasons. Since the club secured mandatory payments up front, it didn't need to worry about strippers' earnings, which could be explained away by idiosyncratic causes: for example, perhaps she was not as talented as the other dancers or did not work as hard. Also, since the club viewed the strippers as self-employed independent contractors rather than employees, it saw stage dancing as a way for strippers to "advertise their product" and entice patrons into buying VIP and table dances.

Under this setup, the strip club's owner-manager appropriated the profit flowing from the dollar dance, which was produced collectively by the strippers. Since Steve wore multiple hats and simultaneously acted as an owner and a manager, he was one person playing two roles. Under different circumstances, one person might not have control over both tasks. The profit generated by strippers went toward paying rent for access to the land and building that the club occupied; covering the costs of marketing advertisements and website maintenance; providing wages for security to bouncers; replacing worn out seats, carpet, and lights; and paying taxes for the enforcement of rules and laws governing the business. In this capitalist arrangement, the owner exploited the strippers and decided what to do with the fruits of their labor. The strippers had little influence over his decisions because they never received the profit and were seen as expendable.

Women's Profits and Payouts

Unlike with stage dances, patrons directly paid strippers for their private VIP and table dance performances. Strippers were the first recipients of the money generated by their own labor. These independent strippers, in effect, rented club space funded by the production and sale of their wares. Similar to hair stylists in salons, this rent assured them access to club facilities. Though Steve did not institute shift fees, strippers still made payments in the form of reduced pay for required stage dances. Stage-dancing revenues, generated through high-cost entrance and drinks, went directly to the club. In private performances, strippers received and distributed their surplus themselves. They were, as a result, not exploited. The presence of both exploitative and nonexploitative class relationships demonstrates how diverse arrangements may overlap in the same society and in the same activity. As Gabriel Fried and Richard Wolff argue, "all capitalist societies so far have contained non-capitalist" processes.[14] In the case of Fried and Wolff's research on corporate and independent trucking, they find that, although both parties have histori-cally clashed and each has experienced ups and downs, these forms of truck-ing nevertheless persist together. In their trucking industry example, neither the capitalist nor the independent trucker is predestined to win the struggle and absorb the other. Likewise, both stage and private dancing coexist in The Lion's Den, albeit with tensions.

Despite the lack of exploitation in private performances, strippers did not distribute their profits in ways of their own choosing. Fried and Wolff explain that there are "pressures upon [truck drivers] from all who can exer-cise power over the distribution" of the profit.[15] For truckers, these pressures include the necessity of paying "taxes and fees to various governmental agencies, to make interest payments to creditors, to pay brokers for arrang-ing shipments, and to buy additional or new equipment for their trucks to enhance their transport's salability."[16] Similar to the truckers in Fried and Wolff's study, patrons' tips not only provided strippers' nightly earnings but also had to cover payments the club required them to make to other club workers—namely, the deejay whom they each "tipped out" a minimum of $10 at the close of their shift. Since the deejays' incomes were linked to strip-pers' incomes, deejays did their best to secure more than the minimum tip out. Deejays used informal pressures to secure better tips from strippers, like openly disparaging low-tipping strippers and rewarding good tippers with leniency and music they enjoyed. While the club's stated reasoning for having strippers tip out the deejay was that the deejay provided performance music for strippers, the real purpose of this arrangement was to secure further rev-enue for the club by transferring funds among workers, rather than requiring the club to pay higher wages. Since the club management considered stage dancing the chance for strippers to secure private dances to show off their wares, it expected the strippers to appreciate and embrace this opportunity as team players.

Strippers were not the only workers in the club whose pay came mainly in the form of cash tips. Though cocktail waitresses were in a distinctly dif-ferent position, as employees within the club, they shared some economic circumstances with strippers. First, despite being paid a small wage of $3.50 per hour, waitresses were largely paid through cash tips. Second, waitresses were compelled by the organization of work within the club to share tip income with other club workers to secure their working conditions. In addition to the economic components of this arrangement, the tipping setup in the club was also gendered—the club required strippers and cocktail waitresses to share a portion of their tips with male workers (deejays and bartenders, respectively). Male workers, by contrast, were not employed in positions that required sharing their earnings with other workers through tip outs.

In contrast to the other workers, strippers earned all of their money through cash tips, and the amount varied widely from night to night. The club clearly made considerable profit off the tipping setup, since it did not contribute more than a minimal payment to cocktail waitresses and $4.50 per hour to deejays. Furthermore, the tipping system created particular dependencies between bartenders and cocktail waitresses and between deejays and dancers. It also served to diminish the economic power that strippers and cocktail waitresses were perceived to have, since other workers made claims on their tips.

Following the Money: The Flow of Profits in The Lion's Den

One way to illustrate the economics of The Lion's Den is to follow the flow of money through the club. As a capitalist enterprise, The Lion's Den had two primary recipients of profit—the club and the strippers. Both received money from patrons directly without any intermediaries. Here I trace payments as they passed from patrons' pockets into the hands of club representatives and strippers. The path of profits has much to tell us about how The Lion's Den was organized economically, as well as who gained and who lost.

The Club's Revenue

The club's revenue came from inflated door fees and drink prices, both of which were charged because strippers performed stage dances with no wages and at reduced pay when compared with private dances. On an average weeknight, the club had approximately fifty patrons: ten who were ages eighteen to twenty, and forty who were over age twenty-one. With their door fees of $7 and $5, respectively, the club brought in $270 at the end of the day. On weekends, this number doubled to $540. Since each of the patrons over twenty-one years of age was required to purchase one drink and typically ordered at least two more rounds, the total number of drinks for each patron was around three. Given that the average drink price was $4.50 (with a range of $3.00–$5.75), the weeknight beverages purchased by patrons totaled approximately $540. On weekends, this number doubled to $1,080. Strippers' drinks were another source of revenue for the club. Since they ordered about four drinks a night, on weeknights six strippers consumed $108 worth of alcohol. On weekends, this number doubled to $216. Bringing together all of these sources, the total weekly revenue was about $9,504.

Once the club received this revenue, it had a number of expenses to cover. The club paid rent, utilities, taxes, insurance, and donations to local police, as well as wages to management and employees; the club also covered costs for advertising, equipment, repairs, bar supplies, and concessions. The remainder of its revenue was its profit. Some expenses must be covered, like those required to maintain the club's lease, secure its business, and provide for its customers. For instance, donations to local police were seen as important since they helped secure police support and benevolence. That said, the club did not equally value all of these expenses. For example, advertising was kept to a minimum, and the club's website was sparse and not often updated. The club also featured few special events. Strip clubs are well known for "amateur nights," for example, but The Lion's Den only sponsored two during my fourteen months there.

To further demonstrate the lack of value directed toward workers, let us look more closely at two of these expenses—repairs and employee pay. For many years, the club retained its splintered stage flooring and wobbly dance poles, as well as the sticky carpet and ripped chairs in the club's main room. The peeling paint and ripped chairs in the strippers' dressing rooms remained as well. Given The Lion's Den's rundown condition, it is clear that the owner-manager had not been allocating revenue toward repairs to the club. The club also paid little to its employees. The highest paid worker, the bartender, received $8.50 an hour, and the lowest, the cocktail waitress, collected $3.50 an hour. Since the club often operated with a staff of four (doorman, deejay, bartender, and cocktail waitress), the club's financial responsibilities to its workers was minimal. To pay a staff of four over the course of one weekday seven-hour shift cost about $147. Weekends, with an added bartender and two more cocktail waitresses, cost $183.50. Total weekly employee pay was approximately $1,959.50, plus $1,042 toward Steve's annual salary of $50,000. Even after paying workers and himself, Steve had approximately $6,502.50 to allocate toward other expenses or keep as profit.

The Strippers' Revenue

Strippers' incomes came from mandatory stage and private performances. Stage performances paid $1 each, while private dances paid between $10 and $20. Stage performance rotations lasted about fifteen minutes per hour, leaving forty-five minutes for strippers to seek private dances. If we assume strippers made approximately $10 for every stage rotation and performed one or two private dances per hour, their average evening earnings were $210. Once we subtract alcoholic drinks ($18 for four) and the club's mandatory $10 tip to the deejay, they made $182 a night. This figure is close to the average last nightly earnings reported by the twenty-one strippers interviewed ($193).

With these profits, strippers must cover many other performance-related expenses. These included purchasing hair styling, tanning, manicures, pedicures, waxing or shaving materials, makeup, teeth whitener, costumes, shoes, baby wipes, perfume, and deodorant. Strippers also provided their own transportation and arranged childcare, if necessary. If we average the two amounts above (my estimate of $182 and the self-reported average of $193), their income is about $187.50. Conservatively estimating strippers' expenses at $5 for tanning (which was typically done on a weekly basis), $10 for gas, $5 toward toiletries, $5 to manicures, hair styling, waxing, and other beauty-industry products purchased monthly or biweekly, and $10 toward new costumes and shoes, expenses tally up to $35 a week, not including childcare costs. After subtracting this estimate of basic employment-related expenses, strippers in The Lion's Den may have made $152.50 a night, or approximately $22 an hour. While these wages are far better than minimum wage, they are only an average. Earnings were hardly reliable; as is the case for workers whose wages are tip based, they may have varied considerably from shift to shift. Moreover, childcare expenses, which were incurred by more than one-quarter (28%) of the strippers interviewed, may be sizeable. Travelers, of course, had their $40 Vixens fee to pay as well.

Comparing the Money Flows

Due to cost cuts in maintenance and labor, the club preserved some of its revenue to allocate toward other expenses and profit. For the most part, its costs for maintenance were zero. The cost of labor over one week was about 14 percent of its revenue. The club was able to maintain low earnings by having employees make claims to other workers' tips. Cocktail waitresses' $20-per-shift tips contributed nearly 20 percent of a bartender's earnings. For deejays, the contributions were even higher. Each stripper's tip out of $10 constituted two-thirds of a deejay's earnings on a weeknight. On weekends, when there were twice as many strippers present, strippers' tips increased to nearly 80 percent of a deejay's pay. Deejays also made every effort to increase strippers' tips beyond the minimum tip out. Strippers similarly paid 13 percent of their average nightly earnings toward drinks and tip out to the bartender, albeit from a smaller financial pie. If cocktail waitresses were involved in the transaction, they were tipped, too. While strippers could cut back on their drinks, many cited alcohol as necessary to perform their job.

Besides tipping out, the economic realities of exploitation and nonexploitation created further difficulties for strippers. The tension between the strippers' types of work—stage and private performances—is readily apparent in strippers' reports denouncing the "dollar dance." Gross differences in pay, coupled with the absorption of their time, made stage performances a liability. The missed earnings from private dances became like a form of rent all strippers had to pay in order to use club space and provide private dances. If the club had decided to add shift fees, the strippers would have, in effect, been charged twice. The Lion's Den also created innovative ways of increasing revenue through a system of fines to strippers for arriving late or missing shifts, further siphoning off their incomes.

Despite being economically nonexploitative, private dancing was not without its problems. Since these performances contributed two-thirds of strippers' earnings on a given night, they could literally make or break a stripper. Not surprisingly, the hypercompetitive nature of seeking and securing private dances pitted dancers against each other in an intense struggle to attract patrons. The attempts of house dancers to scrutinize and discredit new dancers stemmed from this competition. Layla, a traveling stripper, described the house girls' reactions to the Vixens dancers:

The house girls don't like us at all. They can't stand us. They think we're out to steal their business, but it's not even like that. We're just out here to make our own money. We're not trying to take from them. It's all for yourself. If you're not worried about your best friend or anybody else, you're worried about yourself and how much money you're going to make.

Since new dancers, as fresh faces, were positioned to do well during their first few shifts, seasoned dancers recognized the financial risks new workers posed and did their best to challenge them, as the house girls' contempt for the travelers illustrates.

By following the flow of money through the club, one can see the consequences of particular financial arrangements. The bottom line for the owner-manager was to cut back on most costs that might favor workers, like improvements to the physical space or increases in earnings. Strippers experienced sizeable burdens through missed earnings resulting from stage dancing, tip outs to deejays, the purchase of alcohol, and the club's establishment of fines. Moreover, this system pitted workers against each other in multiple ways. Strippers competed with each other for earnings from private dances. Simultaneously, cocktail waitresses and strippers were caught in financial binds because they were also required to tip out a variety of male coworkers. Since male coworkers' wages did not change, the only way they could increase earnings was by leveraging a greater proportion of women's tips and seeking tips directly from patrons. All of these factors came together to form an intensely competitive and economically hostile work environment, with employees and strippers counting and protecting their turf as well as their dollars.

Shift Fees: Supplementing Economic Exploitation

The primary difference between the travelers and the house girls was that traveling dancers were required to provide a portion of their earnings ($40 from each shift) to Vixens, the agency representing them. For six to eight dancers working a two-shift weekend, this represented a total of $480 to $640, or between $720 and $960 for a three-shift weekend. These payments were supposed to cover the cost of the dancers' four-hour commute in a cramped limousine that carried all six to eight women. It also covered the one to two cheap motel rooms the dancers shared. Even when factoring in gas and lodging, the agency was making considerable profit.

Although The Lion's Den did not institute shift fees, it used their absence as a point of leverage. *The Employee/Entertainer Handbook* clearly states this: "Do you realize that all the other clubs that are worth a shit make you PAY to work there?" (emphasis in original).[17] Despite this strong claim, The Lion's Den still managed to seize some of the strippers' earnings without shift fees by charging $10 late fees—fees that were not charged to other tardy club workers. It also incorporated a system of fines for missed shifts. A flier hung in the strippers' dressing rooms announced the fines for missed shifts: strippers "get only five cancellations per year, every one after that will cost you $30." Ostensibly, these fines were to act as a deterrent, but they served another purpose. Roxanne responded:

It's insane. . . . We get fined, and the club is making more money off of us because if you call in sick or if you miss a shift, . . . they're charging $30 for a missed shift. The club gets another 30 bucks for [you] missing your shift, and you don't get to work your next shift until you pay the fee. You get here and you owe money!

In an industry known for paying women more than the average wage in similar jobs, owners and managers were able to leverage this fact to chip away at the strippers' incomes.

The Costs of Being Your Own Boss

In contrast to other club workers, strippers are independent contractors and not eligible for wages, unemployment insurance, or workers' compensation. To ensure this, the club's owner-manager formed a separate company, RealGirls, to act as an agency that placed dancers with The Lion's Den, so strippers were legally understood as self-employed independent contractors rather than direct employees of the club. Whereas strippers working ten to twenty years ago reported being paid by clubs to work—between $20 and $50 per shift—now the clubs seek to seize strippers' earnings. Promoting independent-contractor status for strippers has enabled clubs across the country to begin charging shift fees to strippers. In effect, owners are renting the club space to strippers for their work, with fees ranging anywhere from $20 to $200 per shift.

The Lion's Den is not alone in the practice of classifying strippers as independent contractors. While labor laws vary, most states allow clubs to classify strippers differently from other club workers. However, three states have ruled otherwise: Alaska, California, and Oregon have had court cases challenging such distinctions. In California, the legislature decided against independent-contractor status after a protracted struggle by The Exotic Dancers' Alliance, a San Francisco Bay Area strippers' collective. Governor Gray Davis signed Assembly Bill 2509 into law in 2000, and as of 2001, when the law took effect, California strip clubs must consider all club workers to be employees. Similarly, in the federal cases *Reich v. Priba Corporation* (1995) in Texas and earlier in *Reich v. Circle C Investments* (1993) in Alaska, the courts ruled in favor of understanding strippers as employees.

Strippers, in particular, are kept outside of the club's organization not just by the gendered division of labor but also by the economic organization of the club that situates them as self-employed independent contractors. This organization is the dominant form used by the industry. As independent contractors, the legal understanding is that they work for commission and maintain control over their hours, working conditions, and services. In contrast, if they were employees, they would be paid at least minimum wage, like restaurant servers, and be subject to a greater umbrella of employment law. Under this scenario, their tips would supplement dependable earnings from the club. These contrasts are even more striking when one considers clubs that not only deny wages but charge shift fees. Despite the aforementioned legal challenges in Alaska, California, and Oregon, most clubs continue to classify strippers as independent contractors and deny them wages, benefits, and sick leave.

Gendered and Economic Organization

Rather than focusing primarily on gendered economic inequalities, campaigns against sex work have long adopted a personal-morality framework, such as those espoused in Victorian England at the time of the Contagious Diseases Act, when prostitutes were seen as fallen women who had lost their virtue to vice.[18] Today, some feminists have opposed sex work on moral grounds for the human rights violations seemingly inherent in the way it is organized.[19] Rather than determining outcomes a priori, it is important to look analytically at the labor produced in the clubs, especially given the tendency to impose value judgments on the sex work industry. As Marjolein van der Veen explains in her writing on prostitution, the recognition of economic or class exploitation allows us to understand sex work in terms of the "relations in which sex work is performed."[20] This framework "neither condemns nor valorizes prostitution per se, but begins to construct a new morality around the different exploitative and nonexploitative" dealings within the trade.[21]

The gendered and economic organization of The Lion's Den demonstrates how multifaceted the consequences of strip club work can be. The troubles strippers face are influenced by a myriad of factors, chief among them being the club's organization of work—in the case of The Lion's Den, a gendered division of labor that empowered male workers while disempowering female workers. Next, consider the club's lax policies regarding patrons, which were designed to ensure their return rather than their good behavior. In contrast, strippers were regularly mistrusted and often mistreated. Add to these concerns the club's economic policy of exploiting strippers by seizing their stage performance profits and denying them the benefits of employment. Exploitation brings a heavy financial cost for strippers. To be sure, the strippers at The Lion's Den had to produce private dances to gain enough income for themselves, let alone the other workers they were required to tip out. Alternatively, unlike many other workers, strippers have some control over profits. Using an economic framework, we can see the ways in which nonexploitative private and table dance performances provide some financial control and autonomy to strippers. However, as clubs increasingly require shift fees and introduce fines for rule infractions, they continue to chip away at the margins of strippers' earnings. It should come as no surprise, given these circumstances, that strippers face struggles with their work for which there are no easy solutions.

Repositioning sex work debates around economic issues, rather than emphasizing moral or political ones, as has often been the case, we can see new avenues of understanding and intervention. Consideration of empowerment and disempowerment has often been linked to questions of coercion and consent—issues not readily understood from afar. Grounding evaluations in sex workers' economic and organizational circumstances pushes analysis closer to local meanings and outcomes, the real lived experiences in the industry. Focusing on local meanings allows researchers to capture the messiness and contradictory character of work in settings like The Lion's Den. The everyday economic practices in The Lion's Den constitute a paradox of gender in terms of their outcome—simultaneous empowerment and disempowerment. Strip club work is ubiquitous, with opposing outcomes for women—often including higher pay and lower authority; on-the-job autonomy and strong oversight; and flexible schedules with little job security relative to other jobs.

Though the outcomes are counterintuitive, the process is not. Interpersonally and structurally, we can see how concrete practices (re)produce gendered outcomes. Political struggles over gender are rife with examples where empowerment and disempowerment go hand in hand. Take, for example, the explosion of women into the labor force since the 1970s and '80s.[22] Though women have made strides in various industries, their labor is still largely segregated;[23] their authority is still often blocked by glass ceilings that limit the scope of their influence[24] and glass escalators that more quickly promote men in female-dominated occupations.[25] In light of these examples, strip club work should not be ghettoized and set apart from other types of labor, since it has much in common with other gendered struggles inside the workplace. Further, strip club work may offer insights into future struggles workers may face in other settings, especially as our culture is increasingly based around service work and the commodification of carework and emotional labor.[26]

Gender in this context is a source of antagonism and play, a resource that is wielded and contested, experienced, embodied, and reproduced by strippers, patrons, and the entire cast of The Lion's Den. The stakes for everyone involved can be high. Preserving personal dignity and self-respect may be difficult on all ends. Male coworkers rely on female workers for their incomes. Patrons are paying for attention and performance from strippers. As a result, men are vulnerable to allegations of dependency and buying affection—opinions that are antithetical to the masculine ideals of independence and attractiveness. For women, however, the potential hazards go beyond issues of personal dignity and self-respect. The gendered organization in clubs like The Lion's Den contains so many potential hazards that their form constitutes organizational jeopardy—a context that is highly likely to be hazardous to women. That said, gender dynamics in a club like The Lion's Den do not constitute a zero-sum game. Examining the club's organizational form, we can see disruptions through economic processes—in particular, in women's economic autonomy. Paying attention to the organization and processes that empower and disempower female workers is vital to understanding how working conditions may be understood and improved in strip clubs and other settings.

Postscript

The Lion's Den, 2005–2006

Throughout my participant observation, Steve, the club's owner-manager, was increasingly frustrated with his work. In February of 2003, Steve sold The Lion's Den to Players, a rival area club. After more than a decade in the business, he called it quits and began to work in a totally different field. Many of the workers he employed also left. In an email dialogue with Steve in early 2003, I learned that only two of the people whom I had interviewed or worked with continued employment with Players. Under new ownership, the club transformed in several other ways. Though still called The Lion's Den, its ambiance, reputation, and working conditions were altered dramatically. Women's roles in the club expanded to include a short-term management position, a new waitressing job, and new stripper performances. Expanding opportunities brought more costs than gains, however, and, as a result, the club's gendered organization and gender paradoxes remain unchallenged.

Examining The Lion's Den as a gendered organization encourages questions about whether organizational change might alter men's and women's roles and experiences in the club. For example, it is important to consider whether placing power in the hands of women might mitigate men's verbal and physical abuse of strippers. This postscript provides an opportunity to investigate these issues. In 2006, four years after my participant observation, I revisited The Lion's Den by analyzing over thirteen hundred website postings about the club from Strip Club List (SCL).[1] SCL is a website that allows users to "chat" electronically by identifying themselves with pseudonyms and writing to each other online through the SCL interface. Using SCL's data, in this follow-up I examine the club's continuity, as well as changes in its gendered organization.

Steve's sale of The Lion's Den's to Players had seemingly incongruous outcomes for female workers, particularly strippers. On the one hand, Players' clubs are well known for promoting greater physical contact between strippers and patrons. Strippers in The Lion's Den preferred to set their own boundaries and often resisted physical contact with patrons. Such sexual agency is an important component of strippers' jobs; indeed, their livelihoods depend on it. Moreover, as Laurel Crown and Linda Roberts argue, "sexual agency—the ability to act according to one's will in a sexual realm—is a necessary component of sexual health."[2] Despite worker complaints under Steve's stewardship, The Lion's Den was generally considered by those in the industry to be a *better* place for women to work, primarily because club pressures to have physical contact with patrons were absent. As Steve rhetorically asked in the *Employee/Entertainer Handbook*, "Do you realize that [The Lion's Den] as opposed to ANY other club around will treat you like a human being, rather than a piece of meat?" (emphasis in original).[3]

In contrast, Players was infamous for treating its strippers as "pieces of meat," valuing them primarily because of their bodily offerings to men. Players actively encouraged a competitive environment known for pressuring women to engage in greater physical contact with patrons, including a space for lap dancing, a fully clothed and full-contact performance simulating seated intercourse. At the same time, unlike The Lion's Den, Players also encouraged women to take positions as bartenders and managers, jobs that entail greater oversight of other workers and decision-making for the club. On the surface, such a change has the potential to disrupt the consolidation of male power so firmly in place under Steve's leadership. However, greater authority alongside pressures for women to engage in more physical contact with patrons also seems incompatible. Why would greater authority for women yield *worse* working conditions? One might assume just the opposite: that with greater authority, women could advocate for and bring about more desirable working conditions. To unravel this relationship between authority and working conditions, we must examine the club's organizational structure and broader cultural constructions of gender.

Gendered Organizational Jeopardy and Gender Paradoxes

The Lion's Den under Steve's leadership placed women in jeopardy, structurally and through men's individual and group practices. Drawing on gendered organizational theory,[4] I examine the club's gendered processes, the use of gender and sexuality as organizational resources, and its gendered substructure. In addition to the club's gendered organization, The Lion's Den was constructed as a space in which all men could experience themselves as desirable, connected, and powerful. Under these challenging working conditions,

The Lion's Den produced contradictory outcomes for female workers. On the one hand, strippers struggled with the consequences of being disempowered and devalued in their work, often placed at risk of physical and emotional harm by patrons and coworkers. On the other hand, unlike club employees, strippers labored partially under economically independent conditions. Even considering club exploitation and variable earnings, strippers remained the highest-paid club workers. These factors produce what I have labeled "gendered organizational jeopardy" and "gender paradoxes," respectively. These themes emerged repeatedly during my ethnographic study of The Lion's Den.

Context is important in producing particular gendered outcomes.[5] In the case of The Lion's Den, the context produced oppressive working conditions for women. As well, social norms beyond the club's walls influenced the club's constructions of gender. This feminist sociological analysis suggests that the aggression and violence men exhibited toward women in the club is connected to the broader culture, not something that exists in isolation within the sex industry or within a particular strip club. The patterns of gendered stereotyping and aggression toward women bear striking similarity to analyses of rape culture and rape myths. Rape culture and rape myths, normative understandings about how and why violence toward women is tolerated and even encouraged, are critical to understanding how such violence is perpetuated.

In addition to broader social norms, the literature on rape culture emphasizes the importance context plays in reproducing men's violence against women. For example, Peggy Reeves Sanday's work on college campuses described the importance of context in producing rape-prone environments.[6] Similarly, looking at college fraternities, A. Ayres Boswell and Joan Spade explored high-risk settings,[7] and Stephen Humphrey and Arnold Kahn examined high-risk groups.[8] Drawing together the concepts of rape culture and rape myths with specific attention to context, here I examine why organizational change and women's empowerment may produce continued inequalities and paradoxes of gender.

Rape Culture and Myths

Feminists have responded to America's culture of violence by exploring the practices that support, reproduce, institutionalize, and excuse men's aggression toward women through media images, gender norms, and stereotypes.[9] Particularly in the sex work industry, images of female subservience and male violence against women are standard fare. In Chyng Sun and Miguel Picker's documentary film *The Price of Pleasure*, examining the extent of pornography's violent content, psychologist Ana Bridges and a group of colleagues describe their findings: "The research team examined 304 scenes from the most popular videos released in 2005. They found that 89.8% of the scenes included either verbal or physical aggression. 48% contained verbal aggression, mostly name-calling and insults, while 82.2% contained physical aggression. 94.4% of the aggressive acts were targeted at women."[10]

Taken together, the processes that normalize violence against women have been called "rape culture"[11] and "sexual terrorism."[12] Both terms emphasize the scope and breadth of men's violence toward women as a social problem. While the problem of rape in U.S. culture is widely recognized, there is some disagreement over the particular facts and figures. The prevalence of rape in the United States varies, depending on where the data are drawn: different sources include police and court records, shelter records, self-report surveys, and interview data. Still, most rapes go unreported.[13] As a result, many of the estimates at or above the much-cited 1 in 4 statistic probably underestimate the problem's scope. According to the U.S. Department of Justice:

The most recent and methodologically rigorous studies show that sexual assault still occurs at rates that approximate those first identified more than 20 years ago when Koss, Gidycz, and Wisiewski, 1987, reported that approximately 27.5% of college women reported experiences that met the legal criteria for rape.[14]

While forcible nonconsensual sex acts meet legal definitions of rape,[15] culturally rape is often falsely contested through normative practices of denial and victim/survivor blaming. As psychologist Lynn Phillips argues, "Examples of continued cultural tolerance of male aggression abound, along with a persistent refusal to take women's complaints seriously."[16] For instance, denial may come in the form of rape myths or scapegoating women, like the misperception that wives and sex workers are "un-rapeable."[17] Scapegoating also occurs through victim/survivor blaming, illogically targeting a woman for a man's assault against her. This was chillingly dramatized in *The Accused* (1988), a film that depicts the gang rape of Cheryl Ann Araujo and the subsequent trial of her attackers.[18] Araujo's trial became a touchstone case regarding the victim's status, engendering protests and activist movements regarding protocol at rape trials. When Araujo's real-life case went to trial, the defendants' attorney bombarded her with questions about her choices and clothing, a cross-examination designed to raise doubt in the minds of jurors regarding the defendants' guilt by blaming Araujo.[19] In the end, jurors convicted four of the six men implicated.[20]

To the extent that broader rape culture and associated rape myths foster an environment in which violence against sex workers is expected and excused, strippers labor under particularly arduous circumstances. Hostile environments are produced through norms, institutions, and practices that can be uncovered and understood. Strip clubs foster hostility toward women through a variety of resources. As The Lion's Den exemplifies, strip clubs are spaces where (1) all men can experience dominant forms of masculinity; (2) women are economically dependant on men; and (3) normative stereotyping of strippers, rape culture, and rape myths prevail. The combinations of these factors create an environment in which violence and aggression is possible and, as we have seen, even probable.

Context affects how the broader rape culture is perpetuated or inhibited, as Boswell and Spade found.[21] In their study of fraternities and bars, they found some settings constituted rape-prone environments, while others were more likely to be rape resistant.[22] The rape-prone environments were places where men viewed women with disrespect, as inferior and anonymous.[23] Though some strip club patrons develop regular relationships with strippers, the other characteristics Boswell and Spade found in fraternity houses apply to club strippers. By seeing the ways in which social norms and specific environments converge to enable men's violence and aggression toward strippers, we may learn how violence is perpetuated and how it may be stopped.

The Lion's Den across Time

The Internet has an ostensibly infinite amount of material related to sex work. To further study The Lion's Den longitudinally, or over time, this postscript draws on a new data source from the Internet—a discussion forum found on Strip Club List (SCL, www.stripclublist.com). SCL is one of two major sources for Internet information on strip clubs. The other source is The Ultimate Strip Club List (TUSCL, www.tuscl.com). Both SCL and TUSCL are websites that provide searchable pages for hundreds of strip clubs worldwide.[24] Their focus is on female performers for primarily male patrons.[25] Club owners, patrons, workers, and website staff update the sites with information regarding new, current, and closed clubs; details about club offerings and costs; links to club websites, reviews, and comments; and driving directions. These sites are also a repository of advertising related to adult entertainment.

The main difference between SCL and TUSCL is that TUSCL requires users to register and pay a fee in order to gain full access to website offerings, including club reviews and patrons' comments sections. SCL and TUSCL are particularly useful in situating stripping geographically. Their self-report data include details about club locations around the world. In particular, both websites delineate the size, scope, and organization of stripping. The following section maps regional and national landscapes in detail. Despite the strengths of these sources, there may also be limitations to the use of such data. For example, we cannot know, beyond a person's self-identification, what their "true" identity is. We must trust dialogue and self-disclosure as our source of "truth." These constraints are not unique to Internet research. One must always keep in mind multiple truths when addressing the messiness of qualitative data in various contexts. The Internet, however, poses specific challenges since online content is a researcher's only source of evidence—there is not a physical person to further guide interpretations. The benefits of this kind of investigation are that it is unobtrusive, produced directly by participants, and readily accessible to everyone with access to a computer and the Internet. SCL's scope is illustrated by the diversity in chat participants, who include both "experts" and "novices," capturing well-informed dialogue, as well as point-of-information requests. The range of questions and responses allows for depth of discussion and clarification of basic concepts and rules.

Regional Comparisons

Drawing on Internet material helps situate The Lion's Den geographically relative to other clubs in the region, as well as the broader United States. It also provides the opportunity to reexamine normative understandings of the stripping industry, its density, and its growth. Despite notions of "sex work hubs," the concentration of stripping within particular states or regions runs contrary to popular assumptions, especially when per capita estimates are taken into account. For example, New England states are conventionally not viewed as having dense sex work concentrations, so the findings from SCL and TUSCL may be surprising. Table 1 begins with the New England region, where The Lion's Den is located.

According to 2007 data compiled from SCL and TUSCL, New England has between 94 and 112 strip clubs. Variation in the actual numbers is due

TABLE 1. *New England Strip Clubs, 2007*

Rank	State	No. of clubs in SCL	No. of clubs in TUSCL	No. of clubs per 100,000 adults ≥ age 18*	No. of clubs per 100,000 males ≥ age 18*
1	Rhode Island	15	11	1.9	4.0
2	Connecticut	45	43	1.8	3.7
3	Vermont	4	2	0.9	1.8
4	Maine	8	5	0.8	1.6
5	Massachusettes	37	31	0.8	1.6
6	New Hampshire	3	2	0.3	0.6
7	New England Total	112	94	0.2	0.4

* Population totals calculated in 2007 using SCL data and
U.S. Bureau of the Census American Community Survey Data (2005).
SCL= Strip Club List; TUSCL= The Ultimate Strip Club List

to the self-report structure of the websites, which rely on clubs, patrons, or workers to detail locations. Rather than comparing the gross number of clubs in each state, it is more useful to evaluate state totals relative to the populations they serve. Table 1 includes the number of clubs per 100,000 in the general adult and adult male populations.[26] Adult males are separated out since they are the target audience for strip clubs. Using these calculations, Rhode Island, though it ranks third in terms of sheer number of clubs in the New England region, is first in terms of the number of clubs per 100,000 in the general adult and adult male populations. Connecticut and Vermont, though first and fifth in the number of clubs for the New England region, respectively, rank second and third in clubs per 100,000 in the general adult and adult male populations.

To situate New England clubs relative to the rest of the United States, Table 2 outlines clubs across the country, as of 2007. Both Rhode Island and Connecticut fall within the top twenty states, with the highest strip club saturation relative to their population characteristics. Vermont, Maine, Massachusetts, and New Hampshire, by contrast, round out the bottom of the list. These findings support an understanding of New England as a varied setting in which to explore the stripping industry.

TABLE 2. *United States Strip Clubs, 2007*

Rank*	State	No. of clubs in SCL	No. of clubs in TUSCL	No. of clubs per 100,000 adults ≥ age 18**	No. of clubs per 100,000 males ≥ age 18**
1	West Virginia	83	49	6.0	12.4
2	Washington, D.C.	20	10	5.0	10.7
3	South Dakota	22	12	3.9	8.0
4	Nevada	69	43	3.9	7.8
5	New Jersey	175	123	2.7	5.8
6	Hawaii	23	20	2.4	5.0
7	Wisconsin	96	84	2.4	4.8
8	Wyoming	9	9	2.4	4.8
9	Louisiana	67	57	2.1	4.4
10	Oregon	58	90	2.1	4.4
11	Indiana	94	76	2.1	4.3
12	Iowa	46	35	2.1	4.3
13	Nebraska	26	15	2.0	4.2
14	Ohio	167	139	2.0	4.2
15	Florida	264	212	2.0	4.1
16	South Carolina	60	57	1.9	4.1
17	Rhode Island	15	11	1.9	4.0
18	Kansas	37	33	1.9	3.8
19	Oklahoma	46	48	1.8	3.7
20	Connecticut	45	43	1.8	3.7
21	Kentucky	53	45	1.7	3.6
22	North Carolina	106	97	1.7	3.5
23	Arizona	73	57	1.7	3.5
24	Alaska	8	9	1.8	3.5
25	New York	220	153	1.6	3.3
26	Michigan	110	86	1.5	3.1
27	Maryland	59	62	1.5	3.1
28	North Dakota	7	6	1.5	3.0

TABLE 2. *United States Strip Clubs, 2007 (continued)*

Rank*	State	No. of clubs in SCL	No. of clubs in TUSCL	No. of clubs per 100,000 adults ≥ age 18**	No. of clubs per 100,000 males ≥ age 18**
29	Texas	229	225	1.4	2.9
30	Pennsylvania	126	130	1.4	2.9
31	Missouri	58	45	1.4	2.8
32	Georgia	83	72	1.3	2.7
33	Illinois	118	86	1.3	2.7
34	Montana	9	9	1.3	2.6
35	Tennessee	53	38	1.2	2.5
36	Idaho	12	10	1.2	2.4
37	Minnesota	44	33	1.2	2.4
38	Delaware	7	6	0.1	2.4
39	Coloado	35	27	1.0	2.1
40	Utah	16	14	0.9	1.9
41	Alabama	29	35	0.9	1.8
42	New Mexico	12	11	2.6	1.8
43	Vermont	4	2	0.9	1.8
44	Arkansas	17	12	0.8	1.7
45	California	212	196	0.8	1.7
46	Maine	8	5	0.8	1.6
47	Massachusetts	37	31	0.8	1.6
48	Virginia	31	38	0.6	1.2
49	Washington	21	16	0.4	0.9
50	Mississippi	15	9	0.7	0.7
51	New Hampshire	3	2	0.3	0.6

* Rank ordered by number of clubs per 100,000 males age eighteen or older.
** Population totals calculated in 2007 using SCL data and
U.S. Bureau of the Census American Community Survey Data (2005).
SCL = Strip Club List; TUSCL = The Ultimate Strip Club List;
shaded areas = New England clubs

Much is often made of the so-called core sex industry states: however, places like Florida (264 in the SCL listing), Texas (229), New York (220), and California (212), which are often noted as having the greatest number of strip clubs, do not even fall in the top ten nationwide in terms of their strip club density relative to their populations. Instead, West Virginia tops the list, with approximately twelve strip clubs per 100,000 males age eighteen and over. Washington, D.C., follows close behind, with nearly eleven, and South Dakota and Nevada also lead the pack, with about eight clubs each per 100,000 males age eighteen and over. The importance of looking at these numbers relative to population is that they provide a sense of the industry's scope in particular regions. Wyoming, for example, has relatively few clubs, but those clubs also serve a comparatively small population, making Wyoming fall within the top ten. As a result, stripping is actually more densely distributed outside of the major sites of the sex industry, with the notable exceptions of Nevada (Las Vegas), New Jersey (Atlantic City), and Louisiana (New Orleans).

In an interview-based study of stripping across three main sites (Hawaii; Kentucky; and San Francisco, California), Bernadette Barton examined the size of the industry through TUSCL.[27] Comparing her nationwide 2005 findings with those here from 2007 exposes both increases—Texas (10) and New York (1)—and decreases: California (10) and Florida (2).[28] Comparing Barton's 2005 New England TUSCL numbers with these 2007 TUSCL data, the number of clubs in Connecticut (3), New Hampshire (1), and Rhode Island (1) all increased. Only Maine (1) decreased its number of strip clubs.[29] Massachusetts and Vermont remained consistent in their number of clubs.[30] In sum, the SCL and TUSCL data underscore arguments about continued growth, as well as fluctuation, in the strip club industry.

A Virtual Reentry into The Lion's Den

Postings to SCL are the primary tool used here to explore The Lion's Den four years after my participant observation ended.[31] Given the restrictive setup for TUSCL and its consistently smaller number of club listings,[32] SCL was the logical choice for further analysis. Drawing on more than thirteen hundred postings from the SCL comments section for The Lion's Den, this analysis offers a new glimpse into life and work in The Lion's Den under Players' ownership. Responses were not solicited on this site; rather, individuals' postings were taken together, exported verbatim as text, and explored using HyperRESEARCH qualitative analysis software.[33] Postings fall between January 5, 2005, and July 18, 2006. In this year and a half, participants covered club renovations (both those completed and those still needed), upcoming events, strippers' schedules, workplace organization and change, and, in particular, interactions between patrons and club personnel. The site also includes discussions of the club's pre-Players days.

Revisiting the Past

People who posted to the list provided uniformly negative representations of the past, especially when they referenced The Lion's Den's former owner-manager, Steve. While talk about Steve specifically was not very common, when his name was mentioned, it provoked talk of "disaster" and a "ruined" club. In the quoted texts, online pseudonyms and thread topics are italicized in brackets preceding the quotation.

[*Soon we forget*]: You know it was not too long ago, 2–3 years maybe, not even that long since [Players] bought The Lion's Den. Does anyone remember what a disaster it was back then? Nearly dead. Few customers. Few very poor, at best, dancers. Now there has been some modest remodeling, we have tons of great talent; a decent staff and they actually have customers. No longer is such an area icon at threat of closing due to no business. Two different owners destroyed this place. And Aiden, the new manager, whether you like him or not, has done quite the job reviving the place. Are there issues? Of course, as with any business there always will be. Aiden does a hell of job working through them to improve.

Most of the other topics that people posted about contained debate or at least disagreement, so the lack of controversy here is noteworthy. In either their disinterest or their dislike, respondents were clear that the club was mismanaged under Steve's leadership:

[*Re: Steve*]: Steve managed to catch the tail end of a good run and ruined it. Steve tried to start his own agency and ruined the club so bad he cut part of the stage out. Because of the lack of girls the stage looked empty. So it is actually you that should not form opinions when you are basing success on the fact that Steve was your buddy or that he gave you a few free beers and not on ability.

The issues raised in these posts both confirm and expand on understandings of club workings under Steve's leadership. Frequently empty, the club retained only a small number of dancers and had a high turnover rate. While Steve acknowledged tough times, he never linked renovations to his difficulty filling shifts. Instead, Steve explained the removal of a portion of the stage as an important step in providing space for a new service—table dancing—though the emptiness certainly provides a counterexplanation. Steve described his RealGirls agency as a separate way to hire dancers as independent contractors so the club did not have to employ them. Creation of this agency, however, may also have been a way for Steve to siphon club funds to himself for work he did on behalf of RealGirls (e.g., hiring, overseeing, and firing dancers). While negative comments regarding a former owner-manager's style might be expected, there may be some truth to posters' statements. Moreover, the insightfulness of the posts suggests intimate working knowledge of the club.

Players Takes over The Lion's Den
Club Changes

Players modified The Lion's Den in many ways when it assumed ownership. It expanded business hours; created new club products, jobs, and fees; and fostered a reputation for physical intimacy between strippers and patrons, a practice consistent with its other area venues. The club is now open seven days a week, including Sundays (7:00 PM–2:00 AM). Under Steve, the club was closed one day a week, which gave everyone a mandatory day off. Though the club still does not mandate a dress code or offer feature performers, some changes have an upscale flavor. There is now a Lion's Den Grill that serves pub fare and provides an alternative to the vending machines and visiting outdoor grill trailer. It offers expanded drink options and a new waitressing position, a "shooter-girl," whose work is limited to delivering high-priced novelty shots of alcohol. Similar to the term "babysitting" used by The Lion's Den employees under Steve's direction, the job title "shooter-girl" rings with a paternalistic and infantilizing tone.

Signifying a step toward sophistication, the space in the club once called the VIP Room is now called the Champagne Room. The new space offers patrons champagne and half-hour interactions with strippers for $100. Discussing these changes, a poster writes:

[*Visiting again*]: It had been many years since I have been to The Lion's Den. Late 80s early 90s there was no better place, [however] as of late it was a dump. But I had time so I wandered in and to my surprise [Players] have shown a lot of interest and done wonderful things. I just happen to walk in on a Wednesday and it was amateur night. This place was packed and had at least 20 house girls and 12 girls in the contest. A cute short-haired girl won 1st place. I was hoping to see her dance again but have not, although there are plenty of good-looking nice girls. Who needs stuck up Barbies? There is a champagne room. Who would have thought The Lion's Den with a champagne room? I have spent a lot of time here lately and I am looking forward to the next amateur night.

In addition to the champagne and strippers' performances, the Champagne Room provides an opportunity for patrons to experience close physical proximity, private conversation, and the attention that results from conspicuous consumption. Chatting about the Champagne Room, posters frequently ask what to expect. *Wondering*, a pseudonym for an online poster, writes, "First time to The Lion's Den—want to know more about the champagne room and how it works." In reply to *Wondering*, another poster explains: "The CR [Champagne Room] is pretty simple—just like the rest of the club. You pay the girl, she dances for you. This is not a whorehouse or a massage parlor, if that is what you are asking!" Another roars, "Like Chris Rock says . . . THERE IS NO SEX IN THE CHAMPAGNE ROOM!! It'll be a day when I look in the newspaper and see that this place gets shut down cuz you choose to turn the other cheek" (emphasis in original).

While posters' consensus did not support expectations for additional physical contact in the Champagne Room, the creation of a new "lap dance room" suggests that physical contact is present elsewhere in the club. Katherine Liepe-Levinson outlines lap dance rules: "The patron must remain dressed and seated in his chair at all times, while the dancer must wear underpants. Hand to genital, genital to genital, and oral-genital contacts between patrons are not allowed, but dancers are permitted to caress patron's genitals through their clothing."[34] Numerous posts included reference to both lap dances and the new lap dance room. Despite the possibility of higher earnings through the club's new offerings, postings suggested that business is still slow:

[*HA*]: No girl here makes $900 a night. Some of them don't even make $900 a week. They just aren't hot enough to make that kind of money without giving extras or meeting customers outside of the club. Get real. I have been to The Lion's Den on a regular basis and the lap dance room isn't that busy. Neither is the CR. And I rarely see the same girl go in there more than once or twice a night.

Rather than emphasizing positive changes to the club, the poster revealed some discontent as well as harsh critiques of female workers. The poster's words were echoed by another:

[*Visitor*]: Came into town for the week. Stayed at the inn down the road. The cab ride cost less than [a] round of drinks. Came in Tuesday [and] paid 3 bucks to get in. Good-looking girls, but there were a couple nasty ones too. Kind of slow. Came in Thursday and there were a lot more girls, but still a couple nasty ones. Got charged 5 at the door and the drinks were more expensive. I have never heard of a strip club that upped their drink prices on the weekends along with the cover. So if you are an out-of-towner, go at the beginning of the week. I will say this, I got a great lap dance from a girl named Eve and the waitress on Tuesday has the biggest real boobs of any chic in the place. But she won't do dances, wouldn't even flash. Said it was against the rules.

Physical contact between strippers and patrons was a popular topic in the comments section. For example, *Not a cop* wrote: "Man, I'm not a cop. I'm gonna be in town at the end of the month and I'm just looking for a spot where I could have some extra fun. This site is a resource, so I thought I'd ask." Another poster, *Extra fun in the CR?* asks: "I'm sure some people are going to hate the fact that I am posting this, but take it easy, I'm just asking a question. Do any of the girls here do extra stuff in the Champagne Room? If so could you hit me up with who does, how much they want, etc. It is much appreciated." In response, posters included both the possibility and denial of physical contact. *Action* wrote: "For anyone looking for some hot live action ([blowjobs], sex), try the [other Players clubs]. They charge a little more for the CR, but [you] can pay the hostess extra $$ to keep her mouth shut."

Players has operated other clubs such as The Copa Cabana for years. When asked about the difference between The Lion's Den and The Copa Cabana, Steve repeated a line from his *Employee/Entertainer Handbook*: "I would hopefully guarantee the fact that as opposed to any other bar around here you're [going to] get treated like a human being and not a piece of meat [at The Lion's Den], and I'm [talking] about the dancers." The Copa Cabana has long had a reputation for having conventionally tall, thin, blonde, large-breasted strippers who provide greater physical contact for a younger clientele in a crowded atmosphere. As Steve explained, at The Copa Cabana, the "customer [is usually] younger.... They want to see exactly how much money—how far their dollar will go. And [there] . . . you get put down and picked on by their deejays over the microphone if you do something out of the ordinary. And we try not to do that [*laughs*]." Steve's reference to the differential treatment of customers in The Lion's Den was geared toward a positive representation of and for patrons. In practice, The Lion's Den's lax treatment of patron "indiscretions" (read: verbal and physical aggression), as well as its policy that the "customer is always right," produced hazardous working conditions for strippers. While the teasing and jeers at The Copa Cabana might not have been geared toward patron compliance with club rules, the fact that patrons got called out and may have needed to watch their behavior sits in sharp contrast to practices in The Lion's Den. For better and worse, the differences between the two clubs helped foster The Copa Cabana's status as a foil for former workers, strippers, and patrons of The Lion's Den under Steve's management.

The Copa Cabana's reputation for providing greater sexual intimacy between strippers and patrons was one way for both the club and strippers to increase earnings, despite the risk of police intervention, fines, and shutdowns. Speaking about these practices at The Lion's Den under Players, another poster bluntly asserted:

[*More than stripping*]: I agree a stripper needs to do more than strip to make money in any of the clubs owned by [Players], onstage you need to stick your pussy an inch away from guys' faces. Lots of contact in [the] lap dance area is a must, if you want any customers. So many girls don't mind contact [that] if you do, you will be passed over. And then there's c-room [Champagne Room], this is where the real money is. Management turns a blind eye to any extra services back there, so leave your morals in another state and you too can be talked about on this site.

Reflecting the opposite experience and lamenting the loss of physical contact in other clubs, another poster wrote:

[*Whore House*]: Well another club in the area was only shut down for a week because they lost their liquor license. I wouldn't be surprised if this place had the same thing happen to them. Even the other club [under the same ownership] is cleaning up and it is bullshit! I do not go there anymore because I was so used to getting so much from just a lap dance. Now I don't even get a hand job in the CR with[out] the fucking hostesses interrupting! All of these places will have their fall eventually; it is only a matter of time.

While conducting research in The Lion's Den, I spoke with no one who discussed engaging in sexual contact within the club, and nothing I witnessed suggested otherwise, though gossip about sex acts in the club (particularly in the walled-off VIP Room) was common. SCL posts regarding Players' changes to The Lion's Den simultaneously amplified and negated the possibility of physical contact extending to sexual activity. Still, the presence of the new Champagne Room space and, more importantly, the additional presence of a new lap dance room, certainly imply greater occurrence of physical contact than in The Lion's Den under Steve, the former owner-manager, especially given the added privacy, cost, and language used. While some things change, others remain the same. Despite numerous changes, The Lion's Den continues to face unpredictability regarding strippers working in the club.

Turnover

SCL postings indicated the presence of new dancers and continued change of employees in The Lion's Den. A conversation about specific dancers arose when one poster requested a regular listing of dancers' schedules online: "How about posting the girls' schedules every week here? It would be nice to see the schedules of my favorites every week." In response, a representative of the club wrote, "NEW DANCERS!!!! This Thursday come meet Madison, Alexis and Heather. You can see Mia, Fri, Sat and Sun nights. Jasmine will be on Fri and Sun nights. And Taylor will be there Fri and Sat day shift!" Regular patrons often keep track of strippers' schedules, either through their own diligence or from strippers' reminders. SCL provides another outlet for this information. Seeking particular dancers a respondent replied:

[Schedules]: Thanks for the update on all the new dancers. It would be really cool if you could mention the dancers who are gone. No need to go into the reasons, but it's annoying to come in expecting to see a particular dancer and not know where she is. Much better if we know ahead of time not to expect them, and can start looking forward to the new girls as well as some old favorites who didn't leave. So who's gone?

In response, a club representative mentioned a number of problems related to routinely posting strippers' schedules. Restrictions on the number of characters a poster's message may include would necessitate countless posts to convey all of the information. In addition, scheduling does not always mean attendance. The club worker's response echoed familiar sentiments about unreliable strippers who frequently do not show up for work:

> [*Schedules*]: Anyone familiar with the strip club business knows that dancers are not always the most reliable. Usually somewhere around 1 out of 5 dancers cancel on any given day. Which would mean I would be living on this website to update everyone on cancellations. And if a girl cancels last minute, or just decides not to show, you would waste a trip to the club. But if you ask for a specific girl, I will post her schedule.

Despite indications that there are a greater number of dancers overall under Players' ownership, this posting also suggests that many dancers continue to leave the club. Dancers who are absent may have moved out of stripping work or on to another club.

Club Happenings

One way to attract "new" dancers, increase the roster of house girls, and draw in additional patrons is to provide special events inside and outside of the club. Players launched countless thematic events, including amateur nights, which were listed on the comments pages. During my fourteen months of research, the club featured only two amateur nights. Amateur nights are contests in which dancers perform shortened stage routines competing for "best amateur stripper," as determined by an emcee's interpretation of the loudest audience applause. Cash prizes are awarded to the winners. Rarely do these competitions include real amateurs, but, rather, they involve dancers not currently working in the club. In fact, some performers are seasoned veterans from other clubs. Unlike typical performances, some of the amateurs provide thematic shows. At one of Steve's amateur nights in the spring of 2002, a stripper began her routine in a short, gray wig and an old bathrobe, hobbling around the stage with a cane. As the tempo of the music increased, she shimmied out of her costume and wig to reveal a string bikini, which prompted roaring audience applause. Interspersed with strippers' performances, the emcee also performed standup comedy routines and brief jokes. At one point, he, too, donned an elderly woman's costume; a black-and-white maid's uniform; and a long, curly, white wig. The two images—aging and servitude—drew a cynical parallel to stripping as a service-oriented and age-delimited job. Such events attract big crowds from the novelty and increased advertising.

On the discussion list, an announcement that seemed to come from club personnel provides insights into how amateur nights have changed under Players' ownership:

> Amateur Night: Ladies and Gents. The Lion's Den, unlike other clubs, our payouts are higher. 1st $1000, 2nd $400, 3rd $100. . . . Ladies, time to make the big bucks. VIP dances and champagne rooms, only $20 house fee.

A more provocative ad read:

> This week is full of Booze, Babes, and Boobies!!! This Thursday night is the return of amateur night!!! Get here early! Show starts around 9pm and we'll need to appoint judges! Winner takes all one thousand dollars cash!!! Ladies interested in entering can contact the bar, or come on down before 8pm!!!! (emphasis in original)

Using a different format, the new amateur nights elected judges from the crowd (rather than informally relying on general audience applause). In addition, the prize money doubled. The largest cash prize for Steve's amateur nights was $500, with smaller prizes for second and third place. The central purpose behind such events is to attract a bigger audience and new dancers to the club. While not uncommon in the industry, the presence of amateur nights coupled with discussions of low patronage may indicate ongoing business challenges for Players.

In addition to amateur nights, postings also mentioned fund-raisers such as a benefit car wash:

> The Lion's Den Bikini Car Wash!! To benefit [a local] Hospital. There will be a raffle for some great prizes, including gift certificates to a couple of area restaurants, Bacardi basketball jerseys, poker set, etc. Come have your car washed by some of our finest, enjoy a beer and win some prizes!

In response to the car wash, one poster replied:

[*Carwash*]: I heard about a car wash to benefit the [local] Hospital. Well, on behalf of all [locally affiliated], including myself, keep your money! We don't want it, or need scum like you donating to our philanthropic organization! I also think [one of the women] would have an incentive to steal. She is a single mother who is in her 6th year at [a local college] for an undergraduate degree! LOL.

Strip clubs host charitable events precisely to combat the stereotypes of strip clubs and strippers as unworthy (and untrustworthy), appropriately set apart from mainstream society. Changing their community profile not only provides a source of advertising but may also boost community tolerance and support of clubs and their workers. The limitations of this approach are visible in the posting above, as these events can provoke scorn rather than support. Perhaps because of the potential for fund-raisers to backfire, Steve refrained from organizing them. Despite the absence of such events during my participant observation in the club, Steve mentioned donating large sums of money to local police and fire departments. He explained: "We try to support the city as much as we can. I mean we're always giving to charities, and organizations and stuff like that. . . . We're in the policeman's . . . yearbooks and their balls and all that stuff; we've given them money. The DARE program, . . . we give them a lot of money every year." By contrast, Steve argued, other clubs in the area did not have the same "visibility" and did not seem to be reaching out to their local communities. Contrary to Steve's claim, Players appeared to use the same community outreach approach.

Players also created new events to attract patrons. A post read: "The Lion's Den and Maximum Magazine brings you The Lion's Den Maximum Panty raid. 10 pm till the panties run out. Get a dance from a girl [and] you keep the panties. Maximum Magazine will be on site to uncover the night." Hosting a local adult-entertainment magazine and providing prizes for patrons are two innovative ways Players increases club exposure. The panty promotion also provides a new type of intimacy between strippers and patrons—something tangible from a stripper that patrons can keep. In effect, sending patrons home with strippers' panties provides proof of the interaction between stripper and patron, regardless of the amount of contact. To anyone familiar with the John Hughes film *Sixteen Candles*, the panty raid is strangely reminiscent of Farmer Ted's acquisition of Sam's panties, which he promptly shows to the "geeks" for a fee of $1.

Four years earlier, thematic events like these were beyond the scope of The Lion's Den's resources. Lacking workers to fill even regularly scheduled shifts, Steve stuck mostly to a routine. The only additional events Steve held, besides the occasional amateur night, were holiday buffets (e.g., for Thanksgiving). The Thanksgiving buffet, a longstanding tradition in the club, included a huge spread of food catered from an outside eatery: turkey, mashed potatoes, and pasta in marinara sauce were offered in large aluminum-foil baking pans. The affair was set up on folding tables without tablecloths; patrons dined with plastic utensils, paper napkins, and paper plates. The all-you-can-eat buffet ran most of the evening, necessitating extra cocktail waitresses to manage the greater number of patrons and increased cleanup. These events were all designed to increase revenue. Given the additional costs (upfront materials and labor), they were potentially less effective than other means available, particularly if turnout was low. In part, this may be why clubs often look to workers' earnings to line club pockets.

House Fees

The $20 house fee mentioned above in one of the amateur-night ads is new. Other clubs in the area and nationwide have initiated them, charging strippers from $20 to $200 a shift to work. Not surprisingly, strippers are concerned that shift fees will further chip away at their profits since they already have to pay a portion of their earnings to the deejay (and possibly other club workers). In discussions and interviews during Steve's tenure, dancers raised concern over the institution of a house fee. From the club's perspective, such fees are not just an untapped revenue source; they are evidence of workers' independent-contractor status. Through shift or stage fees, strippers pay to use the club's space just like a hairdresser pays to rent a station at a hair salon. Such fees are designed to prevent dancers from declaring employee status and receiving the associated wages, workers' compensation, and unemployment benefits. Given Players' position in the market, as well as its ownership of many other local clubs, it is uniquely able to implement house fees without fear that dancers will go elsewhere. Indeed, if it has instituted fees at all of its clubs, as it has at The Copa Cabana, which charges $50 a shift, it leaves dancers with no choice but to pay to work. Alongside economic pressures, women experience greater performance-based demands as well.

Women's Work, Women's Woes

Numerous discussions on the SCL website focused on Players' reputation for promoting physical contact between female workers and male patrons. One exchange revolved around the new shooter-girl waitressing position. Shooter-girls serve shots of alcohol. Debate ensued when a poster asked which shooters do private dances and Champagne Room performances. Previously, the club policy under Steve was to allow cocktail waitresses to dance only when they were not waitressing (e.g., during a separate shift). This practice was often violated during daytime shifts, particularly when the club had few patrons and no other dancers present. Under those circumstances, if a cocktail waitress was asked for a VIP performance, she might be given an informal nod to do so. Discussing practices under Players management, *PD* wrote:

> If you want to know if a waitress/shooter will do a private dance for you, your best bet is to ask them. It's not like they are going to get offended or anything. Keep in mind they tend to be picky—I've had shooters do CR's with me that, in theory, *don't* do CR's. I've had others that I know *do* do CR's, turn me down. Also, keep in mind that shooters doing dances is a sore spot for some dancers, so shooters tend to be subtle and quiet about it. (emphasis in original)

The initial poster was not convinced by this response and asked for more:

> [*Thanks I guess*]: Thanks *PD* for your info. I have been reading this board for some time. I have seen a lot of stuff that is pretty unbelievable and seen a lot of people blow your credibility right out of the water. so does anyone have any real info for me? Which ones tend to and which ones don't? (Shooter girls and waitresses that do private dances or champagne room).

Adding to the debate, another poster weighed in with a mixed response and specific suggestions:

> [*WTF*]: *PD* are you a total idiot? You must be one of those 90% that make guys look bad! The shooter/waitresses that won't even consider PD [private dance] or CR [Champagne Room] most certainly do get offended when asked! Your comment, as always, is piss poor! Who cares if the dancers don't like it, everyone is there to make money! To Help: I have seen Ari-

elle do both and Collette do some PD. Not sure on others. Just remember shooter/waitresses usually want more then [*sic*] the dancers (and rightfully so since this is not what they usually do). (emphasis in original)

Finally, the exchange was followed by two punchy comments arguing against shooters and waitresses being offended by private dance requests. The first stated:

[*Reality*]: I'm sorry, if these girls don't want to hear questions, stay away from the customers, and stop begging them to buy shots. Customers buy shots usually to chat up the shot girls, not for gaff cheap gutter vodka shots, for 2/3 the price of an entire drink. It's part of the job, if you don't like it stop pushing shots and get out of a sex club.

The second comment used more offensive language:

[*Thanks*]: To each piece of crap that works in strip clubs. Thanks for scamming guys out their money and then whining like bitches about how terrible the guys are.

The expectation underpinning these posts is that female workers should surely expect explicit requests for erotic services. As the first poster stated, "it's part of the job." Connecting these comments to the discussion of physical contact between strippers and patrons mentioned earlier, there is a common thread: female workers should expect requests for nearly any sexual service. The posturing style of these posts contributes to representations of strip clubs as a space where anything goes. In turn, it is these characterizations of female club workers as "pieces of crap" and "whining bitches" that foster space for performances of verbally and physically aggressive masculinity.

SCL user statements also underpin assumptions linked to rape-prone environments. Boswell and Spade's study found that evidence of rape culture on college campuses rested in part on fraternity men's practices that demeaned and showed disrespect toward women.[35] In particular, "fraternity men most often mistreated women they did not know personally."[36] Website rants that were aggressive toward all female club workers and strippers often targeted unspecified persons, fostering women's anonymity. These posts characterize men's club experiences in terms of their relationships not with women but with other men. As the men jockey for information and one-up each other with tales of greater physical intimacy, they reproduce their homosocial pecking order. As Michael Kimmel argues, "Women become a kind of currency that men use to improve their ranking on the masculine social scale."[37] PD's claims about access to waitress dances are a case in point. The other posters' challenges illustrate the ways in which women are used to chalk the scoreboard. Between stories of special access, take-home panties, and harsh words, The Lion's Den discussions provided men with many tools to design and contest each other's masculinity.

Despite significant alterations to the club, men's behaviors remain largely unchanged. Men's actions expose the broader culture of masculinity built on sexism (as well as homophobia, racism, and ageism) that exists beyond the club's walls.[38] Cultural changes have, at least to some extent, shifted the gender playing field. White, Christian, heterosexual men's patriarchal power and associated advantages are no longer a given. Though clearly for white ethnics, religious and sexual minorities, the disabled, the poor, and others, male supremacy and prestige may not have been present in the first place. Thus, spaces like strip clubs where most men can feel powerful address a particular desire. Kimmel contends:

> As the dawn of the millennium approached and then passed, American men still felt an urgent need to prove their masculinity. The ground may have been shifting under their feet and old structural buttresses eroding or disappearing, but men remained faithful to the traditional recipe for masculinity. And they search again through the time-tested ways men had always searched: self-control, exclusion, and escape.[39]

Anthropologist Katherine Frank explains that strip clubs constitute a form of escape or "touristic practice" for men.[40] As such, men in clubs like The Lion's Den seek respite from day-to-day responsibilities. Likewise, the meaning behind *Playboy* magazine's name capitalizes on a similar theme, which argues, "American men experienced their manhood most profoundly when they were boys at play, not men at work."[41] Rather than ghettoize sex work as set apart from the mainstream, strip clubs are places where meaningful identity formation takes place. This broader sex-for-profit industry shapes identity in particular ways. As Raewyn Connell explains, "The corporate activity behind media celebrities and the commercialization of sex [is] . . . [an] arena of hegemonic masculinity politics, the management of patriarchal institutions."[42] These industries range from "heavy pornography and prostitution to soft-core advertising [that markets] women's bodies as objects of consumption by men."[43] In short, when sexist attitudes construct an environment, it should not be surprising when those sexist attitudes are, in turn, reproduced in that context.

The content of men's discussions on the website indicate a range of behaviors. As some of the examples illustrate, patrons often described affection toward strippers and cocktail waitresses. However, there were many instances of aggressive masculinity on the site. Consider the following post, dubbed "stripper whores":

> [*Junkies*]: Don't buy the excuse that these girls are going to school, and if they were what, community college? Also I have known a few dancers Fran and Trisha . . . who said that they were dancing to pay for school, well they have been in school for like 20 years now, when the hell are they going to graduate? Just don't kiss a hoe on her mouth and wear a condom when she blows you, but when you are ready to ejaculate take it off pull her back by grabbing her hair, and say, "yeah you are going to eat it now bitch!" Then, bust one all over her face and into her mouth. I have done that in the CR before!

In response, another poster replied:

> [*In their face*]: I have played the Howard Stern stupid stripper question game with some of the dancers. Keep it simple, ask math, general knowledge (who the president is), how many states there are, how many senators etc. . . . Maybe they are living up to their best potential by dancing. Like I always say, go with your strengths!! It doesn't take a brain to suck your cock!!

These snide and violent comments were met with counterarguments emphasizing strippers' education. For example:

> [*F.T.*]: Fran hasn't been there in months, so maybe she actually did do it just to pay for school. You know, not all dancers are liars.

Another post read:

> [*Educated dancers*]: I know of 2 dancers currently there getting masters . . . although I believe one of them took this semester off. Just for the record, neither one of them uses drugs . . . or does "extras" . . . let's stop with the sweeping generalizations . . . it is tedious.

Sidestepping part of the argument and encouraging a sensitive approach, this author argued:

. [*To stripper whores*]: Dude, are you out of your mind? The girls are a fantasy—they can be anything they want. The thing to remember—you are in there paying them to be the fantasy. So stop judging them and demeaning them. Some might be in college or grad school, some might just be telling you that. Who the hell cares? Just go, spend some money and enjoy the time and the view.

Only one respondent took the aggressive posters to task:

[*To stripper whores*]: I'm sure he is befuddled by your question . . . most guys/girls (let's not discriminate) who insult dancers here on the board, just do it to make themselves feel better for some sort of inadequacy they feel they have in their lives. And because they don't have the forthrightness to actually say it directly to the individual(s) . . . they just hide behind their computers . . . it is safe in the anonymous computer world!! Honestly, there is no reason to "reward" negative behavior . . . i.e. posting a response to some ludicrous statement.

Though some postings disagreed with the malicious tone of the original author's posts, many of the replies document the routine frequency of men's aggressive posts. Normalizing these kinds of comments fosters dangers and risks similar to those in research on rape-prone environments,[44] high-risk settings,[45] and high-risk groups.[46] Similarly, during my participant observation, men's hostile remarks were minimized to "boys being boys." Both current and former practices send a clear message that men's aggressive behaviors are allowed in The Lion's Den.

In the strongest suggestion of violence, one thread contained posts related to an alleged assault of a female worker by the club's owner. Early in the discussion, a post read:

[*Whoa*]: Why don't you just tell us how they "drugged" you and "assaulted" you? As if we haven't already figured out how easy it is with a dancer who is down on her luck. Oh, BTW [by the way] did you know it is impossible to "assault" the willing? Or those excepting [accepting] $$$ for the dead [deed]?

In response, the following post appeared:

[*To All*]: You are right, every word of it. Ian the owner had me assaulted and I'm not the only woman he did this to over the years. They even went as far as stealing the key to my house and killing my animal. That's what kind of sick f*ck. . . . The owner drugged me so I did not even know what happened.

In support, another poster echoed:

[*Watch out*]: Ian, the owner, has girls assaulted at [The Copa Cabana]. Most of his workers participate in the assaults. This man is sick in his head. [Men who work for him] are puppets for him, they do his dirty work. They pay off people so [no one] will talk. This is not a joke.

This text was followed by another sympathetic statement:

[*Noticed*]: You must have a lot of ex-employees and angry customers bad mouthing and lying about what goes on in these clubs. I highly doubt that all of them are lying. I truly believe that you all are trying to cover up every bit of prostitution, rape, drugs and any corruptions that go on.

These posts underscore violence against women—not necessarily visible within the club, but committed elsewhere through henchmen. Even if the violence described never actually took place, the words (and the stories they reflect) connect perceptions of violence (and associated fears) with the club.

Performances of masculinity, like those described above, are shaped by a club's norms and strategies (or lack thereof) for addressing or constraining them. To draw again on rape culture research, Boswell and Spade's study suggests evaluating the role of context and culture in rape. What they found was that both environment and social norms affected how high-risk and low-risk college fraternities and bars influenced women's danger of being raped. They write: "Rape cannot be seen only as an isolated act blamed on individual behavior and proclivities, whether it be alcohol consumption or attitudes. We must also consider characteristics of the settings that promote the behaviors that reinforce a rape culture."[47] A rape culture is fostered when women are disrespected, anonymous, and perceived as weak, while men are empowered, connected, and (needing to be) seen as tough. Fraternities are often suspected of promoting rape culture on college campuses, but they are not alone. In addition to fraternities, Boswell and Spade found that bars can also foster (and mitigate) rape culture. After looking at different contexts, Boswell and Spade conclude that "some settings are more likely places for rape than others."⁴⁸ In The Lion's Den, it is both the broader culture of violence against women and the particular context produced by Steve and re-created by Players that reinforce particular dangers for women. A hostile environment is further perpetuated by reference to the stripper's animal being murdered. According to a recent study, many women seeking shelter for men's domestic violence have witnessed abuser's threats of cruelty to their animals.⁴⁹ Such acts are central to the power and control abusers seek over their victims.⁵⁰ As well, these acts of cruelty inhibit women's ability to challenge and leave abusive relationships.⁵¹

In response to the alleged rape, two subsequent posts underscored a deep distrust of women working in the club:

[*When*]: Gee, I wonder at what point Strip Club List starts turning over the IP addresses and post times of belligerent, libel and threatening posts to the local authorities? Surely cannot be much longer.

[*Myself*]: Hey just a word to the wise. . . . Be careful of a dancer named Sydney [also known as] Sara from upstate NY, she is working with law enforcement. Tall black girl [with the] real name Caroline.

Connected to the litigiousness of contemporary society, both posts add an air of formality and seriousness to patrons' experiences that may involve brushes with the law, including lawsuits and undercover police presumably working to expose illegal drug use or prostitution in strip clubs. These posts also underscore impressions that strippers are not to be trusted.

When posts specifically address the alleged assault from the perspective of the club's manager and the alleged assault's victim, they evoke central aspects of rape myths. First from the manager:

[*Evidence*]: I can prove beyond a shadow of a doubt that none of this crap has happened! if it had, anyone in their right mind would have gone [to] the authorities and hired a lawyer. They would be on their way to owning the club. They would not be telling tall tales here, as it would totally destroy any [of] their credibility and any chance they would have had getting a conviction. Furthermore, both the authorities and lawyer[s] would have been telling them to keep their mouth shut. All anyone is doing here is creating a case for a libel suit. It will be truly poetic justice to see the

individuals posting this garbage get nailed! In the meantime, they are providing the best free advertising for the clubs ever! (emphasis in original)

The manager's gratitude for the "best free advertising" while he remained
callous and flippant regarding allegations of assault demonstrate his lack
of seriousness when it comes to addressing verbal or physical aggression
toward female workers. Just consider how different the post would read if it
contained, for example, a strong club policy for handling aggressions toward
women. Instead, the manager's reactions were remarkably similar to those
found in Steve's *Employee/Entertainer Handbook,* as well as in my interviews
with club workers. In response, a later poster shouted:

> [*To Aiden*]: I think I know what happened to me and as far as a dark alley
> goes, I'm the one you had to stop a little fight with up stairs in one of the
> other clubs. i think you know i dont bullshit!!!!!!!! besides this has nothing
> to do with you anyway. maybe you should talk to one of your other friends
> who they made up a reason to fire because he tried to help me. i know
> you're all right, but as far as the others go you may not know them as well
> as you think. i have nothing to gain by making things up. i wish this was a
> lie. thanks. Women don't make these things up!!!!!! (emphasis in original)

Echoing a refrain from antiviolence activism, this poster's comment that
"women don't make these things up" recalls other language, like "no means
no," which is designed to take the burden of proof off of victims/survivors and
place it onto assailants. Nevertheless, the manager's reaction was intended to
discredit these earlier claims:

> [*Aiden Management!*]: I personally think this site is exclusively restricted
> to disgruntled employees, customers, and entertainers when it comes to
> negative comments. I assure you that the only reason why I actually enter-
> tain comments from this site is to monitor customers' opinions. Having
> worked for and with all of the names mentioned, you must be completely
> out of your mind! I assure you that I will be back soon, and I hope that
> you, I, and anyone else don't find ourselves together in a dark alley! . . .
> And as for Ian, the owner, he spends 90% of the time watching TV! Get
> your facts straight.

Though we can never know for sure whose story to believe, we can evaluate the impressions about women contained within the text. Management's

malicious remarks about "assault[ing] the willing" and "find[ing] ourselves together in a dark alley" send a message. Taken together, these comments reveal ongoing hostility toward women in The Lion's Den that continues to extend all the way through to management. As well, remarks designed to discredit strippers' allegations of abuse, calling them belligerent, libelous, and threatening posts, attempt to silence discussion like the litigious remarks above. Collectively, these comments reinforce rape culture in The Lion's Den under Players.

In a strange twist of fate, Aiden's hostile comments were concurrent with a major change for the club that could have signaled greater authority for women: the hiring of a woman into a management position. By contrast, Steve maintained a strict segregation of labor by gender in which men held all positions of power and authority. Under Players, the new female manager was Kayla, a bartender, who filled in temporarily. Discussion of her experience provides information on the club's reaction to change in the gendered organization of work. The ensuing dialogue both questions and supports Kayla's efforts. Supportive posts often tied Kayla's work to the full-time manager, Aiden:

[*Funny*]: To be honest, its clear you've never spoken to Kayla if you think she takes all the credit for the bar. The woman bends over backwards to praise Aiden and claim she's just holding down the fort. Dancers aren't supposed to like her—she's the "bad guy." But most—and all the good ones—respect the job she does as manager. They just wish she would stop booking so many girls each night.

In a particularly supportive post, a website participant wrote:

[*To Mr. Grapevine*]: Quite frankly, if one just looks at the talent now in The Lion's Den, it is pretty obvious Kayla has done one hell of a job!!! . . . Aiden and Kayla make a hell of a team. . . . Aiden and his "total teamwork" approach to bring this club back to it former glory has gone a long way. Most true strip club connoisseurs really thought it was way too late for this club to be revived when a rival club bought it. Aiden and Kayla proved them all wrong! (emphasis in original)

There were also derogatory discussions about Kayla, which included her sex life (while lauding Aiden's), threats about exposing skeletons in her closet, accusations of theft from the club, and name calling (e.g., "bitch").

The devices used to demean Kayla (and other women) closely resemble those associated with rape myths—namely, they call her character into question through sexist attacks. The following excerpt exemplifies these kinds of negative postings:

[*I bet*]: Kayla slept with Aiden and maybe a couple of the other staff members. I know her boyfriend used to work there so she obviously has a thing for guys in the strip club. That's probably why he hasn't fired her yet. He's afraid she'll tell. It seems to me that Aiden gets around. Sleeping with the chicks is their initiation. I say—if you can do it man—do it. Go Aiden. I know if I worked there I would bang them all. Well not all—not the linebacker with the blonde hair that dances like she is having a seizure. There's a scary brunette, but the chic can put her feet behind her head so I might consider her with a lot of beer. Just Aiden—for some of those girls—wrap it twice!!!!!!!!

Citing insider knowledge, a club regular contributed:

[*Long Time Patron*]: This is all pretty humorous. A bunch of people bickering over a website. I frequent the bar quite a bit; I will come regardless of who is in charge. I admit I have enjoyed the place a lot over the past 2 years, except for the past stretch, when Aiden left there was a difference. Now, if all of this backstabbing by Kayla is true, there could be a problem. I, like a lot of the regulars, have quite a bit of damaging dirty laundry on her, stuff that is damaging both professionally and personally. It would be a shame if this information was leaked out.

Adding to the list of rumors and innuendo, a poster who appears to have been a worker lamented the loss of income under Kayla's leadership:

[*Can't Wait*]: Cant wait till Aiden comes back!!!!! So many people are done with Kayla and her reign of terror, get that girl a hobby!!!! Once Aiden returns maybe this place will go back to being enjoyable again, and everyone will start making money too. Any night I stop in, all you hear about is no one is making any $$ anymore and how much of a bitch Kayla is!!! Aiden, dude, hurry back!!!! (emphasis in original)

Discussions of Kayla coupled with the stripper's alleged assault by Players' owner provide an ominous view of ongoing mistrust and mistreatment of women in The Lion's Den. These posts illustrate how context fosters a whole range of men's aggressive and sexist behaviors that are associated with club norms reproduced by club patrons and workers, as well as management. Although the gendered division of labor in the club has changed, women's broader experiences have not. The fleeting presence of a female manager does little to disrupt the gendered organization of power in the club. In part, the lack of change may be the result of the gendered organizational change's being temporary. However, more likely, gendered organizational change will take more than simply adding a woman to management's roster.[52]

The Lion's Den and Players: New Directions, Similar Outcomes

Using ethnographic and online chat site research, club practices can be compared over time and context. Although not perfectly equivalent, the new data provide a modest basis for evaluating the gendered organization of work, economic consequences, and broader constructions of gender in The Lion's Den. While there have been changes to the social organization of work and the gendered division of labor, constructions of gender remain largely unchanged. Patrons may be more or less pleased or displeased by the club's setup and services, but the common denominator remains the same: male patrons and workers foster a risky environment for women. Alongside major physical and personnel changes, The Lion's Den continues to reproduce familiar performances of masculinity fostering men's aggression. The website most likely draws from a particular subset of patrons—website users may be disproportionately regular patrons, those with a greater stake in the goings-on in the club, or those who display greater amounts of aggression than an occasional visitor. However, my previous ethnographic research on The Lion's Den suggests that the content of these posts is credible.[53] Furthermore, the analysis of Internet discussions shows that statements about aggression were not restricted to a particular type of man. Rather, various men displayed different performances of masculinity during and across visits to the club and the website. In short, the characterization of the club as a space where men can come in and try on different performances of masculinity—including aggression—holds.

The new performances available to strippers, including exchanges in the Champagne Room and lap dancing, have both positive and negative consequences. As a benefit, these new performances provide additional "products" and sources of income. However, lap dancing in particular places demands on strippers for greater physical contact with patrons. As strippers are compelled to do more in order to compete, new club rules detract from strippers' ability to informally set and collectively regulate their own and others' physical contact boundaries. Instead, club pressures shift the boundaries of stripping work and prostitution much closer. In addition, Players' establishment of a shift fee further taps strippers' financial resources. Nonetheless, strippers remain the first recipients of their profit from private dancing and retain control over their earnings; there were no postings to the contrary. In sum, website posts suggest continued gender paradoxes in which women's economic empowerment and disempowerment go hand in hand.

Reworking Strip Clubs

Given these changes, how might strip clubs create safer environments? The implications of this follow-up research suggest that if female workers desire increased safety and better treatment, solutions need to extend beyond the gendered organization of work. Based on web reports about Players' practices, putting a woman (or even a few women) into a position of power may not be enough to promote change. Change must affect all club workers. Transformations to the club might include greater support of female workers through management's enforcement of club rules and the promotion of positive norms regarding all women in the club. Management would also need to consistently hold aggressive male workers and patrons accountable for their transgressions. If clubs value a steady workforce, they might entice strippers to stick with a club by treating women with respect, understanding strippers as employees, paying them a regular wage, and providing benefits rather than taxing them with shift fees and fines. However, change must also affect patrons. Patrons should be encouraged to treat strippers and other female workers with respect, even in sexual play. This does not rule out playing with power roles, nor does it eliminate the explicit nature of club dialogue. It does, however, necessitate that such exchanges have recognized boundaries. Clubs must insist on behaviors that produce a safe environment for female workers and cultivate a reputation for strict responses in reaction to verbal and physical aggression. Perhaps if all of these tactics are employed simultaneously, they might help manufacture better workplaces.

Transforming the work environment is only one possible approach to changing strip clubs. At the other end of the spectrum, some participants in the sex work debates have called for eliminating clubs, emphasizing the rampant oppression, exploitation, and slavery in the sex industry.[54] Those who favor a more conservative anti-sex-work position might look at the aggression and violence toward women in The Lion's Den, under both Steve's and Players' ownership, and call for greater policing or outright elimination of strip clubs. Prior evidence suggests that policing strategies alone may have a limited effect if police and courts enact them.[55] As with prostitution, isolated efforts to shut down particular clubs will probably shift men's performances to other venues rather than alter their content.[56] Moreover, as analysis of Steve's practices makes clear, policing fails to fully protect women, even in clubs that support less physical contact between strippers and patrons. Outright elimination of stripping seems shortsighted at best. As we have seen from prostitution policies, outlawing sex work simply pushes practices elsewhere or underground, where women face even greater dangers of aggression and violence from men.[57]

Rather than scapegoating one industry or a differentiated set of men, what this research suggests is that we must address the larger social causes of violence and aggression toward women through rape culture and rape myths. The most important problems include continued valorization of hegemonic masculinity; cultural acceptance of discrimination; disrespect of women, racial, and sexual minorities; and a climate of sexual intolerance. There are important reasons to take discrimination and disrespect in this context seriously. Strip clubs provide a guide for unfettered constructions of masculinity. Behaviors that would be sanctioned or prohibited in other work sites, such as objectification of women, unwanted physical contact, and sexually explicit play, are commonplace. Despite legal and social strides made in other settings, the gendered organization of work in clubs like The Lion's Den provides a space for men's aggression and violence. Strip clubs become acceptable spaces for men to scapegoat a subgroup of women they deem expendable. Indeed, the consistency of men's aggression toward women in The Lion's Den four years after my ethnographic research implies that legal and social prohibitions do not extend beyond the particular settings the laws and gentlemanly conventions were designed to address. The fact that men can enter strip clubs with little regard for violence and aggression toward women suggests that we have yet to fully challenge the underlying causes of men's violence toward women. Men, however, are not the enemy. As studies of masculinity make clear, men do not uniformly occupy the same relationships to power; subordinated and marginalized masculinities exist alongside hegemonic forms.[58] Nonetheless, in strip clubs, all men have access to hegemonic performances. Because strip clubs are created for and patronized mostly by men, only with men's cooperation could these spaces be experienced differently.

To make real progress toward women's safety in strip clubs, discrimination and disrespect toward women, as well as racial and sexual minorities, must be addressed. As studies of discrimination demonstrate, we must consider identities through their intersections and relationships to each other.[59] Meaningful gains for all women will not be realized without gains for racial and sexual minorities. Discrimination in access to authority and power makes it difficult for female workers to challenge problematic working conditions. The stereotypes used in The Lion's Den that allege women's inability to be thoughtful, responsible adults are not products of this club or this industry alone. Though sex work is often ghettoized apart from other workplaces, these stereotypes are scripted products of a broader culture of gender inequality.

Finally, it is ironic, given how sex saturates our media, that we simultaneously live in a cultural climate of sexual intolerance inside and outside of the sex industry. This cultural ambivalence is demonstrated by the proliferation of strip clubs and explicit content in mainstream films and television that exist alongside the dominance of abstinence-only sex education. Clearly, sex sells, while sexual understanding does not. Sexual intolerance in The Lion's Den takes the form of institutionalized male homophobia and racism, as well as narrow-minded assumptions about women's roles, femininity, and embodiment. Continuing under Players' leadership, The Lion's Den is a hostile place for those who challenge the convention: strong, white, heterosexual men and compliant women. Some have argued that it is the very sale of sex that promotes intolerance.[60] Debates over sex work's content—sale of self or emotional/erotic labor with similarities to or differences from other emotional and physical labor—provoke heated debate.[61] However, eroticizing the sale of sex and power is not the problem. The problem is that the sex industry continues to promote gender inequality, racism, homophobia, and sizeism, as well as ambivalence about sex and sexuality. Instead, the industry could work toward creating broader norms that de-stigmatize sex for pleasure and fun in its various consensual forms. As well, strip clubs could work to humanize gender, race, bodies, sex, and sexuality. Alongside these kinds of industry and club-based reforms, broader social change may help foster safer spaces for women to work inside (and outside) of the sex industry.

Appendix 1

Researching The Lion's Den

"Is she attractive?" This was the question posed by a student's father upon learning that his son's professor carried out participant observation in a strip club. When the class laughed nervously at the student's comment, I should have responded by asking if this student's father was attractive, but I lacked the comedic timing and worried I might offend him. These kinds of inquiries have become routine, yet they often catch me off guard. There is something about the embodiment of sex work research that makes this study somewhat different from other forms of research I do. For example, I also study nursing assistants, but no one has ever asked me if I was a nursing assistant. No one cares about my physical appearance and how it may or may not relate to that work. Conversely, I am frequently asked if I have worked as a stripper. While this question has some merit, as it relates to insider/outsider debates in qualitative research,[1] it is more often asked in similar fashion to the attractiveness question—for titillation, and not for substance.

Yet, there is something to these questions. They are continual reminders of my experience. As a researcher, I was keenly aware of my physical presence in a potentially dangerous place. Each time I drove to the club, I would run through my list of ethnographer's equipment. Research tools: small notepad, pens, cassette recorder, and tapes—check. Safety items: cell phone, driver's license, credit card, and $20 cash in pocket—check. Everything I needed had to fit on my person since bags left unattended often came back short. Preparation was important so I could be smart about safety. This was, after all, The Lion's Den.

Entry into The Lion's Den

My introduction to this club came from Angela, a stripper and cocktail waitress, whom I met though a common friend while conducting exploratory interviews for this project. During our meeting, Angela mentioned there was an opening at her club for a cocktail waitress and expressed her willingness to vouch for me as a good worker. Gaining access to a research site is often made easier through connections,[2] and The Lion's Den was no exception. Typically, jobs there were passed between friends and acquaintances; jobs were less often given to persons unknown to the club or its workers. Since I had no prior connection to The Lion's Den or experience with strip club work, Angela's recommendation proved invaluable. My easy transition into club work and culture was due, at least in part, to my connection with her. She was well liked and trusted by all, including the club's owner-manager. Early on, I became known as "Angela's friend" or someone "Angela knew" and was tentatively accepted by association until I developed my own presence in the club.

Participant Observation, Interviews, and The Lion's Den's Employee/Entertainer Handbook

As an employee of the club, I worked as a cocktail waitress one seven-hour shift a week (typically on Thursdays, but also on other weekdays and weekends) for fourteen months. In addition to my scheduled shifts, I studied the club at other times for over five hundred hours of observation. Since I disclosed my plan to conduct research when I was hired, I could openly pursue my study. When conducting observations and working in the club, I took field notes both overtly and covertly using a pocket notebook—sometimes behind the bar, in the dressing rooms, or in the bathroom; other times sitting openly in the main room. I also tape-recorded observations while driving home and typed additional notes after each visit. I recorded my observations to produce "thick descriptions" of the club, its occupants, and its culture.[3]

Working in the club in addition to conducting in-depth interviews enabled me to build rapport and mutual trust with my coworkers, a vital part in facilitating interviews.[4] Given my familiarity with the club and its workers, I was able to make knowledgeable decisions regarding interviews, which include a variety of perspectives across age, duration of work, and type of employment. In choosing participants, I relied on informant interviewing that identified key perspectives, since "some interviews are more important than others because the respondent knows more, has better insight, or is more willing to share what he or she knows with the interviewer."[5] I interviewed over one-half of the club's employees: twenty-two women, including twenty-one strippers, five of whom were also working as cocktail waitresses and one who worked solely as a cocktail waitress; nine men employed as deejays, bartenders, bouncers, and doormen, four of whom were also patrons; and the owner-manager of the club. I also interviewed eight of the club's male patrons. These forty interviews were conducted face-to-face and tape-recorded, then transcribed verbatim and coded. See Table 3, beginning next page for the demographics covering all these participants.

I began patron interviews by asking them to describe The Lion's Den to someone who had never been there. Responses included the obvious: "It's a nude bar"; to personal connections: "It's my second home"; to descriptions of the club's offerings: "It's a clean club"; and evaluations: "It used to be one of the best." Asking for patrons' descriptions served as an icebreaker and enabled me to access all sorts of information. Since interviews are always coauthored, semistructured questions helped to promote collaboration and the inclusion of ideas and information previously unknown to me.[6] For example, Jack, the patron who mentioned the club's past reputation, provided a detailed history of famous feature acts, adult-magazine models, and film actresses who appeared at the club. I also learned of his informal work driving feature performers to the airport or helping them carry trunks full of clothing, shoes, and makeup to their dressing rooms. The remainder of the interviews covered club experiences and perceptions, as well as the effect club attendance had on their lives, work, and romantic relationships.

Of the patrons I approached for interviews, only a few declined. Those who did had a common characteristic: they were men who would only agree to speak with me in exchange for dates or nude dances. Though this might have been a ploy to avoid talking, I always explained why I could not fulfill their requests and asked several times for an interview before deciding whether to ask again or move on to another possible participant. This process ensured that I did not prematurely screen out potential interviewees. Recruiting participants entailed a delicate balance since too much persistence might work against my good standing with club management (thus jeopardizing the entire project), especially if I alienated customers during the course of my research. The others who were not included in the interview portion of this research were those men with reputations among the staff of being verbally or physically aggressive. In addition to safety concerns, I knew my time was best spent on more willing participants. Instead of direct questioning, my method for studying difficult and aggressive men was through observations, interactions, and secondhand accounts of their behaviors.

TABLE 3. *Participant Demographics*

Participant	Status	Age	Race	Education	Relationship	No. of children
Amelia	Stripper	21	White, Russian	In college	Cohabiting	
Angela	Cocktail waitress, stripper	21	White, Portuguese	In college	Single	
Charlie	Patron	38	White	Bachelor's degree	Single	
Craig	Patron	32	White	High school diploma	Relationship ending	1
Daria	Stripper	18	White	High school student	Cohabiting	
Darrel	Bouncer	38	African American	High school diploma	Cohabiting	3
Dawn	Stripper	19	White	Some high school	Cohabiting	
Destiny	Stripper	20	African American	In college	Single	
Evangelina	Cocktail waitress	22	White, Greek	Some college	Single	
Faith	Stripper	37	White	High school diploma	Divorced	1
Fiona	Stripper	19	White	Some high school	Single	2
Frank	Bouncer, doorman	56	White	Some high school	Married	2
Jack	Patron	33	White	High school diploma	Single	
Jade	Stripper	24	Latina	In college	Single	
James	Bartender, bouncer, patron	23	White	Some college	Cohabiting	3
Jeff	Patron	56	White	Master's degree	Divorced	2
Jen	Cocktail waitress, stripper	26	White	Some college	Cohabiting	3
Kelly	Cocktail waitress, stripper	29	White	Associate's degree	Maried	1
Layla	Stripper	21	White	Some college	Single	
Leo	Deejay	20	White	In college	Single	

Participant	Status	Age	Race	Education	Relationship	No. of children
Marcus	Deejay, patron	26	White, American Indian	Some college	Cohabiting	4
Marissa	Cocktail waitress, stripper	20	White	High school diploma	Cohabiting	
Marlon	Patron	29	White	In college	Dating	
Mindy	Stripper	19	White	Some high school	Cohabiting	
Ned	Bartender, bouncer	36	White	Some junior college	Single	
Nina	Stripper	18	White	Fashion merchandising degree	Single	
Robin	Stripper	23	White	GED	Single	
Roxanne	Cocktail waitress, stripper	33	White	High school diploma	Divorcing	
Shane	Patron	29	White	High school diploma	Single/ dating	1
Stella	Stripper	22	White	GED	Cohabiting	1
Steve	Owner- manager	36	White	Bachelor's degree	Cohabiting	1
Summer	Stripper	20	White	Some college	Cohabiting	
Tamara	Stripper	25	White	High school diploma	Married	
Ted	Bartender, bouncer, door-man, patron	33	White	In college	Single	
Tess	Stripper	25	White	Some college	Single	2
Tim	Deejay, patron	19	White	In college	Single	
Travis	Deejay	53	White	Bachelor's degree	Married	4
Vivian	Stripper	21	White	GED	Married	4
Walter	Patron	44	White	High school diploma	Separated	3
Winston	Patron	54	White	Some postgraduate education	Divorced, widowed	

Almost all of the club's workers agreed to be interviewed. I approached strippers, cocktail waitresses, bartenders, bouncers, deejays, doormen, and the club's owner-manager. Two strippers declined because they said they feared that an interview might make it difficult for them to face their work. Since at least some of the women were barely coping with the intense demands of stripping, these refusals were not surprising. In other cases, strippers approached me and asked to participate after learning about my project. Many women at The Lion's Den managed their work experiences by talking with others, so interviewing became an extension of conversations they already had within the club. With one exception, all of the male workers in the club happily agreed to an interview. The man who declined was a doorman who was talkative with other men in the club but did not interact with many of the women. The housemom was not included in my sample since her position was limited to scheduling, and she did not spend much time in the club.

Strippers and club workers were first asked to describe their work. Some mirrored back, "It's work, it's a job"; others emphasized the entertainment component; still others highlighted the sometimes-lucrative earnings. Though not always the first item mentioned, the promise of making money came up in all of my conversations. Other structured, or fixed, questions included participants' impressions of the club, relationships with coworkers, and interactions with patrons, followed by more personal questions regarding the effects of strip club work and attendance on their self-concept and interpersonal relationships. Many of the interviews lasted about an hour, though some went more than two. I encouraged participants to actively choose convenient locations for their interviews, so the sites included their homes, local restaurants, and private rooms within the club during slow daytime shifts.

During this time, I also secured access to the club's *Employee/Entertainer Handbook,* a twenty-page document outlining the roles and responsibilities of all club workers.[7] Steve, the club's owner-manager, created the handbook. Its cover features a lion's head, referencing artwork in the club that depicts a lion lying down with his tail in the grip of a buxom woman reclining near the lion's rear. This image prompted me to dub the club "The Lion's Den." Not only does the title reflect club iconography of men as kings of the jungle, but it also captures the club's often-hostile environment for women. At the bottom of the title page is a note informing all to read and prepare to be tested on the handbook's material, though an exam never materialized. Beyond the title page, the *Employee/Entertainer Handbook* reflects management's perspective on workers' performances within the club. It begins with a brief introduction by Steve in which he asks for changes including more professionalism and teamwork from all. He assures readers that following the handbook's instructions will lead to profitability for the club, as well as its workers. Despite the occasional positive spin, the manual's overall tone is sarcastic and harsh, particularly toward strippers. Take, for example, the following passage:

> I have never met a bigger bunch of whiners in my life! Even the customers notice it, and believe me they DON'T want to hear it. . . . NO LONGER will we hear "SIT THE FUCK DOWN" "THERE'S NO MONEY HERE I'M GOING HOME" "THAT'S NOT MY JOB" "I'LL BE UP IN A MIN-UTE" "THAT GUYS AN ASSHOLE" "MY BOYFRIEND BROKE UP W/ ME" "MY RENTS DUE" "I DIDN'T DO THAT" and of course "SORRY STEVE" there probably is 100's of others but I don't have enough paper, I hope you get the point. (emphasis in original)[8]

In sum, I mapped out the gendered organization of work in The Lion's Den through multiple data sources—participant observations, interviews, and club texts, including the handbook and posted notices—all of which allowed me to evaluate the accuracy of my findings and make informed decisions regarding this research.[9] I analyzed the information collected from these sources using a grounded theory approach,[10] which determines that concepts should emerge directly from the data—in this case, transcribed interviews, observational field notes, and text from the handbook and notices. I coded the text from these sources to identify patterns and concepts within and across materials. I then organized these patterns and grouped them together to map out central ideas and theoretical propositions in the research. The main themes were identified based on their overarching frequency and importance across interviews and club texts. In doing so, I paid careful atten-tion to both agreement and divergence with regard to relationships between particular concepts and themes.

Identity, Disclosure, and Experience

When I interviewed for the waitressing position in the early spring of 2001, I made it clear to Steve that I wanted to conduct research. While I knew this acknowledgment might jeopardize my ability to gain access to the club, I believed that ethically and practically a covert strategy would only cre-ate problems. As I had hoped, my decision to spell out my intentions paid off and built a solid foundation on which I could openly pursue my study. I will never be sure why Steve gave me full access to the club and why he participated in my research. I can only speculate that it was the combination of a lack of perceived threat, an insider recommendation from someone he trusted, our shared Midwestern U.S. background, or a particular interest in research that led Steve to support my work. In addition, a climate of informality was ever-present in the club. Five minutes after my initial job interview, I was on the club floor training with Angela as a cocktail waitress. Since The Lion's Den had no uniforms at that time, my casual dress sufficed while I shadowed Angela on her rounds. This quick transition from interview to training was my first indication that The Lion's Den often operated casually with new recruits, quickly changing them into workers because of perpetual labor shortages.

Patrons often asked me why I was working in the club. When asked, I disclosed that I was conducting research. I informed familiar patrons and all of the club's workers about my study. Most responded with mild interest but quickly shifted the conversation to something else, so my introductory explanations were often brief. No one responded negatively to my disclosure. While my participant observation surely influenced the goings-on around me, I did my best to limit my involvement when it might have disrupted recording observations and experiences. At first, when customers and employees made racist and sexist remarks, I had difficulty stopping myself from interrupting in disagreement. After the first couple of instances, I decided not to interrupt but to listen or ask questions so they would not censor themselves during conversations they had with others when I was nearby. I soon learned I had little cause for concern; racist and sexist conversations went on despite any verbal or nonverbal protests I might have made. In short, my presence and response mattered little as a disruption. In fact, antiracist and antisexist responses I made often led to my being dismissed as a college student.

While in some ways I tried not to disrupt, in other ways I know my presence stood out. While I was initially accepted as "Angela's friend," I later developed a persona of my own. For one, due to the cigarette smoke in the club, I wore glasses (rather than contact lenses). Since I was the only female wearing glasses that weren't designed to block out the sun, I was often affectionately called "teacher" or "librarian" and often had the Van Halen song "Hot for Teacher" dedicated to me. The other way I stood out was through my clothing. When I first began working at The Lion's Den there were no required uniforms for club employees, and I arrived in t-shirts and jeans. At about the time the *Employee/Entertainer Handbook* came out, Steve began requiring staff to wear uniforms:

UNIFORMS or reasonable facsimiles thereof are NOT optional. I want to see the men in Black [Lion's Den] shirt, the girls [cocktail waitresses] in Pink tank or crop tops and since the club is going more up-scale I want to see the deejay's dress more upscale. What I don't want to see is hats, ripped jeans, shorts, tank tops etc. (emphasis in original)[11]

In one of very few acts of resistance, I refrained from wearing my uniform until chided into compliance. I eventually adopted a modest version of the club's pastel-pink tank top and black pants. My choice of clothing helped signal my desire to avoid competition with the other women working in the club. While the owner-manager and a bartender would often joke with me, asking "cereal or granola?" as a comment on my modest student dress, the ribbing was always playful and kind. While I was accepted into the club, I did not pass as a conventional worker.

As an outsider, I had the challenge of establishing my own presence but also the advantage of seeing the club through critical eyes that took little for granted. Embodying multiple roles during my research (cocktail waitress, doctoral student, feminist, researcher, girlfriend, and white, middle-class female, to name a few) necessitated self-awareness regarding my identities. I knew that one might be privileged over another at various times, though all were always present.[12] Being open about my work in each context helped, and, as a result, mostly my different roles were not in conflict, though the long late hours took their toll over time. The substantial burdens lay in the physical and emotional demands of the work—the countless trays of drinks I transported with a smile when the club was crowded, as well as the exhaustion that comes with physical and emotional labor. Along with these conventional aspects of service work, I also experienced the overt sexism that was part and parcel of women's work in The Lion's Den. Given the context and my anticipation of these comments, they failed to rattle me.

While I had fears of aggression and violence from men, I did not directly experience any threatening or dangerous encounters during my time in the club. My fears were made ever more real after learning that two women were assaulted during my time in the club. One was digitally raped onstage. I directly confronted the associated contradictions with strip club work—men I knew as polite and benign were characterized by other female workers' reports as aggressive and violent, insensitive and insecure, expressing wide-ranging behaviors on any given shift. Despite these conflicting accounts, I developed sensitivity and compassion for many of the men in the club, in particular, the workers and regular patrons. Some of the regular patrons and employees shared their fears of loneliness, betrayal, and failure with me. As recorded in my field notes, for example, Stuart, who self-identified as a little person, struggled in his interactions with average-sized women. Coming to the club provided a safer space than a conventional bar, precisely because he could anticipate kinder and friendlier treatment. Through such conversations, I began to understand the experience of the club from the patrons' perspectives. I could see the vulnerability some men experienced in their relationships with women. I often heard about men's disappointment with their jobs, financial problems, and beliefs that the club fueled their disillusionment. This knowledge continued to humanize the men for me and enabled me to recognize important differences and similarities among them.

With male coworkers, I experienced a sense of camaraderie; they complimented my hard work and provided a helping hand with patrons or various tasks. I was especially thankful for the help I received cleaning up beer bottles and glasses at the end of my shifts. By and large, I was welcomed into the club's community. I was invited into strippers' homes for interviews, offered help in finding research participants, and always asked how my work was going. The interest of club workers and patrons helped maintain my momentum throughout this project—they were an invaluable source of encouragement and support. I found them to be accessible, generous, frank, and knowledgeable regarding my many, sometimes deeply personal, questions.

Appendix 2

Participant Descriptions of Life and Work

Participants are the lifeblood of ethnographies; without them, research would not be possible. Nonetheless, apart from life-history interviewing, most interview analyses spend little time exploring individual biographies beyond each person's contribution to the research project as a whole. As with many such studies, the individual narratives of participants in this research are considered together in terms of their relationship to concepts and theories. As a result, we learn little about each contributor's personal story. The forty participants in this research warrant individual consideration to explore the important themes in their lives that relate to their work in The Lion's Den. To orient the reader, in this appendix I explore each participant's entrance into the industry, as well as the consequences that work in The Lion's Den had for their lives. These narratives paint detailed pictures of the individuals who contributed to this book. Age and duration of work are as recorded at the time of each interview.

Amelia: After leaving Russia for the United States with a work visa, Amelia first became a housekeeper, laboring hard for little pay. Speaking with a strong Russian accent, this twenty-one-year-old, white, student stripper explained how she began working in the club three to four days a week for several months. Her American boyfriend first introduced her to stripping. Deciding to stay with her boyfriend and begin school, she asked if he would bring her to The Lion's Den: "I wanted to see what this job's about. . . . I'd never been in a strip club, ever." During her first visit, she watched the other strippers and described being "shocked." She explained, "I never thought . . . I would be able do it. . . . I brought my bathing suit [*laughs*]; this was the only thing that I had. And they asked, 'You can do it?' And I said, 'I don't know.' I never did it before. I'd just danced in a disco center." Describing why she continued to work in the club, Amelia emphasized the money and kindness she received from men. She left the job "sometimes for weeks" only to return, "thinking, 'How else can I make this type of money?'" In her words, "It's pretty dirty at this level. . . . I don't see the cream of this society—not the best part, but some of [the patrons] are very nice. Some people brought me Russian CDs and songs. One man taped old movies for me because he knows that I like old movies." Despite her overwhelmingly negative tone, the tension between the costs and rewards of this work were apparent and were no doubt shaped by her citizenship status and a desire to have lucrative work she could balance with college.

Angela: Angela was a twenty-one-year-old, white, single college student who worked as a cocktail waitress and a stripper for a year and a half. "[I] was in debt really, really bad, and my guy friends up here used to go to The Lion's Den. . . . I'd heard of it but I never, never thought of being a stripper. It's just something—I never thought I'd have the self-confidence to do it. It's just something I never thought of." Her friends explained that The Lion's Den had waitresses in addition to strippers, so she decided to check it out. When she arrived at the club, the doorman told her they didn't need any more waitresses. Instead, he suggested she consider dancing. She responded with a laugh, not taking him seriously. He proposed that she stay and watch the goings-on in the club to see for herself if this was something she could do. After watching the dancers, she remarked, "There's no way I would ever get up there and do that!" Ultimately, she joined the club first as a waitress and only later became a stripper. Angela's perspective changed with the increasing money and compliments that eventually drew her onto the stage. She became one of the club's most popular strippers. Despite how lucrative and sometimes self-affirming stripping was, Angela insisted, "I'm not going to be stripping in a year. . . . The plan [is] to find a better job," after she finished school. Stripping was a source of trouble, because her conservative family did not understand or approve of her work. Though she told her friends about her work and insisted she was "not ashamed of it," Angela shared a certain amount of ambivalence. For example, a former boyfriend used to announce her work to others, causing her a good deal of discomfort: "When I was with my ex-boyfriend and I met a few of his friends, he used to say, 'Yeah my girlfriend's in college; she's a stripper.' That used to make me mad. I'm not a stripper—I'm a college student. [Stripping is] my job. It's not who I am." Angela's ambivalence about stripping coupled with her post-college plans made her days in the industry seem numbered.

Charlie: Charlie was a thirty-eight-year-old, white, single man who self-identified as a computer developer by virtue of his enrollment in a computer-training workshop. He described the club he attended two days a week as "a sad place." Asked why, he responded: "Look at the lives of some of the people in here. What they do for the money and stuff like that. . . . It seems like most of them are on their way not into a very profitable or meaningful life." Living with and caring for his ailing mother after his father's death, Charlie made the club a fixture in his life, one that provided a convenient "escape" proximate to his home and work. Candidly, Charlie offered that the club provided a source of comparison that changed the way he viewed his life. "This offers everything I don't want somewhere else [*laughs*]. . . . Maybe I [come into the club] to realize that my life isn't so bad when I take a look at other individuals out there. I mean, granted, I have to take care of my mom. [But] maybe this isn't so bad; I say to look at my life compared to others." Charlie's ambivalence about the club, the strippers, and his patronage resonated throughout his interview.

Craig: Craig was a trailer repairman. He attributed his occasional visits to the club to one of the bartenders, who was a good friend. Despite his personal connections, Craig's interest in the club extended beyond stopping by to see the bartender. He was drawn to the possibility of people watching, as well as the anonymity strip clubs provide. In particular, Craig enjoyed observing interactions between dancers and patrons: "I think that some dancers are extraordinary, and, if they're really good, then they're good at judging their clients. They can get a sense of what everybody wants, because everybody's looking for something different. Sometimes it's as interesting to watch the guys in the bar." Describing himself as a thirty-two-year-old white father of one in a "failing relationship," Craig said strip clubs appealed to him when he "was really depressed" and "always just trying to get out of the house." He explained, "I didn't want to be around anyone I knew, because my friends are weird. They always want to talk when they're depressed, but when I'm depressed they're like, 'Oh look at the time.'" By contrast, strip clubs provided predictable, minimal interactions that also made possible no-strings-attached companionship.

Daria: Daria was an eighteen-year-old, white, high school senior and traveling stripper who had been working two days a week for the past four months. She described herself as someone who was "into drama," making stage work that involved acting a good fit. Daria was drawn to stripping because of connections through her sister, who also worked as a dancer. When she first started, Daria was told she would make lots of money. While the money had been good, she explained that the lure was part fiction and part reality. The money was not always easy, and there was "lots of bad stuff that goes along with it." Asked if any of her friends or family know about her work, she laughed: "Most of my really close friends know. I'm still in high school, so I try to keep it on the down low 'cause, you know kids, a lot of people when you say 'stripper' or 'exotic dancer,' porn comes to mind. I'm not an escort service." In addition to hiding her work from many of her schoolmates, Daria kept her stripping a secret from her parents. Because she had a sister in the industry, she knew her parents would not react positively. They "almost accept" her sister's work because "she has done a lot of stuff," and "it doesn't shock them." There was a different story, however, when it came to Daria: "I would never tell my dad, because he's a strict Roman Catholic, same with my mom. . . . If I had told them, I think my dad would have a heart attack. . . . I hate lying to my dad. I love my dad. If he ever found out, it would break his heart." While chronologically young, Daria presented herself as aged beyond her years.

Darrel: After Darrel lost his job as a security guard, the club provided much-needed paid employment. He described himself as someone who was "trying to get [his] life together." A thirty-eight-year-old, African American bouncer, Darrel had worked in the club three days a week for three months. He concealed the location of his work from his live-in girlfriend. He explained, "I tell her I work at a bar; I call it The Spot Room." When asked, "Is it hard for you?" he replied, "No, believe me, if the truth comes out—I'll say we needed money, I got a job, it's a nice job. I'd prefer a day job, but I can't get that, and you got to get what you can get—can't be picky. I'm happy because all the other bars you go to they don't even need bouncers, or security work, what have you, whatever you want to call it." Darrel's newness and optimism was striking when compared with the cynicism reflected by his long-employed male counterparts. Darrel, by contrast, registered few complaints. He explained with a laugh, "Like I say . . . everybody's crazy, but I love it; it's a good crazy, not a hurtful crazy." That said, he also had serious concerns about working conditions. When asked what he liked least about the work, he explained, "The hours. Like I said, I just need a job, and this is a job. If you're a single man, you've got it made. . . . I'm a family man, and this is a nightmare, but it's a good nightmare to me, because I'm working."

Dawn: Dawn, a nineteen-year-old, white stripper, had been working in the club four days a week for a little over a year. Living on her own since the age of fifteen, Dawn found stripping to be a lucrative way of supporting herself. Initially, she was drawn to the images of stripping in television and film: "Before I started dancing, I wanted to try it. I wanted to go to a dance club and see what it was. I was curious. I wanted to see if it was like what it was on the TV, if it was dramatic. [If] everybody's lifestyle inside the club was dramatic, and if everything was like it was in the movies. It is, in a way, but it isn't." She was adamant that stripping would not be a career; she planned to continue work for another year until her live-in boyfriend finished school. Her relationship and desire for a family seemed to influence this choice. She explained: "If you ever wanted to have a family, you wouldn't want to be a dancer." When asked "Why not?" she replied: "It's not a bad thing, but you want to have a say in your relationship. If you're out there dancing for guys naked and stuff, I feel like you don't have much of a say in the relationship." She continued: "With my boyfriend, he's cool with it. But there's times when I don't want him to go—go out to bars and stuff because I'm not with him. And he's like, 'But you go out and dance for a bunch of guys naked!' And then you think about it, and you're like, I guess I really don't have the place to say. I don't want to feel like that."

Destiny: Destiny, a twenty-year-old, African American, single stripper, had been working in the club two days a week for five months. She worried about her work becoming a "trap." As she explained: "You get a taste of the money, and you're like yea-yea." Despite the lure of economic rewards, stripping was incompatible with the rest of her life, particularly her and her family's religion. She explained: "I pray to God for forgiveness, and God knows I'm not doing it as a living. I'm doing it because I won't get financial aid from the government, and I've got to get the money somehow." Both her religion and personal modesty made the club a challenging place for her. In one story, she explained: "One guy, he said, 'I love Black pussy,' and I'm like, 'Whoa!' When I first started, I almost ran off the stage because I was so shy, and I used to blush." In response, the male club employees advised her "to stop being so shy." They reasoned that, to patrons, "it might be cute at first, or whatever, but after a while, you know they're going to start saying, 'What's wrong with her?'" Angered by their reaction, she said, "You try to get up here with some six-inch heels on, with a string up your butt, and try to move this way and that way and have people cuss at you and try to blow smoke on your coochie and stuff like that. . . . You try to do that for eight hours and see how it takes a toll on you!" Destiny was, for a time, the only African American dancer in the predominantly white club. When asked why she chose to work in a white club, as opposed to a more integrated or predominantly African American club, she explained that it helped her keep her secret and reduced her worries since "not a lot of non-white people come into the club."

Evangelina: Evangelina supplemented her college work-study income by cocktail waitressing. A twenty-two-year-old, white woman, she had been working in the club one day a week for seven months. Though she earned one week's income in one day's work, her life in the club was troubled, both because of the working conditions and because she kept her job a secret. Her boyfriend supported her work in the club but insisted she promise never to dance. While she disliked her boyfriend's double standard, Evangelina also felt that stripping was not for her. When asked if she would recommend her work to others, she offered a laundry list of complaints: "Every Saturday you come in here and the music is so loud, and it's like a cave. It's so dark that you feel like it's nighttime. It could be beautiful out, and you feel like it's a shitty day because you're just in the dark all day long. I'm kind of glad that I only work one day. I feel like if I did that all the time, I'd just have a shitty week." Cynical about men before she began working in the club, Evangelina's feelings became even more entrenched over time. In her words, "I get pissed off at guys. I'm like a guy-hater." Most upsetting to her were "disgusting" men her father's age who propositioned her or brought their sons to the club to meet her.

Faith: Faith, at thirty-seven, was the oldest stripper working in The Lion's Den. A white, divorced mother of one, she was a traveling stripper who had been working two days a week for five months. She started stripping five years before, when she could not find a job, and despite her love for the exercise and dance involved, she wanted to "get done." Although she still conveyed excitement about the physicality of dancing, she explained that she lost her ability to really connect with patrons. To her, what mattered in a performance were "eye contact" and a "smile," two things she could not bring herself to do "right now." Exhausted, she said, "That's why I don't make as much. The head games—I don't do it anymore. I can't. Faith's dead, Faith's gone. She's retired; she doesn't want to do it anymore." Using the third person, Faith distanced herself from the work she had come to dislike in many ways. In her words, "It's just not me because I'm very conservative. I'm thirty-seven, and I've slept with ten people in my whole life. I mean, I married once for eight years, and I was engaged to one for five, so I'm very conservative when it comes to that kind of stuff. Plus, sticking my coochie into some strange guy's face isn't my idea of fun [*laughs*]." When asked why she continued to dance, she explained, "I do this because it's the only way I can make a living as a single mother and have time with my kids."

Fiona: Fiona was a tough-talking, nineteen-year-old, white, single mother of two. She had been working as a traveling stripper two days a week for five and a half months. Early in her interview she exclaimed that she stripped because she "like[s] fucking with people!" Though at times maintaining this sense of humor, Fiona's strong dislike of men was palpable through her descriptions of patrons: "I didn't think guys were that bad until I started being a dancer. Men are fucking pigs—that's all there is to it. It just took this job to make me realize it." Elaborating, she continued: "Get some dirty old man in here, 'Look at that young pussy!' 'I like young pussy!' 'I'd like to take you home with me.' 'You're young enough to be my daughter!' Shit like that. Just sick, perverted old men come in the place." Despite her aversion, as a stripper Fiona needed to pay attention to men's "little fetishes," "strange little quirks," and "what turns them on, what turns them off" because "in a job like this, . . . if you let the little things slip by, then you're not right, you lose money." While putting up a tough front, Fiona softened when she described the difficulties of her work: "It's hard going from being [Kathy] at home, having my life here, coming down to [another state] and playing somebody totally different."

Frank: Frank, a white doorman and bouncer, was out of work until a friend talked with the former owner about hiring him. Eight years later, he was a fixture during daytime shifts, working as a doorman six days a week. Asked about his work, he offered: "I enjoy my job! One reason—I get a lot of people in here, and I enjoy talking with them." Frank was upbeat and had a fatherly presence in the club. For new dancers, Frank acted as a coach, some-times sitting at the stage and providing instructions on how to move. Since the club was often quiet when he worked, he developed his own batch of regular patrons. A family man with two children, Frank was happily married to a woman who "trusted" him and knew he would not "cheat on her." Rather than sharing worries about strip club work, Frank and his wife had more practical concerns: "She'd mainly like me to get a job with more security, like with insurance. But now she just got a job with insurance, so we're all set. That covers that problem." The club provided an important opportunity since Frank, at age fifty-six, did not see other job options, given that he had "only a few years to retire." He lamented the age discrimination he experienced as an older worker: "Nobody wants to train you for a job now to keep me for four or five years or three years, you know. It's not worth it to them, and you can't blame them. They say they're not going to discriminate. They are." In addi-tion to his concerns about health insurance, Frank was heavily focused on his physical health. He often discussed weightlifting with other men in the club. His interest in staying healthy prompted him to arrive at work each day with a cooler full of bottled water. Since most other employees drank soda and alcoholic drinks from the bar, his healthy practices stood out.

Jack: Jack first came to The Lion's Den for his twenty-first birthday. At age thirty-three, this white patron replied, "It's my second home, basically." As a regular patron, he said, "[I spend] more time than I should, anywhere from three to four days a week or nights. It's like a family to me. I mean, I know all the bartenders, all the deejays, and everybody, the waitresses. To me, they're like a family, and I don't mind doing them favors if they're needed." While never an employee—Jack was a factory worker—he was compensated in cash, drinks, and free entry for providing assistance to various club workers. This informal exchange fostered Jack's feelings of the club as "home" and the workers as "family." It also gave Jack special access to performers without having to pay. Years ago when the club brought in feature performers (porn and adult-magazine stars who gave special stage shows), Jack assisted in a number of ways. In all, he felt like he spent more time in the club than he should. He openly remarked, "Well, let's put it this way, instead of doing something productive at one point in time, I sit here and half the time I drink beer and just hang out. I don't do anything." Nevertheless, over the years he cited some changes: "With time, it changes. I got older. With age, you always change a little. My habits are still the same, but you get a little wiser and a little dumber in certain aspects. I don't sit at the stage. How am I dumber? I still come."

Jade: Lured into stripping by friends who found it lucrative, Jade, a Latina dancer, found stripping to be a mixed bag: "It's true sometimes, but like I said, sometimes you get bad days when you don't even make that much. [My friends] made it seem like you could get a lot of money all the time. They did make a lot of money, actually. So I believed them." Jade joined the club after injuring her back in a car accident and having trouble finding suitable work. In The Lion's Den, she was able to skip shifts when she suffered chronic pain, without losing her job. She was regularly working four days a week. Despite the job's flexibility, keeping it a secret from her mother and brothers was a continual source of worry: "Sometimes I feel like . . . telling my mother, but I . . . fear that she'll get mad, and she won't want to ever see me again. . . . She would never approve of me doing this. She sees this as prostitution. . . . I feel that what I do with my life should be up to me because I'm not a baby anymore. I'm twenty-three, but it's my mother and I understand [*laughs*]." She continued: "Sometimes it bothers me because I feel like I'm doing something wrong, but then again I think that I need money." The money she made stripping helped finance her college tuition.

James: James first came to strip clubs when he was "really underage." At twenty-three, this white bartender and bouncer explained, "I was never really big into these types of clubs. I used to come here because my friends wanted to come here. I hang out in strip clubs now because I know people that work in them; that's the only reason why I hang out here." Two years before, he took over working as a bartender four days a week, a job he liked because he got to listen to patrons' problems. First working in the club as a bouncer, James still filled in bouncing on Wednesday nights. Overall, the job worked out well since he lived close by, and it had not caused much trouble in his relationship. In his words, his girlfriend had been to the club once and "has no problems with me working here at all." Nevertheless, her friends presented a different perspective, telling her, "He's got to be cheating on you!" In response, he snorted, "Why? Just because I work in a strip club? I mean it's just a job. At any job you can cheat. . . . All my friends ask my why I don't, and it's like, first of all I'm afraid of disease, and I'd never bring anything home. Seriously, I'm wicked paranoid." Though his emphasis on disease rather than cheating might not have brought comfort to his girlfriend, the job had been important in supporting his growing family. The bottom line, he explained, was that his girlfriend "knows I need a job, and I need to make money—we have three kids."

Jeff: Jeff visited the club twice a week, "because it's like *Cheers!*" Indeed, in The Lion's Den, everyone soon knew Jeff's name. The draw for him was the ease of interaction he had with others. By contrast, in other bars, he explained, "You might be here, and you'd be serving us beer, but you've got twelve other customers, and you've got to hustle tables, so you really don't have the time" to visit. "If you come [here] on your own, even the doorman will come over and talk with you. There will be social interaction if I want social interaction." As a fifty-six-year-old, white, divorced man with two grown children, Jeff found companionship in the club that he easily accessed by himself: "There are a couple of other places I can go where there's sports on the TV, but you don't go on your own; you probably don't stay on your own." Regular patronage was not without its hazards for Jeff. An engineer, his preference was for strippers with a college background, like himself. Women who viewed dancing as a "career" and those who were "uncomfortable" onstage made him less "comfortable" because they highlighted how tough the job was emotionally and physically, especially over time.

Jen: Jen never imagined she would work as a stripper. When she was a child, her father owned a strip club. Though she did not live with her dad, she continued to hear a great deal about stripping from her mother: "All I ever heard was what whores strippers were and very, very negative stuff about them, continually." Her mother's stories were influential. In her words, "I was so brainwashed by my mother so I could not see any good in it at all." At nineteen, she needed money for school and could not find other work, so she planned to "try it for the summer." "Once I started waitressing, I saw these girls and I was like, 'Wow, they're not that bad.' But, I do not advise anybody to get involved in the industry, either. Very negative atmosphere, negative environment, really breaks you down. I don't know any dancers who are happy." Now twenty-six, this white cocktail waitress and stripper had been working for three to four days per week for almost seven years to put herself through college. She first worked in The Lion's Den as a cocktail waitress, a job she landed through a friend who worked in the club. However, at the time of our interview, the friend was no longer working there. Like other dancers, Jen opted to work in another state to avoid club interactions with people she knew. She explained: "At this point, everybody knows that I'm a dancer, but there's a big difference between them knowing it and giving me a dollar to look at me. It's kind of personal."

Kelly: Kelly started working in the club because she "needed money." After getting married and having a child, she decided to quit stripping: "Giving up dancing—I wanted to give it up anyway, but I danced to that point where it burns you out after a while. Like I said, it's good for a while, the money's good, but sometimes it can't be all about money [*laughs*]." Though Kelly liked dancing and the money associated with it, she found the emotional labor draining. When she decided to leave, she was concerned about its being a permanent decision. "I left, ... got married, and had my son. ... I didn't want to quit and then say I'm going to come back. I wanted to make sure my life was good enough that I would not have to come back. But my husband makes very good money, so I had that option ... if I wanted to stay home [or] I wanted to work." Later deciding to take a part-time job outside of the stripping industry, she struggled with rationalizing the cost of daycare since it ate up most of her earnings. When she and her husband learned about an opening for a cocktail waitress, she decided to come back. At twenty-nine, this white dancer's return to strip club work made sense because, in her words, "I already danced so I already knew what I had do and stuff to deal with the people and everything. ... So I [cocktail waitress] because I make good money, and I don't have to work a lot." She had been working in the club three days a week for the past four years.

Layla: Layla began stripping because she heard she would "catch on quick" and make "so much [money] a year." Over two months, this twenty-one-year-old, white stripper learned quickly that stripping was hard work and did not guarantee a certain level of earnings. Layla's ambivalence about her work went beyond the ups and downs in income. On the one hand, she reasoned, "I know that my work is clean. I know that I ain't doing anything wrong by what I'm doing." On the other hand, she admitted, "I wouldn't be doing this if I didn't have to—I wouldn't be, 'cause I've always looked at strippers and been, like, 'Eeew.' But I'm doing it now, so [*pause*] it's definitely made me more comfortable with myself." In addition to more personal comfort, she described her family as "all cool" with her stripping. When Layla told her family about her job as a stripper, her mother's only request was that she work in another town: "I was all worried because my mom is really Christian and stuff like that. I finally told them, and she's cool with it. She doesn't care. She's like, 'It's your own business.' She just asked that I don't do it in her hometown, you know, obviously, but that's about it. She understands because I've got to take care of myself." Stripping two days a week was helping Layla pay for college.

Leo: Leo "took this job because [he is] a real deejay." At age twenty, this white deejay found club work matched his college schedule: "I work in nightclubs and whatnot, and I was really bored during the day in the summer, and I was like, 'I just want to deejay; I don't want to do anything besides that.' This is the only place I can do it." Asked how working in The Lion's Den had affected his life, Leo explained: "There's different impacts. . . . I dated on a girl for a year and a half. I met her in between. . . . She didn't like the image of it." Leo recognized that his ex-girlfriend was not alone in her negative impressions of the stripping industry: "I don't feel sleazy about what I do, but, image-wise, it is kind of sleazy, not by my views, but by society's views. I've lied about it many a time." Having worked in the club for eight months, Leo had concerns about how a strip club job would play out on his résumé. Continuing his refrain about others' impressions of strip clubs, he puzzled, "I'm in school now, and I'm supposed to make something of myself, and it's kind of one of those things you have to wonder if it's really a good investment in your future." Leo's worries were somewhat unusual since men did not often share fears about the club's stigma impacting their lives. Despite concerns about the general public's learning about his job, he told his parents, though not his sisters: "My mom and dad know I work here, but my sisters don't; they're very young, and I'm very overprotective of them."

Marcus: Once out of work, Marcus, a twenty-six-year-old, white and American Indian deejay, got his job in the club through his girlfriend, who was working as a stripper. The club needed a deejay, and he had some experience, which, coupled with an insider recommendation to the manager, got him hired. A year and a half later, alongside deejaying in another club, Marcus worked four days a week in The Lion's Den. Since taking the job, his girlfriend quit stripping and "hasn't danced in a long time." Both Marcus and his girlfriend shared some unease about working in the club: "Especially when my girlfriend was pregnant, she was definitely edgy about me being around thirty different naked women a week, . . . but, for the most part, it's not too bad. She doesn't dance, and I don't dance [*laughs*]." It was particularly difficult for Marcus when patrons were rude to his girlfriend: "You know, some of the comments you hear said, you want to jump up and punch the guy in the mouth, but you can't. If it was in a regular bar, and you were drinking, and you were sitting at the bar, and somebody says [something foul] to your girlfriend, you would, but because it's there you've got to let it slide." Marcus's family also knew about his work. His dad "works about a mile away, and he gets out at, like, midnight. He'll stop in real quick [and] shoot the shit. Sometimes one of my friends will buy him a beer, and he'll chug it down in five minutes and go home, or my mom will flip on him." His mother's worries stemmed from her fears about alcohol consumption and drunk driving.

Marissa: Marissa was a patron of the club before becoming a stripper. "I used to come every once in a while with my guy buddies and just have a good time. It was good, clean, legit fun." At age twenty, this white stripper found that working three days a week, as she had done for the past year and a half, meshed well with her attitude and lifestyle. Though Marissa began by both stripping and occasionally cocktail waitressing in the club, she recently quit stripping. While her friends were supportive of her work in the club, they showed greater support once she quit dancing: "First they were like, 'Oh great, dance—that's awesome! It's cool!' But after I quit dancing, [they said,] 'Oh that's awesome, that's even better, that's great that you stopped dancing! You know, it makes you look so much better now you can da da da.' A lot of people have a lot more respect for you once you stop dancing." Like her friends, Marissa's live-in boyfriend also expressed relief over her quitting. They met in the club through one of the deejays. Given how they met, Marissa explained, "He didn't really mind too much [that I was stripping]. But after I quit dancing, he was psyched. . . . I think it comforted him a little bit that I wasn't showing off my goods anymore [*laughs*]." Her openness with friends did not extend to family. She kept her work a secret from her father: "My father would never know. I would never tell him. My mom found out through one of my friends. I think one of my friends just flipped out and told her one day. She knew, but she wouldn't tell me she knew." Like others in the club, Marissa found that keeping her work a secret was a difficult task.

Marlon: Marlon, a twenty-nine-year-old, white man, was an occasional patron who frequently dated strippers. Drawing on a connection through one of the strippers he dated, Marlon began visiting The Lion's Den, as well as other strip clubs in the area. Though Marlon's girlfriend was a stripper, she was not a dancer in The Lion's Den. He asserted that he did not mind watching his girlfriend strip, though he did so on an infrequent basis. In his words, "I don't care if a girl—if my girlfriend is sitting on some guy's lap. If my girlfriend's working, she's over there sitting on some guy's lap, and he's got his hands on her legs—big deal, that's what she's there for. That's how I see it. I don't like to see it, but I've just got to look away and laugh, and that's exactly what I've always done." He has introduced his friends to many of the women he has met: "A lot of my friends don't understand how I can do that. They get a girlfriend that I've set them up with, and they're like, 'Dude I can't deal with this!' And I'm like, 'Then let her go.' Most people can't really deal with that. I think maybe it's a matter of control, I don't know. You know, trying to have a level of control over your partner's life." Marlon's libertarian politics and familiarity with stripping enabled him to keep his jealousies in check when negotiating interactions with women in the industry. He credited his perspective to his parents: "That's something else my parents gave me. You do what you want to do, and you let everybody else do what they want to do."

Mindy: Mindy began stripping to pay off debts. She was adamant that her work in the club was only short term. At age nineteen, this white stripper had been working four to five days a week for four months: "When I tell people what I do for a living I don't necessarily tell them I'm a stripper." For Mindy, there were career and short-term workers in this job. Short-term workers "do it to get themselves through school or to straighten out bills." She fell into the latter group, who did not want to strip for "the rest of [their lives]." That said, the list of items she hoped to purchase, coupled with her debt, hinted at the possibility of a longer run in the club: "I do it just to get my bills straight for now. I don't plan on doing it for the rest of my life. In September, I plan on going back to school. I've gotten kind of far behind on bills—got a couple grand in bills I got to pay back. I want to get my apartment straight so I can get nice things for that and get a car, kind of get my life together." When asked if dancing had affected her relationship with her live-in boyfriend, Mindy explained: "Not really. He doesn't really like me doing what I'm doing, but he supports what I do, because he met me when I was already dancing, so he can't really say anything. He's never gotten in my face; he'll never start any arguments, because I don't want to do this for a long time."

Ned: Ned had worked in the club longer than anyone else. At age thirty-six, this white male worker had been bartending and bouncing five days a week for thirteen years. Ned's connection to the club came from a friend who was working there: "Actually I didn't want to come up here, but a friend said, 'Come on up. I work here. I'll buy you a couple beers.' But I didn't want to come up there. I'd never been in a place like that, so I didn't want to come up to begin with." Ned decided in the end to visit the club, and his size made an impression on the boss, who told his friend they were in need of workers. The boss asked, "Where's that big guy you were with the other night? Tell him to come up!" As Ned explained, "I haven't left since [*laughs*]; that was thirteen years ago." Working in the club, Ned put on a different persona. He was friendly and talkative but explained, "Out of the club I'm the opposite. You won't hear me talking so much. I'm more reserved." Living with his mother and working five days a week, Ned had a difficult time meeting someone to have a relationship with: "I have no time, I'm serious. I don't go out. I don't drink no more, so I don't know what to do. All my times at the club and then my days off are people's days to go to work, so it's tough to do anything." When asked if his work changed anything about his life, he laughed and said, "Yeah, I have no life!" Though he brought on board countless friends in need of a job, he wouldn't recommend his work: "I don't think I would. Not anymore, anyway."

Nina: Nina began stripping to help support her roommates' two children, and at age eighteen she had been working two days a week for a month and a half. Throughout this time, her size had been an important issue. In particular, this white dancer battled constant emphasis on weight loss from the group of strippers she traveled with. She tried to focus on "just [looking] forward": "When they tell me to lose weight, I don't get sad or feel horrible. I just think, okay, just a little bit more to go and then maybe they'll be congratulating me instead of saying all the time, 'You have to look better and be better.'" Nina expressed the many troubles she had with her job: "You know, it's degrading. Nobody wants to do this for a job. We do it because we want to get paid. Nobody likes to stand up there naked and feel like a piece of meat, but that's what we do for money." While money was her primary reason for stripping, Nina had not found the work lucrative. Like all traveling strippers, Nina had to pay out both her host club and her employer, but she did so from a much smaller total. Her reported last shift earnings ($100) were considerably less than the average ($200). This was perhaps due to her inexperience and physical size—she was considerably larger than all of the other dancers in the club. She described herself as "hard" but "strong," less sensitive to men's comments but still "creeped out" by the patrons. The most positive aspect of her work was the camaraderie she felt with some of her fellow female travelers. Asked if her family and friends knew about her work, she explained, "They know it's exotic dancing, but they don't know what I do. I don't think they know that it's completely nude and stuff like that, but they kind of know. . . . I tried to hide it from them at first, but eventually you can't. I can't lie to my family. I'm too close to my parents."

Robin: Though not a newcomer to the industry, Robin had the enthusiasm of someone new—this despite having worked six days a week for two months consecutively. By and large, this twenty-three-year-old, white dancer had boundless energy and described stripping as a good fit, because it was something she enjoyed. Though Robin's family was initially uncomfortable with her new line of work, after spending time in the club, her mother and sister accepted her stripping: "Yeah, my mom actually washes my clothes. . . . She said, 'It's your body; you can do what you want. You're an adult. I don't approve of it.' But now if my mom were to call and I'm not onstage, she'll stop in, . . . because she's working up the road, . . . and have lunch with me, and when it was time for me to go up onstage, she'd leave." The club became such a part of her family's life that her younger sister was now dating a regular patron. While Robin was happy about her sister's new boyfriend, she was protective regarding her sister's sexual explorations: "My sister said, 'That's fucked up that my boyfriend saw you naked before he saw me naked!' And I was like, 'Whoa!' And she's like, 'He hasn't seen me naked yet. I'm just saying, eh, that's gross.'"

Roxanne: Roxanne started dancing at age eighteen because of, in her words, a "boyfriend who cost me a lot of money." After six years, she was one of the longest-working strippers in the club, but at thirty-three, this white dancer was ready for a new job. Her family "knew" about her work but "thinks [she's] retired." Over time, she also began filling in as a cocktail waitress. When asked if she would consider telling her family about waitressing, she replied dryly, "They wouldn't care; they don't want me at any strip club." Later in the interview, Roxanne explained: "My parents said no self-respecting man would let their girlfriend dance, and I think that's very true." In agreement, she asserted, "Because if you're with somebody, you're with them, and I don't think you can have a relationship with somebody and come into the club and have guys hitting on you and making comments to you." Roxanne's expressed her concern about stripping: "The club has affected [my relationships] a great deal, which is part of the reason that I'm separated and getting divorced because of this place and the static that it's put in our relationship." Asked what she meant by "static," she explained that the "atmosphere of people is very immature," and that created "problems that impacted [her] marriage." With plans laid out for an office job, it was unclear whether Roxanne would continue working in the club much longer.

Shane: Shane had been attending the club five days a week for a number of years, "because it's my family here," he said. He explained: "I've been hanging here for a long time. . . . I knew some people before I started coming. I knew [a bartender] a little bit, and [a doorman] a little bit, and I moved into the area, so I just started hanging out here and getting to know everybody." Despite his regular patronage, Shane believed stripping work created troubles for women: "I don't really think the job that these girls are doing is a very respectful job for them. A lot of these girls are stuck in doing this. They'll come in saying, 'I'm only going to do it for a couple months during the year,' and then they do it for three, five, eight years, whatever. And then by the time they get out, they're a little too old to be starting a new job, or they have no experience in other things. So I really don't think it's a good thing for girls to do." At age twenty-nine, this white, factory-worker father of one also greatly disapproved of stripping work due to the difficulties it might pose for kids: "Like my girlfriend did it for like a year. . . . She had a kid, and now she understands you don't want a kid growing up—kid's three years old, 'Where's mommy?' 'Mommy's going to work.' 'Where's mommy work at?' 'Mommy works at a bar.' 'Oh, what kind of bar?' You know, you don't want that." Without being asked, Shane raised the issue of contradictions between his regular patronage and his belief about dancing's negative impact on women: "I can't really even say anything because I come here all the time. Me saying that it's bad what girls are doing—it's a bad place, but I hang out here all the time. So it's like being a hypocrite in that sense." When asked about how he dealt with the contradictions, he emphasized that he did not sit at the stage but visited to "hang out with his friends" and that now he "know[s] everybody, and it's a safe haven."

Stella: Stella had been stripping in the club four days a week for a year and two months. Asserting that she stripped to make money, Stella described her family's poverty as a child: "We were very poor. I used to always wear not even my sister's clothes [but] her friends' clothes. I'd go to school, be so embarrassed, because they'd be like, 'Your sister was supposed to give me that back last Wednesday!' And I'm like [*looks down, shaking her head*] all in front of everybody." Stella, whose sister Tess also worked in the club, was introduced to stripping by their eldest sister, who had since quit dancing. Stella's family knew about her work. She explained that her mom "doesn't complain . . . because she knows when she needs money to borrow, I have it. My brothers will joke around about my job, 'Oh bring some of your stripper friends over,' and I'm like, 'You wouldn't have a chance' [*laughs*]!" Stella began stripping because it fit well with raising her daughter. After dropping out of school at seventeen due to poor grades and lack of interest, she "went to a young teen parent program, got [her] GED": "and I want to do something with it, I'm gonna do something." At age twenty, this white stripper wanted to be a massage therapist but, due to the prohibitive cost of daycare, planned to wait until her child was old enough to be in school. Though stripping worked well with parenting, it caused friction in her relationship with her live-in boyfriend. Despite meeting Stella in the club, her boyfriend battled jealousy: "He doesn't come in here anymore, because he doesn't like to see me [with other men]. He doesn't like to see me dressed like that. He knows that I need the money right now, but he still throws comments at me once in a while."

Steve: Steve, a white man in his mid thirties, had been the owner-manager of The Lion's Den for the past eight years. Recruited because of his management experience by the former owner, Steve explained that he got his job "through mutual friends": "I've got a lot of friends in the beer and liquor industry, and [the former owner of the club] approached one of the distributors [to see] if they knew of good managers, and then they hooked us up together; here I landed!" Describing his work, he said, "I'm a fireman. I'm the person who waits for little fires to arise here and there, and I'm the person who puts it out. I have no problem telling anybody I don't know what I do for a living. My job is to look at the past, predict the future, and manage the pain." As a thirty-six-year-old father of one, working in the club changed a lot about Steve's life. His six-day-a-week schedule caused him to be "on call twenty-four seven": "My phone doesn't stop ringing. . . . My girlfriend gets irritated with people calling the house, . . . but, like I tell her, I'd rather answer a stupid question than fix a stupid mistake." Steve, who had been divorced twice, believed his job played a major role in the stress on his intimate relationships, between "the hours involved" and suspicions that he was there "to get laid." Protesting these impressions, he asserted, "I'm here to run a business. I hardly ever look at the girls naked. To me they're just like wallpaper. Maybe my first week in the business it was, 'Oh this is kind of weird stuff,' but now it's just like a naked person and a clothed person is basically the same thing to me." Nevertheless, Steve had dated a dancer in the past: "Um hum. I was stupid. That will never happen again [*laughs*]. I got involved with one of the dancers, and that was absolutely the wrong thing to do. It was like four years ago, and there's still ramifications to this day for it. . . . It was the biggest mistake I ever made." While his work in the club had a negative impact on his intimate dating and marital relationships, the same had not happened to his relationship with his parents, who remained supportive and "open-minded" after visiting the club.

Summer: Summer, a self-described "tomboy" who never wore makeup outside of the club, began stripping for the money. Summer traveled with other strippers from a nearby state. The only family member who knew about her work was her sister, whom she introduced to stripping. Summer explained: "My sister dances with me. . . . Well, she's going to college. She just wanted to do it so she has money for college and stuff." Though her parents knew about her work, they did not know about her sister's: "Nope. It's undercover [*laughs*]! It would be my fault. It's always been my fault. [*In a high-pitched tone, mimicking her mother*] '[E-MI-LY] it's all your fault!'" When she told her parents, they did not provide much of a response: "I told my dad about it, and he said, 'I don't want to hear about it.' I told my mom about it. She didn't like it at first, but I took her out for dinner the other day, and I was talking to her about it, and she was . . . very interested. I just talked to her about it. She listened, and she didn't say anything." In terms of the impact stripping had on her life, despite only being twenty, this white stripper explained, "I feel a lot older. I've lost like twenty-five pounds since I started dancing. I didn't know how to put makeup on before." After working in the club twice a week for five months, Summer believed she had "gotten to know men a little bit better": "I grew up with all sisters. I see what they act like now, and I see— it's funny." Despite the ups and downs with money, dealing with men, and being in competition with other strippers, Summer asserted, "Someday I'll look back and smile about it."

Tamara: Tamara's first impression of the club was "disappointing." After growing up as a child with dance lessons and taking belly dancing as an adult, she hoped for more performance in strip clubs. Drawing on her background in holistic health and massage therapy, along with her love of dance, Tamara believed her work had a "healing component." By contrast to her hope for dance and personal connection, "Here girls go around naked more. They're more flashers than anything else. You'll go to the guy and be like, 'Boobies—oh my god!' And then you put everything back on and go to the next guy, like, 'Boobies!'" Despite her dissatisfaction, stripping fit well with her life because, in her words, "I don't like working more than like twenty to thirty hours a week. So I wanted something that was good, fast money, fun, without a lot of hours to it." Her boyfriend (now husband) knew about stripping from women he had dated in the past. Following his recommendation, Tamara visited a club where some of her friends worked and decided to try it herself. Three years later, at age twenty-five, this white dancer lamented that she had "gotten stuck being a dancer." Accustomed to the money and the hours, she found it difficult to "put more effort" into getting a "real job."

Despite working once a week, Tamara did not describe stripping as an "easy job." She explained: "I have a hard time getting to work. I cancel a lot, and before work I'm always huffy or irritated, and I don't want to go. When I'm there, I'm fine. But when I get home, I'm exhausted. I don't always feel good about being a dancer, mostly because I don't like that I'm doing something that my parents wouldn't be proud of."

Ted: Ted was a regular patron before landing a job as a bartender. Though he first started going to the club infrequently, as he got to know one of the dancers, he started attending more regularly and talking with one of the bartenders: "I was a customer, and instead of sitting at the stage all the time, I went up and stayed with the bartender. One weeknight . . . someone was leaving, and he asked me if I wanted [his position]. Apart from me not having any bartending experience, I got the job. I never was a bartender before." Ted had been working two days a week for the past year and three months. Being in the club added some pleasure to his life: "Even me, when I was a customer, I really didn't have a job. . . . I was going to school, but I had some income, and you do with what you've got to make your life worth living, I guess, bearable. In my case a strip club is adequate, I guess." When asked if working in The Lion's Den has changed anything about his life, Ted replied: "I guess working there has changed me a little bit. I guess for the most part, one of the reasons I don't go very often anymore is because I'm there all the time, and I see them, and the emphasis—I don't know if I want to say the emphasis is different—but it's monotonous I guess." Ted was unusual as a male worker, because he kept his job a secret, particularly from his mother. He explained: "She'd have a heart attack [*laughs*]. . . . My mother thinks I work at a regular bar in a nearby town. . . . She's very religious, Catholic, and she thinks everything that's wrong in this world is because nobody has morals." At age thirty-three, this white man hoped to conclude work in the club once he finished his bachelor's degree.

Tess: Like her sister Stella, Tess, also a white dancer, emphasized her family's poverty while they were growing up: "We were very poor. I've had a job since I was fourteen years old." When Tess lost her job after being framed for a drug sale, she was unable to find other work and decided to begin stripping at age twenty-five. The job was never a good fit for her: "I don't like being naked in front of people I don't know. . . . I'm not even an exhibitionist in front of the person I'm with. I was with this guy six years, and he was lucky if he saw me naked. So it's totally not me, but I know I have to do it to make the money I have to make. It's very hard, and it sucks for me big time." Tess was probably more inclined to try and stick with stripping in a familiar place like

The Lion's Den, where both of her sisters danced. While one of her sisters quit during the time I was conducting research, her other sister, Stella, continued. Tess expressed some concern over being the "good girl" in the family who fell on hard times. After losing her other job, she had been stripping three to four days for the past few weeks to "take care of two children, pay for school, and pay for all [her] bills." While she lamented, "This is, like, the only way I can do it," Tess was hopeful she would be able to stop after four months.

Tim: Tim, a white, male deejay, described his job jubilantly: "It's fun. Probably the fact that I get to hang out with cool people, play music, watch TV, being under twenty-one and working in a strip club is pretty much like a dream job . . . for a teenage [nineteen-year-old] guy. . . . I don't have to pay to get in. I get paid to be there!" Tim's introduction to the club came from a friend: "I used to come with him and just hang out during the day while he was working, and I started hanging out [at the club] more and more. You know, but I live five minutes away, so I'd rather come hang out with my friend while he's working than sit at my house and watch TV." Asked how he got this job, he explained: "My boss hooked me up with a deejay job, and then his schedule this semester conflicted with his hours [at the club] and mine didn't, so he had me start working here like on Fridays during the day. I've been doing that ever since and covering his shifts when he's not around or busy." Five months later, Tim continued to juggle deejaying two days a week alongside his college courses. While he did not actively conceal his work, he also did not advertise it. He had gotten mostly neutral to positive responses from friends and family. His mother and her boyfriend "really don't mind": "I don't want it to sound trashy, but my mom will go out with her boyfriend [to another nearby strip club], so they accept that kind of thing. They're just like, 'You do what ever you want. If you're making money and you're happy, go for it.' That kind of thing." His male friends and uncles were excited by the news, in part because they were patrons too. His female friends provided the only contrast, often saying, "Oh, it's gross."

Travis: For Travis, a fifty-three-year-old, white, male worker, the idea to deejay in a strip club came from his wife of thirty-one years, who had danced in another club years before. Prior to working in The Lion's Den, Travis was employed as a deejay on the radio and for weddings. As weddings began to seem like too much work, and he "got really tired of hauling [equipment] all around," he began to consider alternatives. Given his experience, he and his wife discussed club work. Relaying the story, he explained: "We talked about that one day, and she says, 'Why don't you pick up a club gig or something? You could just do that for a couple of nights a week and then maybe do a wedding on a Sunday or something when you feel like it.'" His connection to The Lion's Den came through a friend who ran another club. Travis explained to his friend that he was considering club work. Immediately his friend asked if he would "consider a couple of nights" working in his club. At the time, Travis had never been to a strip bar. Twelve years later, he found that the consistency of three days a week of club work fit well with his family life. Remembering his hours deejaying, Travis explained: "I really don't like being on the road. I've got kids at home. I got a wife at home. I've got a home life. I got a life." Working in the club allowed him to have a live audience and stay put.

Vivian: Vivian worked as a stripper so her husband could be a stay-at-home dad before her kids entered school. She explained: "I'd rather spend the three days away from my family doing this, hanging out in a bar watching naked ladies dance, than sitting behind a secretary's desk for forty hours a week." At age twenty-one, this white dancer did not plan to strip for long: "Some of the women who've been in there for a long time, they're like, 'Oh, you'll never leave. You'll be addicted to the money. Girls don't leave this and go to college.' I'm like, 'Well, there's a different story here. You can change your career path anytime you want.'" Vivian's husband was supportive of her work since it enabled him to stay at home with their two kids. Asked about the rest of her family and friends, she explained that most knew about her work, with the exception of her father-in-law and mother-in-law: "I told my husband he could tell his mom. I asked him to. I'm like, 'You need to tell her; I wouldn't mind if you told her while I was gone.' I love his mother. I wouldn't want to lose that respect. I know she's had a hard time with other family members stripping in the past." Even though she kept stripping a secret from only two people, she explained: "I really have to watch what I say. I can't comment on how the weather was down here this weekend. . . . 'What? What were you [*trails off*] . . . ?" After two months as a traveling stripper, Vivian was still weighing the pros and cons of her work.

Walter: Walter's interview differed from the others in that he provided only short responses, not the lengthy narratives characteristic of the other participants. After suffering a stroke a few years earlier, Walter's speech was soft and hesitant, and his bodily movements were visibly slow. Shortly after the stroke, he separated from his wife, who retained custody of their three children. Living on his own at age forty-four and working as a store clerk, this white patron found that the club provided a place where he could experience friendly interactions with men and women who might not have responded as favorably under other circumstances. He visited the club four times a week because, in his words, "I like to see the nude girls. . . . It offers a relaxation for me, a place to go. [It] offers socializing for the regulars." He first came to the club before it offered nude dancing: "I used to come in when I was little—nineteen. It was a bar. Stopped coming for about three years." In The Lion's Den, Walter typically sat in the corner, consistently joined by the doorman and other regular patrons. His verbal interactions with the dancers were minimal, and though he purchased VIP dances, his focus was most often on watching rather than talking, since conversation was especially difficult for Walter alongside the loud music and background noise in the club.

Winston: Describing what drew him to strip clubs, Winston explained, "It's cheaper here [*laughs*]. You can go to a topless or a strip club and look at the strippers, and you can have all the fantasies in the world one way or another. . . . The girl's nice as long as the money's there. Then off you go. You have a fantasy that lasts for about as long as it will." At age fifty-four, this white patron explained that he had been around the block with women: "I've been married twice and divorced once and lost my first wife to cancer, so I've kind of been through it." Once again single and dating, Winston found that visiting the club a couple of days a week wreaked havoc on his relationships. He explained candidly, "When [women I dated] knew that I would come here once a week just to see Frank or stop off at the strip club, that was it. They don't want to have anything to do with me." The problem for the women he dated, he surmised, was wondering whether stripping was prostitution. He explained, "When you say prostitution, people always think bad. We're puritanical." For Winston, the parallel between stripping and prostitution was not only warranted; the logic was simple: "This is sex. You're selling sex. Prostitution is selling sex." Rather than singling out stripping, Winston also drew a parallel between prostitution and marriage: "It's the same thing with a guy. [They say,] 'I never paid for sex.' Well, you got married, and you were married for ten years, and you got divorced, and it cost you $100,000 to get divorced. How much did those five blowjobs you got in ten years cost you [*laughing*]? You didn't think you paid for sex, but wait." As his relationships waxed and waned, strip clubs provided an important source of fantasy and sexuality in Winston's life.

Notes

PREFACE

1. All names are pseudonyms, and some identifying details have been altered to protect the anonymity of participants.
2. I explore both my research questions and experiences in more detail in appendix 1.
3. Price 2000.

INTRODUCTION

1. Kernes 2007; Kirk 2002; Schlosser 1997.
2. Schlosser 1997.
3. Ehrenreich and Hochschild 2002; Hondagneu-Sotelo 2001.
4. Bernstein 2007.
5. Frank 2002.
6. Frank 1998, 2002, 2003; Pasko 2002; Ronai and Cross 1998; Ronai and Ellis 1989; Wood 2000.
7. U.S. Bureau of the Census 2000.
8. Ibid.
9. I use the terms "stripper," "striptease dancer," "nude dancer," "dancer," "performer," and "entertainer" interchangeably in this text. Out of all of those labels, the term "stripper" may have the most obvious derogatory connotations. Euphemistic terms like "dancer" may seem more palatable, but they are also less accurate. The women I interviewed argued they "don't really dance." Instead, they remove their clothes rather quickly and pose or writhe nude in front of patrons. Given the shape of the stage and the number of women performing simultaneously, the club is not really designed for dance per se. In addition, the women I interviewed used the term "stripping" to describe their work.
10. Meridian 1997.
11. Frank 2002.
12. Ibid.
13. "Club Listings" 2001.
14. Ibid.
15. U.S. Bureau of the Census 2000, 2003.
16. Ibid.
17. U.S. Bureau of the Census 2003.
18. Ibid.
19. Ibid.

20. U.S. Bureau of the Census 2000.

21. Ibid.

22. U.S. Bureau of the Census 2003.

23. Ibid.

24. Boles and Garbin 1974a; Carey, Peterson, and Sharpe 1974; McCaghy and Skipper 1972; Sweet and Tewksbury 2000a, 2000b.

25. Lion's Den 2001.

26. Ibid., p. 3.

27. Hochschild 1983.

28. Different states have varying regulations for nudity in strip clubs. Most clubs regulate nudity alongside alcohol. For example, Connecticut allows both fully nude and topless strip clubs to operate, but only topless clubs are allowed to serve alcohol. Laws regulating nudity and alcohol are often in flux at the state and local levels. For example, in 2004 Ohio reversed its allowance of alcohol and full nudity in strip clubs. In the 2008 Ohio Sixth Circuit court decision in *J. L. Spoons Inc. v. Dragani*, the courts upheld this restriction and ruled that limiting nudity in strip clubs does not curtail First Amendment rights.

29. Acker 1990; Acker and Van Houten 1992.

30. Barton 2006.

31. Eneck and Preston 1988.

32. Chapkis 1997; Walkowitz 1982.

33. Walkowitz 1982, p. 24.

34. Dines and Jensen 2004; Dines, Jensen, and Russo 1998; MacKinnon 2005; Sheffield 1994.

35. Barton 2006; Egan 2006; Frank 2002.

36. Barton 2006; Langley 1997; Query and Funari 2000.

37. Lusty Lady 2009.

38. Koopman 2003.

39. Chapkis 1997; Dines and Jensen 2004; Dines, Jensen, and Russo 1998; Raphael 2004; Sanchez 1997.

40. Acker 1990, 1992; Acker and Van Houten 1992.

41. Lorber 1995, p. 5.

42. Bordo 2004; Brumberg 1997; Gimlin 2002; Thompson 1996; Wolf 1992.

CHAPTER 1

1. Steinem 1984.

2. Ibid., p. 70.

3. Miller 1986.

4. For earlier approaches to the study of stripping specifically, see Carolyn Rambo's work (formerly Ronai): Ronai 1992a, 1992b, 1994, 1998; Ronai and Cross 1998; Ronai and Ellis 1989.

5. Chapkis 1997, p. 222.

6. For examples, see Bruckert 2002; Egan 2006; and Frank 2002.

7. Naples 2003.

8. "Club Listings" 2005.
9. Caldwell 2005, p. 282.
10. Allen 1991; Jarrett 2000.
11. Allen 1991, p. 205.
12. Jarrett 2000.
13.Allen 1991.
14. Ibid.
15. Ibid.
16. D. Scott 2003.
17. Jarrett 2000, p. 60.
18. Ibid., p. 67.
19. D. Scott 2003.
20. Quoted in Jarrett 2000, p. 68.
21. Allen 1991; Jarrett 2000; D. Scott 2003.
22. Allen 1991.
23. Caldwell 2005.
24. Quoted in Goldberg 1986, p. 1.
25. Peiss 1986.
26. Snyder 1991, p. 130.
27. Ibid.
28. Shteir 2004, p. 213.
29. Ibid., p. 286.
30. Ibid., p. 323.
31. Shteir 2004; Jarrett 1997.
32. Jarrett 1997.
33. Shteir 2004.
34. Posner and Silbaugh 1996.
35. Foucault 1990, p. 4.
36. Shteir 2004, pp. 308–309.
37. Tucker 1997.
38. Ibid.
39. Ibid.
40. Hanna 1998, 1999.
41. Hanna 1998.
42. Friend 2004; Gopnik 2001.
43. Brick 2005; Kershaw 2004.
44. Yancey 2003.
45. Aerobic Striptease website, http://www.aerobicstriptease.com/ (accessed September 30, 2008).
46. Sheila Kelley's S Factor website, http://www.sfactor.com/Press/index.asp (accessed September 30, 2008).
47. Levy 2005, p. 26.
48. Eaves 2002; Langley 1997; Query and Funari 2000.
49. Brooks 1997; Dudash 1997.
50. Baldwin 2004; Bosse 2004; Nygaard 2003; Romano 2004; Weldon 2005.

51. Allen 1991.

52. Johnson 2002.

53. Allen 1991.

54. Male stripping for female audiences has also undergone mainstreaming. Bachelorette parties at Chippendales-like clubs and with male strippers for hire are now standard fare. Celebration of male striptease performances has been captured in the media through popular films like *The Full Monty* (1997).

55. Johansmeyer 2009, p. 1.

56. Query and Funari 2000.

57. Cited in Schlosser 1997.

58. Bose and Whaley 2009.

59. Quoted in Weinberg 2004, p. 11.

60. Bose and Whaley 2009.

61. Hochschild 1983.

62. Kang 2009.

63. Ibid., p. 255.

64. Bose and Whaley 2009.

65. Ronai 1992a.

66. Lorber 1995.

67. Hyde 2005; Lorber 1995.

68. Lorber 1995, p. 6.

69. Ibid.

70. Carey, Peterson, and Sharpe 1974; Forsyth and Deshotels 1997; McCaghy and Skipper 1969, 1972; Reid, Epstein, and Benson 1995; Ross, Anderson, Herber, and Norton 1990; Salutin 1971; Skipper 1970, 1971; Thompson and Harred 1992; Thompson, Harred, and Burks 2003.

71. Carey, Peterson, and Sharpe 1974; Ross, Anderson, Herber, and Norton 1990; Skipper 1970.

72. Frank 1998, 2002, 2003; Pasko 2002; Ronai and Cross 1998; Ronai and Ellis 1989; Wood 2000.

73. Blumer 1969.

74. Ferguson 1984; Vance 1984.

75. Barton 2002.

76. Dworkin 1997; MacKinnon 1987.

77. Ferguson 1984; Vance 1984.

78. Chapkis 1997, p. 82.

79. Foucault 1990; G. Rubin 1984; Hochschild 1983.

80. Barton 2002, 2006.

81. Frank 1998, 2002, 2003; Pasko 2002; Ronai and Cross 1998; Ronai and Ellis 1989; Wood 2000.

82. Acker 1990.

83. For examples, see Bruckert 2002; DeMichele and Tewksbury 2004; Lewis 2006; Price 2000; Prus and Irini 1980; Raphael 2004; Tewksbury 1994.

84. Acker 1990, p. 142.

85. Ibid., p. 141.

86. Britton 2000; Dellinger 2004; Trautner 2005.

87. Britton 2000, p. 428.

88. Hallett 2003, p. 131.

89. Acker 1990.

90. West and Zimmerman 1987.

91. Acker 1990; Alvesson and Billing 1997; Britton 1997.

92. Acker 1990, 1992.

93. Acker 1990, 1992; Collins 1990; Crenshaw 1995.

94. Acker 2006, p. 441.

95. Ibid., p. 443.

96. Bruckert 2002; Frank 2002; Schiff 2001; Trautner 2005.

97. Frank 2002.

98. Schiff 2001, p. 16.

99. Ibid.

100. Ibid., p. 13.

101. Meridian 1997.

102. Collins 1990.

CHAPTER 2

1. Hoffman 2006.

2. Ibid.

3. Pasko 2002, p. 49.

4. Wesley 2002.

5. Thompson, Harred, and Burks 2003, p. 569; see also Maticka-Tyndale, Lewis, Clark, Zubick, and Young 2000.

6. Sweet and Tewksbury 2000a.

7. Barton 2002, 2006.

8. DeMichele and Tewksbury 2004.

9. Lewis 2006.

10. Acker 1990, 1992.

11. Lion's Den 2001, p. 2.

12. Acker and Van Houten 1992, p. 28.

13. Ibid., p. 20.

14. DeMichele and Tewksbury 2004, p. 555.

15. Price 2000.

16. Acker 1990, pp. 146–147.

17. Lerum 2004.

18. Connell 1995; Connell and Messerschmidt 2005.

19. Acker 1990.

20. Ensler 2005.

21. Cancian 1986; Chodorow 1978; Hochschild 1983.

22. Fenstermaker and West 2002; West and Fenstermaker 1995.

23. Acker 1990; West and Zimmerman 1987.

24. Acker 1990; Dellinger 2004.

25. Acker 1990, p. 146.

26. Acker 1992, p. 255.

27. Lion's Den 2001, pp. 7–8.
28. Ibid., p. 2.
29. Ibid., p. 8.
30. Acker 1992.
31. Acker 1990, 1992.
32. Acker 1990.
33. Ibid., p. 255.
34. DeMichele and Tewksbury 2004, p. 539.
35. Hoffman 2006; Mayer 2009.
36. Hoffman 2006.
37. Hoffman 2006; Mayer 2009.
38. Connell 1995; Gruber 1998.

CHAPTER 3

1. Beller 2004, p. 85.
2. Ibid.
3. According to *Advertising Age,* a marketing trade journal, *Men's Health* is one of the most widely circulated men's magazines.
4. Frank 2002, p. 85.
5. Frank 2002, 2003; Wood 2000.
6. Frank 2003.
7. Erickson and Tewksbury 2000.
8. Wood 2000, p. 27.
9. Jhally 2007.
10. Liepe-Levinson 2002, p. 185.
11. Lion's Den 2001, p. 3.
12. Loe 1996.
13. Ibid., p. 405.
14. Barton 2002.
15. Frank 1998, p. 188.
16. Ibid.
17. Eaves 2002, p. 292.
18. Simmel and Levine 1971, p. 122.
19. Selfe and Burke 2001, p. 236.
20. Chapkis 1997, p. 98.
21. Weitzer 2005.
22. Egan 2006; Frank 2002.
23. Egan 2006, p. 141.
24. Ibid.
25. Frank 2002.
26. Bernstein 2007, p. 7.
27. Ibid.
28. Goffman 1959, p. 83.
29. Connell 1995, p. 215.

30. Kimmel 1990, p. 231.

31. Goffman 1959, p. 91.

32. Kimmel 2000, p. 225.

33. Allison 1994.

34. Ibid., p. 154.

35. Connell 2000, p. 31.

36. Erickson and Tewksbury 2000, p. 290.

37. Sanchez 1997.

38. L. Rubin 1994, p. 193.

39. Ibid.

40. Holsopple 1998; Maticka-Tyndale, Lewis, Clark, Zubick, and Young 2000; Raphael 2004.

41. Lion's Den 2001, p. 5.

42. Sanchez 1997, p. 566.

43. Posner and Silbaugh 1996, p. 5.

44. Ibid.

45. Bruckert 2002, p. 93.

46. Boles and Garbin 1974b, p. 142.

47. Barton 2007; Holsopple 1998; Maticka-Tyndale, Lewis, Clark, Zubick, and Young 2000; Sweet and Tewksbury 2000a.

48. M. Scott 2006.

49. Ibid.

50. Raphael 2004; Sanchez 1997.

51. Raphael 2004.

52. Black 1993.

53. Scully 1990; Scully and Marolla 1985.

54. Miller and Schwartz 1995, p. 9.

55. Sanchez 1997, p. 576.

56. G. Rubin 1984.

57. Pascoe 2007, p. 82.

58. Ibid.

CHAPTER 4

1. Barton 2006; Egan 2006; Frank 2002.

2. Coltrane 1998; Gerstel and Gallagher 1994; Hays 1996; Hochschild 1983.

3. Foner 1994; Kang 2009.

4. Chancer 1993, p. 165.

5. Lion's Den 2001, p. 9.

6. Hochschild 1983, p. 55.

7. Bell, Sloan, and Strickling 1998, p. 355.

8. Hochschild 1983, p. 35.

9. Ibid.

10. Leidner 1993.

11. Ibid., p. 26.

12. HandsomeRocus 2008.
13. McNair 2002, p. 88.
14. Jhally 2007.
15. Risman and Schwartz 2002, p. 20.
16. Ensler 2000.
17. de Beauvoir 1957, p. 267.
18. Wolf 1992.
19. Bordo 1997, p. 343.
20. Gimlin 2002.
21. Urla and Swedlund 1995, p. 305.
22. Ronai 1992a, p. 315.
23. Ibid.
24. Collins 1990; King 1988.
25. Hochschild 1983.
26. Lewin 1984, p. 95.
27. Hochschild 1983, p. 187.
28. Price 2000.
29. Barton 2006.
30. Ibid., p. 22.
31. Goffman 1974.
32. Ibid.
33. Ibid.
34. Ibid., p. 95.
35. Reid, Epstein, and Benson 1995, p. 287.
36. Ronai and Cross 1998.
37. Matson 1995, p. 220.
38. Price 2000.
39. Lewis 1998, p. 63.
40. Sweet and Tewksbury 2000a, p. 155.
41. Price 2000.
42. Pasko 2002, p. 61.
43. Ronai 1992b, p. 121.
44. Goffman 1959.
45. Ibid.
46. Hochschild 1983.
47. Ibid., p. 133.
48. Chapkis 1997, p. 82.
49. Paules 1991, p. 39.
50. Smith, Cox, and Saradjian 1999.
51. Adler and Adler 2007, p. 549.
52. Ibid.
53. Barton 2006, p. 91.
54. Ibid., p. 109.
55. Chapkis 1997.
56. Ibid.

CHAPTER 5

1. Carpenter 2001; Flint 1996; Kuntz 1997; Maticka-Tyndale, Lewis, Clark, Zubick, and Young 2000; Pendleton 1998.

2. Barton 2002; Egan 2006; Frank 2002.

3. MacKinnon 1987, p. 172. See also Barry 1995.

4. MacKinnon 1987, pp. 48–49.

5. Carey, Peterson, and Sharpe 1974; Forsyth and Deshotels 1997; McCaghy and Skipper 1969, 1972; Reid, Epstein, and Benson 1995; Ross, Anderson, Herber, and Norton 1990; Salutin 1971; Skipper 1970; Skipper and McCaghy 1971; Thompson and Harred 1992.

6. Detman 1990, 241.

7. Carey, Peterson, and Sharpe 1974; Ross, Anderson, Herber, and Norton 1990; Skipper 1970.

8. McCaghy and Skipper 1972, p. 370.

9. More recent research challenges these understandings of deviance, as discussed in chapter 4. Ronai and Cross argue that strippers use "narrative resistance" to construct a positive sense of self in spite of a stigmatized job. While these coping strategies certainly have particular forms for strippers, they are used more generally by those facing society's normative values: "The working mother is told that she should be at home; the father is told that he should do more for his kids; the striptease dancer is told that stripping is wrong" (Ronai and Cross 1998, p. 117).

10. Wesley 2002, p. 1182.

11. Salutin 1971, p. 20.

12. Quoted in Chapkis 1997, p. 22.

13. Resnick and Wolff 1987.

14. Fried and Wolff 1994, p. 103.

15. Ibid., p. 105.

16. Ibid.

17. Lion's Den 2001, p. 8.

18. Walkowitz 1982.

19. Barry 1995.

20. van der Veen 2000, p. 123.

21. Ibid.

22. Toossi 2006.

23. Bose and Whaley 2009.

24. Baxter and Wright 2000.

25. Williams 1992.

26. Bernstein 2007.

POSTSCRIPT

1. "Club Listings" 2006a, 2006b.

2. Crown and Roberts 2007, p. 386.

3. Lion's Den 2001, p. 8.

4. Acker 1990, 1992; Acker and Van Houten 1992.

5. Britton 1997, 2000.

6. Sanday 1996.

7. Boswell and Spade 1996.

8. Humphrey and Kahn 2000.

9. Boswell and Spade 1996; Brownmiller 1975; Jhally 1999; Sheffield 1994.

10. Sun and Picker 2008. See also Wosnitzer and Bridges 2007

11. Boswell and Spade 1996.

12. Sheffield 1994.

13. U.S. Department of Justice 2006.

14. U.S. Department of Justice 2009.

15. Posner and Silbaugh 1996.

16. Phillips 2000, p. 12.

17. Miller and Schwartz 1995.

18. Niemi 2006.

19. Ibid.

20. Ibid.

21. Boswell and Spade 1996.

22. Ibid.

23. Ibid.

24. "Club Listings" 2006a.

25. Using SCL's terminology, it lists information for fifteen "gay" clubs and one "lesbian" club ("Club Listings" 2006a).

26. U.S. Bureau of the Census 2006.

27. Barton 2006.

28. Ibid.

29. Ibid.

30. Ibid.

31. "Club Listings" 2006a.

32. "Club Listings" 2006b.

33. ResearchWare 2005. All names and any identifying information have been changed.

34. Liepe-Levinson 2002, p. 159.

35. Boswell and Spade 1996, p. 142.

36. Ibid.

37. Kimmel 2007, p. 78.

38. Kimmel 1994, 2006, 2007.

39. Kimmel 2006, p. 221.

40. Frank 2002, 2003.

41. Kimmel 2006, p. 167.

42. Connell 2005, p. 215.

43. Connell 2002, p. 6.

44. Sanday 1996.

45. Boswell and Spade 1996.

46. Humphrey and Kahn 2000.

47. Boswell and Spade 1996, p. 143.

48. Ibid.

49. Flynn 2000.

50. Yllö 1998.
51. Flynn 2000.
52. Britton 2000; Kanter 1993.
53. Price 2008.
54. Dozema 2009; Walkowitz 1982.
55. Chapkis 1997; Dozema 2009; Walkowitz 1982.
56. Weitzer 2000.
57. Chapkis 1997.
58. Connell 1987, 2000, 2002, 2005; Connell and Messerschmidt 2005.
59. Acker 2006.
60. Chapkis 1997.
61. Ibid.

APPENDIX 1

1. Naples 1996.
2. Lofland and Lofland 1995, p. 37.
3. Geertz 1973.
4. Oakley 1981.
5. Zussman 1992, p. 243.
6. Berg 2004.
7. Lion's Den 2001.
8. Ibid., p. 8.
9. Denzin 1989.
10. Glaser and Strauss 1967.
11. Lion's Den 2001, p. 1.
12. Frank 2002; Johnson 1999; Maher 1997; Ronai 1998.

References

Acker, Joan. 1990. "Hierarchies, Jobs and Bodies: A Theory of Gendered Organizations." *Gender & Society* 4:139–158.

———. 1992. "Gendering Organizational Theory." Pp.248–260 in *Gendering Organizational Analysis*, edited by A. J. Mills and P. Tancred. Newbury Park, CA: Sage.

———. 2006. "Inequality Regimes: Gender, Class, and Race in Organizations." *Gender & Society* 20:441–464.

Acker, Joan, and D. R. Van Houten. 1992. "Differential Recruitment and Control: The Sex Structuring of Organizations." Pp. 339–359 in *Gendering Organizational Analysis*, edited by A. J. Mills and P. Tancred. Newbury Park, CA: Sage.

Adler, Patricia A., and Peter Adler. 2007. "The Demedicalization of Self-Injury: From Psychopathology to Sociological Deviance." *Journal of Contemporary Ethnography* 36:537–570.

Allen, Robert Clyde. 1991. *Horrible Prettiness: Burlesque and American Culture.* Chapel Hill: University of North Carolina Press.

Allison, Anne. 1994. *Nightwork: Sexuality, Pleasure, and Corporate Masculinity in a Tokyo Hostess Club.* Chicago: University of Chicago Press.

Alvesson, Mats, and Yvonne Due Billing. 1997. *Understanding Gender and Organizations.* Thousand Oaks, CA: Sage.

Baldwin, Michelle. 2004. *Burlesque and the New Bump-n-Grind.* Denver, CO: Speck.

Barnes v. Glen Theatre, Inc. 501 U.S. 560 (1991).

Barry, Kathleen. 1995. *The Prostitution of Sexuality.* New York: New York University Press.

Barton, Bernadette. 2002. "Dancing on the Möbius Strip: Challenging the Sex War Paradigm." *Gender & Society* 16:585–602.

———. 2006. *Stripped: Inside the Lives of Exotic Dancers.* New York: New York University Press.

———. 2007. "Managing the Toll of Stripping: Boundary Setting among Exotic Dancers." *Journal of Contemporary Ethnography* 36:571–596.

Baxter, Janeen, and Erik Olin Wright. 2000. "The Glass Ceiling Hypothesis." *Gender & Society* 14:275–294.

Bell, Holly, Lacey Sloan, and Chris Strickling. 1998. "Exploiter or Exploited: Topless Dancers Reflect on Their Experiences." *Affia* 3:352–368.

Beller, Thomas. 2004. "What I Learned at the Strip Club." *Men's Health*, September, pp. 84–88.

Berg, Bruce L. 2004. *Qualitative Research Methods for the Social Sciences.* New York: Pearson Education.

Bernstein, Elizabeth. 2007. *Temporarily Yours: Intimacy, Authenticity, and the Commerce of Sex.* Chicago: University of Chicago Press.

Black, Donald. 1993. *The Social Structure of Right and Wrong.* San Diego: Academic Press.

Blumer, Herbert. 1969. *Symbolic Interactionism: Perspective and Method.* Berkeley: University of California Press.

Boles, Jacqueline, and Albeno P. Garbin. 1974a. "The Choice of Stripping for a Living: An Empirical and Theoretical Explanation." *Sociology of Work and Occupations* 1:110–123.

———. 1974b. "The Strip Club and Stripper-Customer Patterns of Interaction." *Sociology and Social Research* 58:136–144.

Bordo, Susan. 1997. "Material Girl: The Effacements of Postmodern Culture." Pp. 335–358 in *The Gender and Sexuality Reader,* edited by R. N. Lancaster and M. di Leonardo. New York: Routledge.

———. 2004. *Unbearable Weight: Feminism, Western Culture and the Body.* Berkeley: University of California Press.

Bose, Christine E., and Rachel Bridges Whaley. 2009. "Sex Segregation in the U.S. Labor Force." Pp. 233–242 in *Feminist Frontiers,* edited by V. Taylor, N. Whittier, and L. J. Rupp. Boston: McGraw-Hill.

Bosse, Katharina. 2004. *New Burlesque.* New York: D.A.P/Distributed Art Publishers.

Boswell, A. Ayres, and Joan Spade. 1996. "Fraternities and Collegiate Rape Culture: Why Are Some Fraternities More Dangerous Places for Women?" *Gender & Society* 10:133–147.

Brick, Michael. 2005. "Moving In on New York Laps: Texas Strip Club Owner Plans a Flagship." *New York Times,* January 21, p. 1.

Britton, Dana M. 1997. "Gendered Organizational Logic: Policy and Practice in Men's and Women's Prisons." *Gender & Society* 11:796–818.

———. 2000. "The Epistemology of the Gendered Organization." *Gender & Society* 14:418–434.

Brooks, Siobhan. 1997. "Dancing toward Freedom." Pp. 252–255 in *Whores and Other Feminists,* edited by J. Nagle. New York: Routledge.

Brownmiller, Susan. 1975. *Against Our Will: Men, Women and Rape.* New York: Fawcett Columbine.

Bruckert, Chris. 2002. *Taking It Off, Putting It On: Women in the Strip Trade.* Toronto: Women's Press.

Brumberg, Joan Jacobs. 1997. *The Body Project: An Intimate History of American Girls.* New York: Random House.

Caldwell, Mark. 2005. *New York Night.* New York: Simon and Schuster.

California Assembly Bill 2509. 2000. 110th Sess. (September 28). Pp. 2–9 in *Labor Code,* Chapter 876.

California v. LaRue. 409 U.S. 109 (1972).

Cancian, Francesca M. 1986. "The Feminization of Love." *Signs* 11:692–709.

Carey, Sandra Harley, Robert A. Peterson, and Louis K. Sharpe. 1974. "A Study of Recruitment into Two Deviant Female Occupations." *Sociological Symposium* 8:11–24.

Carpenter, Susan. 2001. "Are Strip Clubs Dancing Around the Law?" *Los Angeles Times,* April 23, p. 1.

Chancer, Lynne Sharon. 1993. "Prostitution, Feminist Theory, and Ambivalence: Notes from the Sociological Underground." *Social Text* 20:143–172.

Chapkis, Wendy. 1997. *Live Sex Acts: Women Performing Erotic Labor.* New York: Routledge.

Chodorow, Nancy J. 1978. *The Reproduction of Mothering: Psychoanalysis and the Sociology of Gender.* Berkeley: University of California Press.

City of Erie v. Pap's A.M. 529 U.S. 277 (2000).

"Club Listings." 2001. Strip Club List [SCL]. At www.scl.com (accessed August 2001).

———. 2005. Strip Club List [SCL]. At www.scl.com (accessed January 29, 2005).

———. 2006a. Strip Club List [SCL]. At www.scl.com (accessed July 18, 2006).

———. 2006b. The Ultimate Strip Club List [TUSCL]. At www.tuscl.com (accessed July 18, 2006).

———. 2007. The Ultimate Strip Club List [TUSCL]. At www.tuscl.com (accessed June 1, 2007).

Collins, Patricia Hill. 1990. *Black Feminist Thought: Knowledge, Consciousness, and the Politics of Empowerment.* New York: Routledge.

Coltrane, Scott. 1998. *Gender and Families.* Thousand Oaks, CA: Pine Forge.

Connell, R. W. 1987. *Gender and Power: Society, the Person, and Sexual Politics.* Palo Alto, CA: Stanford University Press.

———. 1995. *Masculinities.* Berkeley: University of California Press.

———. 2000. *The Men and the Boys.* Berkeley: University of California Press.

———. 2002. *Gender.* Malden, MA: Blackwell.

———. 2005. *Masculinities,* 2d ed. Cambridge, UK: Polity.

Connell, R. W., and James W. Messerschmidt. 2005. "Hegemonic Masculinity: Rethinking the Concept." *Gender & Society* 19(6):829–859.

Crenshaw, Kimberlé Williams. 1995. "Mapping the Margins: Intersectionality, Identity Politics, and Violence against Women of Color." *Stanford Law Review* 43:1241–1299.

Crown, Laurel, and Linda Roberts. 2007. "Against Their Will: Young Women's Nonagentic Sexual Experiences." *Journal of Social and Personal Relationships* 24(3):385–405.

de Beauvoir, Simone. 1957. *The Second Sex.* New York: Knopf.

Dellinger, Kristen. 2004. "Masculinities in 'Safe' and 'Embattled' Organizations: Accounting for Pornographic and Feminist Magazines." *Gender & Society* 18:545–566.

DeMichele, Matthew T., and Richard Tewksbury. 2004. "Sociological Explorations of Site Specific Control: The Role of the Strip Club Bouncer." *Deviant Behavior: An Interdisciplinary Journal* 25:537–593.

Denzin, Norman. 1989. *The Research Act: A Theoretical Introduction to Sociological Methods.* Englewood Cliffs, NJ: Prentice Hall.

Detman, Linda A. 1990. "Women behind Bars: The Feminization of Bartending." Pp. 241–256 in *Job Queues, Gender Queues: Explaining Women's Inroads Into Male Occupations,* edited by Barbara F. Reskin and Patricia A. Roos. Philadelphia: Temple University Press.

Dines, Gail, and Robert Jensen. 2004. "Pornography and Media: Toward a More Critical Analysis." Pp. 369–379 in *Sexualities: Identities, Behaviors and Society,* edited by M. S. Kimmel and R. F. Plante. New York: Oxford University Press.

Dines, Gail, Robert Jensen, and Ann Russo. 1998. *Pornography: The Production and Consumption of Inequality.* New York: Routledge.

Dozema, Jo. 2009. "Forced to Choose: Beyond the Voluntary v. Forced Prostitution Dichotomy." Pp. 517–525 in *Feminist Frontiers,* edited by V. Taylor, N. Whittier, and L. J. Rupp. Boston: McGraw-Hill.

Dudash, Tawnya. 1997. "Peepshow Feminism." Pp. 98–118 in *Whores and Other Feminists*, edited by J. Nagle. New York: Routledge.

Dworkin, Andrea. 1997. *Intercourse*. New York: Simon and Schuster.

Eaves, Elisabeth. 2002. *Bare: On Women, Dancing, Sex, and Power*. New York: Knopf.

Egan, R. Danielle. 2006. *Dancing for Dollars and Paying for Love*. New York: Palgrave Macmillan.

Ehrenreich, Barbara, and Arlie Hochschild. 2002. *Global Woman: Nannies, Maids, and Sex Workers in the New Economy*. New York: Metropolitan Books.

Eneck, Graves E., and James D. Preston 1988. "Counterfeit Intimacy: A Dramaturgical Analysis of an Erotic Performance." *Deviant Behavior: An Interdisciplinary Journal* 9:369–381.

Ensler, Eve. 2000. *The Vagina Monologues*. New York: Dramatist's Play Service.

———. 2005. *The Good Body*. New York: Random House.

Erickson, David John, and Richard Tewksbury. 2000. "The 'Gentleman' in the Club: A Typology of Strip Club Patrons." *Deviant Behavior: An Interdisciplinary Journal* 21:271–293.

Faludi, Susan. 1999. *Stiffed: The Betrayal of the American Man*. New York: Morrow.

Fenstermaker, Sarah, and Candace West. 2002. *Doing Gender, Doing Difference: Inequality, Power, and Institutional Change*. New York: Routledge.

Ferguson, Ann. 1984. "Sex War: The Debate between Radical and Libertarian Reminists." *Signs* 10(1):106–112.

Flint, Anthony. 1996. "Skin Trade Spreading across US: High Tech Fuels Boom for $10b Industry." *Boston Globe*, December 1, p. A1.

Flynn, Clifton P. 2000. "Woman's Best Friend: Pet Abuse and the Role of Companion Animals in the Lives of Battered Women." *Violence against Women* 6:162–177.

Foner, Nancy. 1994. *The Caregiving Dilemma: Working in an American Nursing Home*. Berkeley: University of California Press.

Forsyth, Craig J., and Tina H. Deshotels. 1997. "The Occupational Milieu of the Nude Dancer." *Deviant Behavior: An Interdisciplinary Journal* 18:125–142.

Foucault, Michel. 1990. *The History of Sexuality*. London: Penguin.

Frank, Katherine. 1998. "The Production of Identity and the Negotiation of Intimacy in a 'Gentleman's Club.'" *Sexualities* 1:175–201.

———. 2002. *G-strings and Sympathy: Strip Club Regulars and Male Desire*. Durham, NC: Duke University Press.

———. 2003. "'Just Trying to Relax': Masculinity, Masculinizing Practices, and Strip Club Regulars." *Journal of Sex Research* 40:61–75.

Fried, Gabriel F., and Richard D. Wolff. 1994. "Modern Ancients: Self-Employed Truckers." *Rethinking Marxism* 7:103–115.

Friend, Tad. 2004. "Naked Profits: The Employees Take Over a Strip Club." *New Yorker*, July 12, pp. 56–61.

Geertz, Clifford. 1973. *The Interpretation of Cultures*. New York: Basic Books.

Gerstel, Naomi, and Sally Gallagher. 1994. "Caring for Kith and Kin: Gender, Employment, and the Privatization of Care." *Social Problems* 14:519–539.

Gimlin, Debra. 2002. *Body Work: Beauty and Self Image in American Culture*. Berkeley: University of California Press.

Glaser, Barney G., and Anselm Strauss. 1967. *The Discovery of Grounded Theory: Strategies for Qualitative Research*. Chicago: Aldine.

Goffman, Erving. 1959. *The Presentation of Self in Everyday Life*. Garden City, NY: Doubleday.

———. 1974. *Stigma: Notes on the Management of Spoiled Identity*. New York: J. Aronson.

Goldberg, Gerald Jay. 1986. "4 Brothers—Count 'Em—4." *New York Times*, March 30, p. 1.

Gopnik, Adam. 2001. "The Naked City: The New Burlesque versus the Old Smut." *New Yorker*, July 23, p. 30.

Gruber, James E. 1998. "The Impact of Male Work Environments and Organizational Policies on Women's Experiences of Sexual Harassment." *Gender & Society* 12:301–320.

Hallett, Tim. 2003. "Symbolic Power and Organizational Culture." *Sociological Theory* 21:128–149.

HandsomeRocus. 2008. "Grand Theft Auto: Vice City 100% Walkthrough" (v9.5), http://faqs.ign.com/articles/611/611234p1.html (accessed June 30, 2008).

Hanna, Judith Lynne. 1998. "Undressing the First Amendment and Corsetting the Striptease Dancer." *Drama Review* 42:38–69.

———. 1999. "Toying with the Striptease Dancer and the First Amendment." *Play and Culture Studies* 2:37–55.

Hays, Sharon. 1996. *The Cultural Contradictions of Motherhood*. New Haven, CT: Yale University Press.

Hochschild, Arlie Russell. 1983. *The Managed Heart: Commercialization of Human Feeling*. Berkeley: University of California Press.

Hoffman, Claire. 2006. "Joe Francis: 'Baby, Give Me a Kiss.'" *Los Angeles Times*, August 6. At http://www.latimes.com/features/printedition/magazine/la-tm-gonewil-d32aug06,0,5620406.story (accessed March 3, 2009).

Holsopple, Kelly. 1998. "Stripclubs according to Strippers: Exposing Workplace Sexual Violence." At http://www.uri.edu/artsci/wms/hughes/stripc2.htm (accessed February 3, 2005).

Hondagneu-Sotelo, Pierette. 2001. *Domestica: Immigrant Workers Cleaning and Caring in the Shadows of Affluence*. Berkeley: University of California Press.

Humphrey, Stephen E., and Arnold S. Kahn. 2000. "Fraternities, Athletic Teams, and Rape: Importance of Identification with a Risky Group." *Journal of Interpersonal Violence* 15:1313–1322.

Humphreys, Laud. 1970. *Tearoom Trade: Impersonal Sex in Public Places*. Chicago: Aldine.

Hyde, Janet Shibley. 2005. "The Gender Similarities Hypothesis." *American Psychologist* 60:581–592.

Jarrett, Lucinda. 1997. *Stripping in Time*. London: Pandora.

———. 2000. *Stripping in Time: A History of Erotic Dancing*. London: Pandora.

Jhally, Sut. 1999. *Killing Us Softly 3: Advertising's Image of Women*. Northampton, MA: Media Education Foundation. Film.

———. 2007. *Dreamworlds 3: Desire, Sex and Power in Music Video*. Northampton, MA: Media Education Foundation. Film.

Johansmeyer, Tom. 2009. "Dirty Sexy Money: Is Porn Recession-Proof?" *Atlantic*, January/February, p. 1.

Johnson, Merri Lisa. 1999. "Pole Work: Autoethnography of a Strip Club." *Sexuality and Culture* 2:149–157.

———. 2002. *Jane Sexes It Up: True Confessions of Feminist Desire*. New York: Four Walls, Eight Windows.

Kang, Miliann. 2009. "The Managed Hand: The Commercialization of Bodies and Emotions in Korean Immigrant-Owned Nail Salons." Pp. 253–265 in *Feminist Frontiers,* edited by V. Taylor, N. Whittier, and L. J. Rupp. Boston: McGraw-Hill.

Kanter, Rosabeth Moss. 1993. *Men and Women of the Corporation.* New York: Basic Books.

Kernes, Mark. 2007. "Analyzing the 'Adult Film Industry' Report: Health Study Rife with Errors." *Adult Video News,* November 5. At http://business.avn.com.

Kershaw, Sarah. 2004. "Life as a Live! Nude! Girl! Has a Few Strings Attached." *New York Times,* June 2, p. 1.

Kimmel, Michael S. 1990. *Men Confront Pornography.* New York: Crown.

———. 1994. "Masculinity as Homophobia: Fear, Shame, and Silence in the Construction of Gender Identity." Pp. 119–141 in *Theorizing Masculinities,* edited by H. Brod. Thousand Oaks, CA: Sage.

———. 2000. *The Gendered Society.* New York: Oxford University Press.

———. 2006. *Manhood in America: A Cultural History.* New York: Oxford University Press.

———. 2007. "Masculinity as Homophobia: Fear, Shame and Silence in the Construction of Gender Identity." Pp. 73–82 in *Gender Relations in Global Perspective,* edited by N. Cook. Toronto: Canadian Scholars' Press.

King, Deborah. 1988. "Multiple Jeopardy, Multiple Consciousness: The Context of Black Feminist Ideology." *Signs* 14:42–72.

Kirk, Michael. 2002. "American Porn." *Frontline.* Boston: WGBH Educational Foundation.

Koopman, John. 2003. "Lusty Lady Becomes First Worker-Owned Strip Club." *San Francisco Chronicle,* June 26, p. A17.

Kuntz, Tom. 1997. "Word for Word: A Strippers' Union Contract." *New York Times,* April 20, p. 1.

Langley, Erika. 1997. *The Lusty Lady.* New York: Scalo.

Leidner, Robin. 1993. *Fast Food, Fast Talk: Service Work and the Routinization of Everyday Life.* Berkeley: University of California Press.

Lerum, Kari. 2004. "Sexuality, Power and Camaraderie in Service Work." *Gender & Society* 18:756–776.

Levy, Ariel. 2005. *Female Chauvinist Pigs: Women and the Rise of Raunch Culture.* New York: Free Press.

Lewin, Laurie. 1984. *Naked Is the Best Disguise: My Life as a Stripper.* New York: Morrow.

Lewis, Jacqueline. 1998. "Learning to Strip: The Socialization Experiences of Exotic Dancers." *Canadian Journal of Human Sexuality* 7:51–66.

———. 2006. "'I'll Scratch Your Back if You'll Scratch Mine': The Role of Reciprocity, Power and Autonomy in the Strip Club." *Canadian Review of Sociology and Anthropology* 43:297–311.

Liepe-Levinson, Katherine. 2002. *Strip Show: Performances of Gender and Desire.* New York: Routledge.

Lion's Den. 2001. *Employee/Entertainer Handbook.* Author's collection.

Loe, Meika. 1996. "Working for Men: At the Intersection of Power, Gender, and Sexuality." *Sociological Inquiry* 66:399–421.

Lofland, John, and Lyn H. Lofland. 1995. *Analyzing Social Settings: A Guide to Qualitative Observation and Analysis.* New York: Wadsworth.

Lorber, Judith. 1995. *Paradoxes of Gender.* New Haven, CT: Yale University Press.

Lusty Lady. 2009. "A Brief History of the Lusty Lady Theater." http://www.lustyladysf. com/history/ (accessed December 23, 2009).

MacKinnon, Catharine A. 1987. *Feminism Unmodified: Discourses on Life and Law.* Cambridge, MA: Harvard University Press.

———. 2005. "Pornography as Trafficking." *Michigan Journal of International Law* 26:993–1012.

Maher, Lisa. 1997. *Sexed Work: Gender, Race, and Resistance in a Brooklyn Drug Market.* New York: Oxford University Press.

Maticka-Tyndale, Eleanor, Jacqueline Lewis, Jocalyn P. Clark, Jennifer Zubick, and Shelley Young. 2000. "Exotic Dancing and Health." *Women and Health* 31:87–108.

Matson, Heidi. 1995. *Ivy League Stripper.* New York: Arcade.

Mayer, Vicki. 2009. "Soft-Core in Prime Time: The Political Economy of a 'Cultural Trend.'" Paper presented at the annual meeting of the International Communication Association, New York City, May 5.

McCaghy, Charles H., and James K. Skipper, Jr. 1969. "Lesbian Behavior as an Adaptation to the Occupation of Stripping." *Social Problems* 17:262–270.

———. 1972. "Stripping: Anatomy of a Deviant Life Style." Pp. 362–373 in *Life Styles: Diversity in American Society,* edited by S. D. Feldman and G. W. Thielbar. Boston: Little, Brown.

McNair, Brian. 2002. *Striptease Culture: Sex, Media and the Democratization of Desire.* New York: Routledge.

Meridian, Reese. 1997. "Special Report: It's a Black Thing . . . Or Is It?" *Exotic Dancer Bulletin,* Fall, pp. 52–54.

Miller, Eleanor M. 1986. *Street Woman.* Philadelphia: Temple University Press.

Miller, Jody, and Martin D. Schwartz. 1995. "Rape Myths and Violence against Street Prostitutes." *Deviant Behavior: An Interdisciplinary Journal* 16:1–23.

Naples, Nancy. 1996. "A Feminist Revisiting of the 'Insider/Outsider' Debate: The 'Outsider Phenomenon' in Rural Iowa." *Qualitative Sociology* 19:83–106.

———. 2003. *Feminism and Method: Ethnography, Discourse. Analysis, and Activist Research.* New York: Routledge.

Niemi, Robert. 2006. *History in the Media.* Santa Barbara, CA: ABC-CLIO.

Nygaard, Sandra. 2003. "Bawdy Beautiful New Burlesque Shakes Up San Francisco." November 7. At http://www.sfgate.com/cgi-bin/article.cgi?file=/gate/archive/2003/11/07/burlesquesf.DTL (accessed January 31, 2005).

Oakley, Ann. 1981. "Interviewing Women: A Contradiction in Terms." Pp. 30–61 in *Doing Feminist Research,* edited by H. Roberts. London: Routledge and Kegan Paul.

Pascoe, C. J. 2007. *Dude, You're a Fag.* Berkeley: University of California Press.

Pasko, Lisa. 2002. "Naked Power: The Practice of Stripping as a Confidence Game." *Sexualities* 5:49–66.

Paules, Greta Foff. 1991. *Dishing It Out: Power and Resistance among Waitresses in a New Jersey Restaurant.* Philadelphia: Temple University Press.

Peiss, Kathy. 1986. *Cheap Amusements: Working Women and Leisure in Turn of the Century New York.* Philadelphia: Temple University Press.

Pendleton, Jennifer. 1998. "Strippers Sue Area Clubs over Treatment." *Los Angeles Times,* December 15, p. 1.

Phillips, Lynn M. 2000. *Flirting with Danger: Young Women's Reflections on Sexuality and Domination.* New York: New York University Press.

Posner, Richard A., and Katharine B. Silbaugh. 1996. *A Guide to America's Sex Laws.* Chicago: University of Chicago Press.

Price, Kim. 2000. "Stripping Women: Workers' Control in Strip Clubs." *Current Research in Occupations and Professions, Unusual Occupations* 11:3–33.

———. 2008. "'Keeping the Dancers in Check': The Gendered Organization of Stripping Work in The Lion's Den." *Gender & Society* 22:367–389.

Prus, Robert C., and Styllianoss Irini. 1980. *Hookers, Rounders, and Desk Clerks: The Social Organization of the Hotel Community.* Toronto: Gage.

Query, Julia, and Vicky Funari. 2000. *Live Nude Girls UNITE!* New York: First Run Features.

Raphael, Jody. 2004. *Listening to Olivia: Violence, Poverty and Prostitution.* Boston: Northeastern University Press.

Reich v. Circle C Investments, Inc. 998 F.2d 324 (5th Cir. 1993).

Reich v. Priba Corporation. 890 F. Supp. 586 (N.D. Tex. 1995).

Reid, Scott A., Jonathan S. Epstein, and D. E. Benson. 1995. "Does Exotic Dancing Pay Well but Cost Dearly?" Pp. 284–288 in *Readings in Deviant Behavior,* edited by A. Thio and T. C. Calhoun. New York: HarperCollins.

ResearchWare. 2005. *HyperRESEARCH.* Randolph, MA: ResearchWare.

Resnick, Stephen A., and Richard D. Wolff. 1987. *Knowledge and Class: A Marxian Critique of Political Economy.* Chicago: University of Chicago Press.

Risman, Barbara, and Pepper Schwartz. 2002. "After the Sexual Revolution: Gender Politics in Teen Dating." *Contexts* 1:16–24.

Romano, Tricia. 2004, "Bombshells Away! The New Burlesque Hits Gotham." At http://www.villagevoice.com/news/0310,romano,42328,1.html (accessed January 31, 2005).

Ronai, Carol Rambo. 1992a. "Managing Aging in Young Adulthood: The 'Aging' Table Dancer." *Journal of Aging Studies* 6:307–317.

———. 1992b. "The Reflective Self through Narrative: A Night in the Life of an Exotic Dancer Researcher." Pp. 102–124 in *Investigating Subjectivity: Research on Lived Experience,* edited by Carolyn Ellis and Michael Flaherty. Newbury Park, CA: Sage.

———. 1994. "Narrative Resistance to Deviance: Identity Management among Strip-Tease Dancers." *Perspectives on Social Problems* 6:195–213.

———. 1998. "Sketching with Derrida: An Ethnography of a Researcher/Erotic Dancer." *Qualitative Inquiry* 4:405–420.

Ronai, Carol Rambo, and Rebecca Cross. 1998. "Dancing with Identity: Narrative Resistance Strategies of Male and Female Stripteasers." *Deviant Behavior: An Interdisciplinary Journal* 19:99–119.

Ronai, Carol Rambo, and Carolyn Ellis. 1989. "Turn-ons for Money: Interactional Strategies of the Table Dancer." *Journal of Contemporary Ethnography* 18:271–298.

Ross, Colin A., Geri Anderson, Sharon Herber, and G. Ron Norton. 1990. "Dissociation and Abuse among Multiple-Personality Patients, Prostitutes, and Exotic Dancers." *Hospital and Community Psychiatry* 41:328–330.

Rubin, Gayle S. 1984. "Thinking Sex: Notes for a Radical Theory of the Politics of Sexuality." Pp. 3–44 in *The Lesbian and Gay Studies Reader,* edited by H. Abelove, M. A. Barale, and D. M. Halperin. New York: Routledge.

Rubin, Lillian B. 1994. *Families on the Fault Line: America's Working Class Speaks about Family, the Economy, Race and Ethnicity.* New York: HarperCollins.

Salutin, Marilyn. 1971. "Stripper Morality." *Transaction* 8:12–22.

Sanchez, Lisa E. 1997. "Boundaries of Legitimacy: Sex, Violence, Citizenship, and Community in a Local Sexual Economy." *Law and Social Inquiry* 22:543–580.

Sanday, Peggy Reeves. 1996. "Rape-Prone Versus Rape-Free Campus Cultures." *Violence against Women* 2:191–208.

Schad v. Borough of Mount Ephraim. 452 U.S. 61 (1981).

Schiff, Frederick. 2001. "Nude Dancing: Scenes of Sexual Celebration in a Contested Culture." *Journal of American Culture* 22:9–16.

Schlosser, Eric. 1997. "The Business of Porn." *U.S. News and World Report* 122:42–50.

Scott, David A. 2003. *Behind the G-String: An Exploration of the Stripper's Image, Her Person and Her Meaning.* Jefferson, NC: McFarland.

Scott, Megan. 2006. "Exotic Dancers Face Real Dangers." *Desiree Alliance.* At http://www.desireealliance.org/Exoticdancersfacerealdangers.htm (accessed October 20, 2009).

Scully, Diana. 1990. *Understanding Sexual Violence: A Study of Convicted Rapists.* Boston: Unwin Hyman.

Scully, Diana, and Joseph Marolla. 1985. "Riding the Bull at Gilley's: Convicted Rapists Describe the Rewards of Rape." *Social Problems* 32:251–263.

Selfe, David, and Vincent Burke. 2001. *Perspectives on Sex, Crime and Society.* London: Routledge-Cavendish.

Sheffield, Carole J. 1994. "Sexual Terrorism." Pp. 1–22 in *Women: A Feminist Perspective,* edited by Jo Freeman. Mountain View, CA: Mayfield.

Shteir, Rachel. 2004. *Striptease: The Untold History of the Girlie Show.* New York: Oxford University Press.

Simmel, Georg, and Donald Nathan Levine. 1971. *On Individuality and Social Forms: Selected Writings.* Chicago: University of Chicago Press.

Skipper, James K., Jr. 1970. "Stripteasers: The Anatomy and Career Contingencies of a Deviant Occupation." *Social Problems* 17:391–405.

———. 1971. "Stripping: Anatomy of a Deviant Lifestyle." Pp. 362–373 in *Life Styles: Diversity in American Society,* edited by S. D. Feldman and G. W. Thielbar. Boston: Little, Brown.

Skipper, James K., Jr., and Charles H. McCaghy. 1971. "Stripteasing: A Sex Oriented Occupation." Pp. 275–296 in *Studies in the Sociology of Sex,* edited by J. M. Henslin. New York: Appleton-Century-Crofts.

Smith, Gerrilyn, Dee Cox, and Jacqui Saradjian. 1999. *Women and Self Harm: Understanding, Coping and Healing from Self-Mutilation.* New York: Routledge.

Snyder, Robert W. 1991. "Vaudeville and the Transformation of Popular Culture." Pp. 133–146 in *Inventing Times Square: Culture and Commerce at the Crossroads of the World,* edited by W. R. Taylor. Baltimore: Johns Hopkins University Press.

Steinem, Gloria. 1984. *Outrageous Acts and Everyday Rebellions.* New York: Holt.

Sun, Chyng, and Miguel Picker. 2008. *The Price of Pleasure: Pornography, Sexuality and Relationships.* Northampton, MA: Media Education Foundation. Film.

Sweet, Nova, and Richard Tewksbury. 2000a. "Entry, Maintenance, and Departure from a Career in the Sex Industry: Strippers' Experiences of the Occupational Costs and Rewards." *Humanity and Society* 24:136–161.

———. 2000b. "What's a Nice Girl Like You Doing in a Place Like This? Pathways to a Career in Stripping." *Sociological Spectrum* 20:325–343.

Tewksbury, Richard. 1994. "A Dramaturgical Analysis of Male Strippers." *Journal of Men's Studies* 2:325–342.

Thompson, Sharon. 1996. *Going All the Way: Teenage Girls' Tales of Sex, Romance, and Pregnancy*. New York: Hill and Wang.

Thompson, William E., and Jackie L. Harred. 1992. "Topless Dancers: Managing Stigma in a Deviant Occupation." *Deviant Behavior: An Interdisciplinary Journal* 13:291–311.

Thompson, William E., Jackie L. Harred, and Barbara E. Burks. 2003. "Managing the Stigma of Topless Dancing: A Decade Later." *Deviant Behavior: An Interdisciplinary Journal* 24:551–570.

Toossi, Mitra. 2006. "A New Look at Long-Term Labor Force Projections to 2050." *Monthly Labor Review* 129(11):19–39.

Trautner, Mary Nell. 2005. "Doing Gender, Doing Class: The Performance of Sexuality in Exotic Dance Clubs." *Gender & Society* 19:771–788.

Tucker, Dana M. 1997. "Preventing the Secondary Effects of Adult Entertainment Establishments: Is Zoning the Solution?" *Journal of Land Use and Environmental Law* 12(2):383–431.

Urla, Jacqueline, and Alan C. Swedlund. 1995. "The Anthropometry of Barbie: Unsettling Ideals of the Feminine Body in Popular Culture." Pp. 277–313 in *Deviant Bodies,* edited by Jennifer Terry and Jacqueline Urla. Bloomington: Indiana University Press.

U.S. Bureau of the Census. 2000. *Demographic, Social, and Housing Characteristics*. Washington, DC: Government Printing Office.

———. 2003. *American Community Survey: Public Use Microdata Sample (PUMS)*. Washington, DC: Government Printing Office.

———. 2005. *American Community Survey: Public Use Microdata Sample (PUMS)*. Washington, DC: Government Printing Office.

———. 2006. *American Community Survey: Public Use Microdata Sample (PUMS)*. Washington, DC: Government Printing Office.

U.S. Department of Justice. 2006. "Criminal Victimization in the United States." Table 91: Personal and Property Crimes. Washington, DC: U.S. Department of Justice, Bureau of Justice Statistics.

———. 2009. "Rape and Sexual Violence." National Institute of Justice. http://www.ojp.gov/nij/topics/crime/rape-sexual-violence/ (accessed April 3, 2009).

Vance, Carole S. 1984. *Pleasure and Danger: Exploring Female Sexuality*. London: Pandora.

van der Veen, Marjolein. 2000. "Beyond Slavery and Capitalism: Producing Class Difference in the Sex Industry." Pp. 121–141 in *Class and Its Others,* edited by J. K. Gibson-Graham, S. A. Resnick, and R. D. Wolff. Minneapolis: University of Minnesota Press.

Walkowitz, Judith R. 1982. *Prostitution and Victorian Society: Women, Class, and the State*. New York: Cambridge University Press.

Weinberg, Daniel H. 2004. "Evidence from Census 2000 about Earnings by Detailed Occupation for Men and Women." Table 4: Twenty Occupations with the Highest Percentage of Female Workers. Washington, DC: U.S. Bureau of the Census, May.

Weitzer, Ronald. 2000. *Sex for Sale: Prostitution, Pornography, and the Sex Industry*. New York: Routledge.

———. 2005. "New Directions in Research on Prostitution." *Crime, Law and Social Change* 43:211–235.

Weldon, Jo. 2005. "Burlesque at G-Strings Forever." At http://www.gstringsforever.com/burlesque.html (accessed January 31, 2005).

Wesley, Jennifer K. 2002. "Growing Up Sexualized: Issues of Power and Violence in the Lives of Female Exotic Dancers." *Violence against Women* 8:1182–1207.

West, Candace, and Sarah Fenstermaker 1995. "Doing Difference." *Gender & Society* 9(1): 8–37.

West, Candace, and Don H. Zimmerman. 1987. "Doing Gender." *Gender & Society* 1(2):125–151.

Williams, Christine L. 1992. "The Glass Escalator: Hidden Advantages for Men in the 'Female' Professions." *Social Problems* 39:253–267.

Wolf, Naomi. 1992. *The Beauty Myth: How Images of Beauty Are Used against Women.* New York: Random House.

Wood, Elizabeth Anne. 2000. "Working in the Fantasy Factory: The Attention Hypothesis and the Enacting of Masculine Power in Strip Clubs." *Journal of Contemporary Ethnography* 29:5–31.

Wosnitzer, Robert, and Ana J. Bridges. 2007. "Aggression and Sexual Behavior in Best-Selling Pornography: A Content Analysis Update." Paper presented at the annual meeting of the International Communication Association, San Francisco, May 23.

Yancey, Kitty Bean. 2003. "Stripping's New Side." *USA Today,* October 27. http://www.usatoday.com/life/2003-10-27-strip-clubs_x.htm (accessed October 1, 2008).

Yllö, Kersti A. 1998. "Through a Feminist Lens: Gender, Power and Violence." Pp. 609–618 in *Families in the U.S.: Kinship and Domestic Politics,* edited by Karen V. Hansen and Anita Ilta Garey. Philadelphia: Temple University Press.

Zussman, Robert. 1992. *Intensive Care: Medical Ethics and the Medical Profession.* Chicago: University of Chicago Press.

Index

abolitionism. *See* sex work, eradication/ elimination of

Accused, The (film), 168

Acker, Joan, 42–43, 63

acting, 105, 137 (*see also* identity, fake; stripper(s), charade of genuine interest in patrons); surface *vs.* deep, 104–5

Adler, Patricia, 141–42

Adler, Peter, 141–42

adult entertainment. *See* sex work industry

affection. *See* physical contact with patrons

affirmation, men seeking, 69–79

African American strippers, 119. *See also* interviewees, Destiny; race of employees

age, norms around, 113–14, 117; and career longevity, 117; stigma toward aging strippers, 116–18

aggression, men's, 179, 189; performances of verbal and physical, 88–96

alcohol consumption, 6, 13, 17, 62, 103, 107, 157. *See also* drink fees

alienation, 126–30, 137. *See also under* identity, fake; identity problems; stripper(s); stripping labor

Allen, Robert C., 30

Allison, Anne, 85

amateur nights, 181–82, 184

amateur stripping, 36–37

Araujo, Cheryl Ann, 168–69

archetypal roles, 110

Assembly Bill 2509, 161

"babysitting" strippers, 37, 50, 61, 176. *See also* housemoms; stripper(s), constantly monitored by male workers

Backwoods, 4

"bank," 13

Bare (Eaves), 76

Barnes v. Glen Theatre, Inc., 33, 92

bartenders, 7, 52, 109 (*see also* interviewees); demographics, 202–3t; female, 166, 193; wages, 17–18, 157

Barton, Bernadette, 41, 142

bathing routine after working, ritualized, 135–37, 141

Bazooms, 74

Beautiful Blondes, 29

beauty, standards of, 113–17, 120–22

Beller, Thomas, 68

Benson, D. E., 127

Bernstein, Elizabeth, 79

bisexuality, 97

bodies at work, 113–20

body image, 121–22

body labor, 38. *See also* stripping labor

body types, ideal, 113–20, 122

Boles, Jacqueline, 96

Bordo, Susan, 114

Boswell, A. Ayres, 167, 169, 190–91

bouncers, 7, 51, 63, 94 (*see also* interviewees); demographics, 202–3t

breast augmentation surgery, 115

Bridges, Ana, 168

Britton, Dana, 42

Bruckert, Chris, 96

Burke, Vincent, 78

burlesque, 30–31; "new," 34, 36

Caldwell, Mark, 29

California Assembly Bill 2509, 161

California v. LaRue, 33
Canadian strip clubs, 96
Champagne Room (CR/c-room), 176–80, 185, 188, 195
Chancer, Lynn Sharon, 103
Chapkis, Wendy, 28–29, 40–41, 78–79, 137
charitable events, 182–83
City of Erie v. Pap's A.M., 33, 92
"Closing Time," 17
club fliers, 160–61
club listings. *See* Strip Club List; TUSCL
club regulars (regular patrons), 86–87
club texts, analysis of, 102, 205. *See also* club fliers; *Employee/Entertainer Handbook*
cocktail waitresses, xi, 15, 53–54 (*see also* interviewees; patrons, relations with female workers); contrasted with strippers, 53–54, 112; demographics, 53–54, 202–3t; emotional labor demanded of, 15; propositioned by patrons, 66, 67, 186, 201; wages, 8, 9, 17, 18, 155–56
collective liability, 96
Columbian Exposition, 30
Combat Zone, 32
compartmentalization of home and work life, 107–8, 120–21, 131–33, 135 (*see also* acting); keeping stripping a secret, 120, 123–26
competition between strippers, 56, 123, 146, 159, 160, 166. *See also under* Lusty Lady theater; stripper(s), distrust and lack of solidarity among
Connell, Raewyn, 81, 88, 187
content analysis. *See* club texts
contract dancers, 13. *See also* traveling dancers
cooch dance, 30–31
Copa Cabana, 178, 179, 185
costumes, 110–11
cover charge, 10. *See also* door fees
Cross, Rebecca, 131
Crown, Laurel, 166
cultural capital, 44
cycle of abuse perspectives, 151, 152; problems with, 151
cynicism, 120, 126–30, 137

"Dancer Daily Report, The," 50
dances, types of, 148. *See also* lap dancing; private dances
dancing, transformative possibilities of, 131
dating strippers, 59–60, 72–73, 77–78, 201
Davis, Gray, 161
de Beauvoir, Simone, 113
deejays, 7, 50–51 (*see also* interviewees); demographics, 202–3t; tipping system and, 155, 156, 159
DeMichele, Matthew, 51
denial, 120
distrust, xii
division of labor. *See* gendered organization of strip club work
"dollar dances," 9, 147, 153, 154, 159. *See also* tips
domestic violence, attitudes toward, 90
door fees, 6, 10, 87, 147, 149, 153, 156, 178
doormen, 51, 109 (*see also* interviewees); demographics, 202–3t
double standard, sexual, 111
Dreamworlds 3 (Jhally), 71
drink fees, 147, 149, 153–54, 157, 178
drug use, 61, 95, 103, 189, 190. *See also* alcohol consumption
Dworkin, Andrea, 40

Eaves, Elisabeth, 76
economic exploitation, 146, 150, 152–54, 162–63 (*see also specific topics*); supplementing, 160–61
economic rationale for stripping, 9, 126–30
Egan, Danielle, 79
emotional labor, 103–9, 137; of bartenders, 109; Chapkis, Wendy, on, 40–41; of cocktail waitresses, 53, 109; emotional toll of performing, 48, 74, 104–9; impact on patrons, 75; Lion's Den's expectation of, 15, 103–4; setting limits around, 132; in various occupations, 38, 103, 109
emotion management, 104
Employee/Entertainer Handbook, 10, 62, 192, 204–5; quotes from, 15, 50, 61–62, 73–74, 93, 103–4, 178, 205–7

employees, 6–8. *See also* interviewees; *specific topics*

empowerment, of women, 2; *vs.* disempowerment, 163. *See also under* sex workers; stripper(s)

entry price. *See* door fees

Epstein, Jonathan S., 127

Erickson, David John, 70, 88

ethnography. *See* interviews; participant observation

Exotic Dancers' Alliance, 161

exploitation, notions of, 150–52. *See also specific topics*

eye contact, 106–7

"fag," 97

Faludi, Susan, 45

family members. *See* compartmentalization of home and work life

female-dominated occupations, 38, 39

femininities, presentation of, 141

feminist perspectives, 28, 40, 41, 103, 150, 151, 152, 162, 167

feminized workplaces, 38

fines, system of, 160–61

First Amendment, 33, 34, 92–93

Foucault, Michel, 32, 41

Frank, Katherine, 44, 69, 75, 79, 187

fraternity men, 186

"free rider" problem, 153–54

Fried, Gabriel, 155

friendships, 130

Garbin, A. P., 96

gay men, 97

gender and sexuality as organizational resources in Lion's Den, 43, 57–61

gendered job titles, 63. *See also specific job titles*

gendered organizational context, 62–65

gendered organizational jeopardy, 21, 43, 64, 100, 103, 164, 167

gendered organizational logic, 42

gendered organizational theory, 21, 63, 166

gendered organization of strip club work, 42–46, 193–95, 205; gendered and economic organization, 18–19, 162–65

gendered paradoxes, 21, 39–41, 145–46, 166–67

gendered processes, 43, 49, 50; in The Lion's Den, 20, 43, 49–57

gendered substructure of The Lion's Den, 43, 61–62

gender exploitation, 150, 151

genitalia, female, 58, 111, 112. *See also* stripper(s), refusing to undress

Girls Gone Wild DVD series, 47–48, 64

Goffman, Erving, 80, 123–24

good-girl/bad-girl dichotomy and hierarchy, 54, 112

group connectedness among patrons, performances of, 79–88

Guys Gone Wild DVD series, 64

"healing work," stripping as, 130

Hefner, Christie, 20

Hefner, Hugh, 20, 81

heterosexuality. *See* masculinities performed by male patrons

hierarchy, social, 57, 137 (*see also* gendered organizational jeopardy; gendered paradoxes); among patrons, 83–85; good-girl/bad-girl, 54, 112

Hochschild, Arlie, 40–41, 104, 121, 137

Hoffman, Claire, 47

holiday buffets, 184

homoeroticism, 97

homophobia, 97

hostess clubs *vs.* strip clubs, 85–86

"Hot for Young Teacher" (Van Halen), xii

Hotties, 4

house fees, 182, 184

"house girls," 57

housemoms, 55–56

humor, 138

Humphreys, Laud, 27–29

identifying as an object of desire, 121–23

identity, fake, 91–92, 124, 137

identity problems, 48, 102, 131

income. *See* wages

inequality regimes, 43

interaction-based perspectives, 40–42, 62–63

interviewees: Amelia (stripper), 57, 74, 202t, 209–10; Angela (cocktail waitress), x, 75, 121–22, 199–200, 202t, 206, 210; Charlie (patron), 59–60, 71–72, 124, 202t, 210–11; Craig (patron), 69–72, 97–98, 202t, 211; Daria (stripper), 128, 132, 134, 202t, 211–12; Darrel (bouncer), 51, 202t, 212; Dawn (stripper), 202t, 212–13; demographics, 202–3t; Destiny (stripper), 57, 107–8, 125, 128, 136, 202t, 213; Elsie (stripper), 133; Evangelina (cocktail waitress), 58, 126, 143, 202t, 213–14; Faith (stripper), 95, 96, 131, 144, 202t, 214; Fiona (stripper), 92, 105, 108, 138, 139, 143, 153, 202t, 214–15; Frank (bouncer, doorman), ix–x, 51–52, 58, 86, 147, 202t, 215; identity, disclosure, and experience, 205–8; Jack (patron), 87, 202t, 215–16; Jade (stripper), 119, 202t, 216; James (bartender, bouncer, patron), 59, 202t, 216–17; Jeff (patron), 14, 69, 202t, 217; Jen (cocktail waitress, stripper), 56, 122, 139, 202t, 217–18; Kelly (cocktail waitress, stripper), 15, 53, 202t, 218; Layla (traveling stripper), 129–30, 133–34, 159, 202t, 218–19; Leo (deejay), 50, 59–61, 81, 202t, 219; Marcus (deejay, patron), 50, 138, 203t, 219–20; Marissa (cocktail waitress, stripper), 58, 94, 106, 203t, 220; Marlon (patron), 203t, 220–21; Mindy (stripper), 89, 94–95, 108, 122–23, 128, 132, 203t, 221; Ned (bartender, bouncer), 87, 203t, 221–22; Nina (stripper), 117–18, 203t, 222–23; Robin (stripper), 16, 76–77, 92, 106–7, 122, 138–39, 203t, 223; Roxanne (cocktail waitress, stripper), xii, 54, 58, 86, 96, 102, 105–6, 113, 115–17, 136–37, 140, 147–49, 203t, 223; Shane (patron), 92, 97, 98, 203t, 223–24; Stella (stripper), 74–76, 107, 121, 129, 203t, 224–25; Steve (owner-manager), ix–xii, 1, 9–10, 20, 37, 44–45, 50, 55, 61, 143, 157, 165, 175, 176, 180–85, 197, 203t, 204–6, 225; Summer (stripper), 135, 203t, 226; Tamara (stripper), 56, 74, 88–89, 91–92, 94, 101–2, 104–5, 108, 110, 115, 118, 124–25, 127, 130–34, 153–54, 203t, 226–27; Ted (bartender, bouncer, door-man, patron), 52, 77–78, 88, 106, 203t, 227; Tess (stripper), 60, 76, 107, 134, 203t, 227–28; Tim (deejay, patron), 203t, 228; Travis (deejay), 59, 203t, 228–29; Vivian (stripper), 108–9, 117, 125–26, 203t, 229; Walter (patron), 203t, 229–30; Winston (patron), 60, 203t, 230
interviews, 200–201, 204–5
Ivy League Stripper (Mattson), 131

Jarrett, Lucinda, 30
Jhally, Sut, 71, 110

Kang, Miliann, 38
Kelley, Sheila, 34–35
Kimmel, Michael, 85, 187

labor, 150, 151. *See also* body labor; emotional labor; stripping labor
"lap dance room," 177, 178
lap dancing, 166, 195. *See also* private dances
larger strippers, 117–18
late fees, 160
lawsuits, 191
Layden, Mary Ann, 96
Leidner, Robin, 109
lesbian strippers, 97
Levy, Ariel, 35
Lewin, Laurie, 121
Lewis, Jacqueline, 49
libertarian perspective, 152
Liepe-Levinson, Katherine, 71, 177
Lion's Den, 20 (*see also specific topics*); across time, 169–71, 174–76; antagonism toward strippers, 146; compared with other strip clubs, 5, 6, 20, 49, 75, 165–66 (*see also* Copa Cabana); descriptions and characterizations of, 201; distrust and lack of solidarity in, xii; employees, strippers, and club management, 6–10 (*see also* interviewees); expenses, 157, 158; inside, 5–6; layout, 11f; overlapping organizational aspects of, 18; physical conditions, 101; Price-Glynn's introduction and entry into, ix, 199–200, 205–6; relations with

surrounding community, 4–5; research-
ing, xi, xii, 1, 3, 199–208; revenue, 156–57
(*see also* profit(s)); revisiting, 175–76;
rules, 93; situating, 3–6; tour of, 10, 12–19;
a typical shift, 12–19; virtual reentry into,
174–75. *See also* Strip Club List
Lion's Den Grill, 176
Live Nude Girls UNITE! (Query and
Funari), 34
Live Sex Acts (Chapkis), 28, 40–41
Loe, Meika, 74
loneliness. *See* affirmation, men seeking
Lorber, Judith, 21, 39
Lusty Lady theater, 19–21, 34, 35, 37

MacKinnon, Catharine, 150, 151
male bonding and identification. *See* group
connectedness; masculinities performed
by male patrons
Managed Heart, The (Hochschild), 41, 137.
See also Hochschild, Arlie
management and owners, corporate,
145–46, 175–76 (*see also* interviewees,
Steve); allegations of violence by, 189–93;
female managers, 166, 195
Marxist perspectives, 150
masculinities performed by male patrons,
69–70, 97, 186–90, 197; consequences of
men's behavior, 98–100; hegemonic, marginalized and subordinated, 81, 88, 187
Maticka-Tyndale, Eleanor, 48
McCaghy, Charles, 151
McDonald, Mark, 30
media, 34
menstruation, 115
methodology, 25–26. *See also* club texts;
interaction-based perspectives; interviews; participant observation; sexual
subcultures; Strip Club List
Miller, Eleanor, 26–29
Miller, Jody, 96
Minsky Brothers, 31
money flows, 75–78, 127–29 (*see also* tips;
wages); and the genuineness of stripper-
patron interactions, 75–78; worker comparisons, 158–60

morality, 162–63. *See also* economic exploitation; exploitation
music videos, 109–10

New England strip clubs, 170–71, 171t
nude performance, erotic, 109–13
nudity, 57; state regulations for, 232n28

Oprah Winfrey Show, 34–35
organizational disempowerment of
strippers. *See* gendered organizational
jeopardy

Paglia, Camille, 152
participant observation, 200–201, 204–5
Pascoe, C. J., 97
Pasko, Lisa, 135
patron interviews, 201. *See also*
interviewees
patrons, 68–70, 135 (*see also* interviewees;
specific topics); asking out strippers and
waitresses, 72, 77–78, 201; club rules and,
93; demographics, 5, 202–3t; ejected,
94; female workers expected to cater
to the needs of, 15; hired as workers, 6,
87–88; outliers and exceptions, 97–98;
personal *vs.* impersonal exchanges
with, 76–79; possessive behavior toward
strippers, 76–77; regular, 14–15, 86–87;
relationships with strippers, 75 (*see also*
dating strippers); relations with female
workers, 18–19, 25–26; rude behavior, 16,
48, 83–84, 135, 179, 186 (*see also* sexual
aggression; stripper(s), devaluation of);
watching television, 139
Paules, Greta Foff, 140
peep shows, *vs.* strip clubs, 35. *See also*
Lusty Lady theater
Phillips, Lynn, 168
physical contact with patrons, 56, 57, 94,
165–66, 186 (*see also* private dances;
sexual aggression; sexual contact with
patrons); at Copa Cabana, 179; after
Players' takeover of Lion's Den, 177, 178;
with waitresses, 54. *See also* cocktail
waitresses, propositioned by patrons

Playboy Corporation, 80–81

Players (taking over Lion's Den), 165; club changes, 176–80; club happenings, 181–84; house fees, 184; new directions, similar outcomes, 195–96; turnover, 180–81; women's work and women's woes, 185–95

pole tricks, 16–17

police, 4, 5, 93, 157; undercover, 191

pornography, 71, 81; violent content, 168

power. *See specific topics*

Pretty Woman (film), 131

private dances, 147–49, 154, 155, 158, 159, 185–86. *See also* lap dancing

private lives of strippers, 137. *See also* compartmentalization of home and work life; stripper(s), relationships with men

professionalism, xi, 28, 130, 131

profit(s) (*see also* tips): in adult entertainment, 2; flow of, 156–61; performances, power, and, 147–50; women's profits and payouts, 154–56

prostitution, 27–28, 78–79, 132. *See also* sex work

pseudonyms, strippers choosing, 91–92, 124, 133

Query, Julia. See *Live Nude Girls UNITE!*

race and class dynamics, 43–46, 118–20

race of employees, 5, 7, 118–20

racist dialogue, 90–91

Railton (location of Lion's Den), 3–5

rape, 94, 95, 207

rape culture and myths, 96, 167–69, 186 (*see also* sexual aggression); Strip Club List and, 190–94

Raphael, Jody, 96

RealGirls, 161, 176

red-light districts, 32, 33

regular patrons (club regulars), 14–15; core group of, 86–87

Reich v. Circle C Investments, 161

Reich v. Priba Corporation, 161

Reid, Scott A., 127

rejection, fear of female, 67, 71, 72

Risman, Barbara, 111

Roberts, Linda, 166

role playing, 110. *See also* acting; stripper(s), fake identities and fabricated backgrounds

Ronai, Carol Rambo, 116, 117, 131, 135

Rubin, Gayle, 40, 41

salaries. *See* wages

Salutin, Marilyn, 152

Sanchez, Lisa, 93, 96

"sandbox," 10, 51

San Francisco, 35

Schad v. Borough of Mount Ephraim, 34

schedules, posting strippers', 180–81

Schiff, Frederick, 44

Schwartz, Martin D., 96

Schwartz, Pepper, 111

SCL. *See* Strip Club List

Scott, Megan, 96

Scully, Diana, 96

secondary (harmful) effects, 32–34, 93

Selfe, David, 78

self-employment. *See* stripper(s), costs of being independent contractors

self-esteem, 121–23, 134. *See also* identity problems

self-injurious behavior, 136–37, 141, 142

separation. *See* compartmentalization of home and work life

sex radical feminism, 40, 41. See also Chapkis, Wendy

sexual agency, 166

sexual aggression, 68, 92, 94, 179, 188, 207 (*see also* aggression; rape); by club owner, 189–92

sexual arousal, 133

sexual contact with patrons, 57, 179, 180. *See also* Champagne Room; physical contact with patrons

"sexualization of the public sphere," 109–10

sexual subcultures, researching, 26–29. *See also* Lion's Den, researching

sexual terrorism. *See* rape culture and myths

sex wars, 28, 40. *See also* feminist perspectives

sex work, 2–3, 151, 162; eradication/ elimination of, 34, 196, 197 (*see also* Supreme Court decisions); gender roles in, 20–21

sex workers, 78–79; disempowerment, 20–21 (*see also* empowerment); exploited as workers, 151; reasons for seeking services of, 78; stereotypes of, 19. *See also* stripper(s), stereotypes of

sex work industry, 198; abuse in, 26; research on, 27–29; third-party control over, 19–20

S Factor workout, 34–35

shaving, 114, 115

shift fees, 149–50, 160–61, 184

"shooter-girls," 176, 185, 186

showers, after-work, 135–37, 141

Shteir, Rachel, 31

Simmel, Georg, 78

Skipper, James, 151

"sleepers," xii

social class. *See* race and class dynamics

Spade, Joan, 167, 169, 190–91

Spoiled Identity (Goffman), 123–24

"spread shows," 16, 111

Sprinkle, Annie, 27–29

stage, physical condition of, 101–2

stage dancing, 146–49. *See also specific topics*

status characteristics, 44

Steinem, Gloria, 25

stereotypes: of sex workers, 19; of strippers, 40, 58–61, 113

Stiffed (Faludi), 45

stigmatization, 123–24; of male employees, 60–61; of strippers and stripping, 59, 111, 112. *See also* stripper(s), devaluation of; stripping, devaluation of

Street Woman (Miller), 27–28

Strip Club List (SCL), 29, 165, 169–74, 180 (*see also* Players); revisiting the past on, 175–76

strip clubs, 23 (*see also specific topics*); fostering hostility toward women, 169; geographic distribution, 170–71, 171–73t, 174; providing an escape, 71–72, 187; rea-

sons for studying, 1; regional comparisons, 170–71, 171–73t; reworking, 196–98; in United States, 171, 172–73t

strip club work, stripping, 19–22

stripper(s), 8–9, 56–57 (*see also specific topics*); authority over their work, 138–40; challenges facing, 55–56; charade of genuine interest in patrons, 76–79, 92 (*see also* acting); constantly monitored by male workers, 49–51; costs of being independent contractors, 146, 149, 150, 154, 161–62; cultivating desire while fending off advances and fixation, 78, 106; de-eroticization, 135; demographics, 202–3t; devaluation of, 58–61, 94–96, 101–2, 111–13, 141, 166, 186, 188, 189, 194–95 (*see also* patrons, rude behavior; rape culture and myths); distrust and lack of solidarity among, xii, 56–57, 140, 144, 159, 160 (*see also* competition between strippers; Lusty Lady theater); education, 188, 202–3t; empowerment, 138–40 (*see also* Lusty Lady theater); estrangement, 48 (*see also* alienation); expenses, 158; fake identities and fabricated backgrounds, 91–92, 124 (*see also* pseudonyms); fear and anxiety, 106–7; lack of protection of, 94, 101, 179; length of career, 19, 39; physical appearance, 10, 113–14; physical expectations, 113; power and influence, 56; preparation for work, 104–5; protecting themselves, 55–56; reasons for working as a, 9, 121–22, 126–27; refusing to undress, 57; relationships with men, 133–34, 138–39; reprimanding patrons, 139–40; resistance, 138–40; risks faced by, 37; stereotypes of, 40, 58–61, 113 (*see also* sex workers, stereotypes of); stripping their power, 140–42; suspected of indiscretions, 57; tales of distress, 60; terminology, 231n9; transitioning to and from work, 135–37, 141 (*see also* compartmentalization of home and work life); turnover rate, 140, 180–81; violence between, 140 stripping (*see also specific topics*): amateur, 36–37 (*see also* amateur nights); devaluation of, 58, 141; as "healing work," 130; history, 31; impact on strippers' relationships with men, 133–34, 138–39; keeping it a secret, 120, 123–26; legal context, 32–34; and mainstream culture, 34–35; *vs.* other types of sex work, 104; over time, 29–32; paradox of, 37–39; as "performance," 41; in popular representations, 29–37; positive and negative aspects, 123, 127, 138; positive psychological effects of, 121–22; in scholarly representations, 40–42

stripping industry, 2, 141 (*see also specific topics*); assumptions about, 1–2. *See also* stripper(s), stereotypes of

stripping labor, how women manage, 120–21; creating personal boundaries, selectivity, and acts of oppression, 131–34; cynicism and alienation, 126–30; denying involvement, 123–26; identifying as an object of desire, 121–23; transforming the work, 130–31; washing work away, 135–37, 141

Supreme Court decisions, 33–34, 92–93
surgery, cosmetic, 115
surveillance, 49, 53, 63, 93
Sweet, Nova, 48, 134

table dances, 148, 154
tampons, 115
tanning, 115, 158
Tearoom Trade (Humphreys), 27
television programs, cable, 34
Tewksbury, Richard, 51, 70, 88, 134
theft, xii
Thompson, Lydia, 29
Thompson, William, 48
tipping system, 7–8, 155, 156, 158–59; deejays and, 155, 156, 159
tips, 76–77, 128; for bartenders, 7, 17–18; as "gift" *vs.* payment, 75–76; size/quantity of, 17–18, 57, 82, 113, 127, 128, 139, 149, 153; for talking to patrons, 76, 77; used by strippers as means of taking control, 140; for waitresses, 8, 17, 18, 82, 83, 156, 158

Tokyo hostess clubs, 85–86
touching. *See* physical contact with patrons
traveling dancers (travelers), 13, 150, 160. *See also* amateur nights; interviewees; Vixen dancers
TUSCL (The Ultimate Strip Club List), 169–74

uniforms, 206–7
unionization. *See* Lusty Lady theater

vaginas, 112. *See also* genitalia
Vance, Carole, 40
van der Veen, Marjolein, 162
violence (*see also* aggression; sexual aggression): domestic, 90; in pornography, 168; between strippers, 140
VIP performances (private dances). *See* lap dancing; private dances
VIP Room, 12, 135, 148, 149, 176. *See also* Champagne Room
Vixen dancers, 143–44, 159, 160

wages, 7–9, 39, 113, 157, 158, 161 (*see also* economic rationale for stripping; money flows; profit(s); tips); after Players' take over of Lion's Den, 177; of bartenders, 17–18, 157; of cocktail waitresses, 8, 9, 17, 18, 155–56; dangers of focusing on, 129–30; of traveling strippers, 144–45, 150
waitresses, 140. *See also* cocktail waitresses
washings, ritualized, 135–37, 141
Wesley, Jennifer, 151
Winfrey, Oprah, 34
Wolff, Richard, 155
women at Lion's Den (*see also specific topics*): ranking and dichotomizing, 54; roles, 20, 55
Wood, Elizabeth Anne, 71
workers. *See* employees
working conditions, unsafe, 101–3

zoning of strip clubs, 32

About the Author

KIM PRICE-GLYNN is Assistant Professor of Sociology and Urban and Community Studies at the University of Connecticut.